Volume 10

SHORT-TERM VISUAL INFORMATION FORGETTING

SHORT-TERM VISUAL INFORMATION FORGETTING

A.H.C. VAN DER HEIJDEN

Routledge
Taylor & Francis Group

LONDON AND NEW YORK

First published in 1981

First edition published in 2014 by Psychology Press

Published 2016 by Routledge
2 Park Square, Milton Park, Abingdon, Oxfordshire OX14 4RN
711 Third Avenue, New York, NY 10017

First issued in paperback 2016

Routledge is an imprint of the Taylor and Francis Group, an informa business

British Library Cataloguing in Publication Data
A catalogue record for this book is available from the British Library

ISBN: 978-1-84872-321-4 (Set)
ISBN 13 : 978-1-138-99615-1 (pbk)
ISBN 13 : 978-1-84872-358-0 (hbk)

Publisher's Note
The publisher has gone to great lengths to ensure the quality of this book but points out that some imperfections from the original may be apparent.

Disclaimer
The publisher has made every effort to trace copyright holders and would welcome correspondence from those they have been unable to trace.

Short-term
Visual Information
Forgetting

A.H.C. van der Heijden
University of Leiden

ROUTLEDGE & KEGAN PAUL
London, Boston & Henley

First published in 1981
by Routledge & Kegan Paul Ltd
39 Store Street,
London WC1E 7DD,
Broadway House,
Newtown Road,
Henley-on-Thames,
Oxon RG9 1EN and
9 Park Street,
Boston, Mass. 02108, USA
Printed in Great Britain by
Billing & Sons Ltd
Guildford, London, Oxford and Worcester

ISBN 0 7100 0851 1

To Annie, Carin and Ellen

Contents

Acknowledgments

The experimental work reported in this study has been possible through the skilled and dedicated co-operation of the following students: G. Damming-Nyrees, T. Creyghton, J. Frankhuizen, G. Glazenborg, W. La Heij, W. Kleijn. R. van Leeuwen, H. Menckenberg, G. van Meurs, J. Mulder, E. Raaymakers, P. van der Steen, and L. Uhlaner. Many of the theoretical ideas expressed in this work have taken shape during the stimulating interaction with these students. Interesting discussions with Dr R. Visser and Dr G. Wolters have also contributed to the development of these ideas. Precious suggestions for the improvement of the manuscript have been provided by Prof. G. Flores d'Arcais, Prof. J. van de Geer, Dr A. Sanders and Dr P. Vroon. Mrs I. Janse-van der Erf, Mrs M. van Sprang-van Beek and Miss M. Versluys have not only provided skilful typing work both at different stages during the preparation of the manuscript and for the present final version of it, but also valuable help at various moments of the planning and execution of the work here reported.

Figures

Figures

Tables

Author's note

Each chapter of the present study is preceded by an introduction, which has been written as a summary of the content of the chapter as well as an overview of the topics to be discussed.

The reader might find it useful to start with the general introduction and then read all the chapter previews together beforehand, as a way of gaining an overall understanding of the theoretical ideas, the structure and the specific lay-out of this work.

Introduction

This study deals with some aspects of visual information processing. In this expression, the term processing has the same meaning as the term cognition in Neisser's (1967) book 'Cognitive Psychology'. It refers to 'all the processes by which the sensory input is transformed, reduced, elaborated, stored, recovered, and used' (cf. p. 4). The term information is not used in its technical or mathematical sense (Attneave, 1959). As used in the present context it can be taken to stand for 'sensory input', or even for '. . . that aspect of the content of the stimulus that the experimenter is interested in studying or manipulating' (Haber and Hershenson, 1974, p. 161), but also for 'the representation of the sensory input within the nervous system', or, for 'that what is transformed, reduced, elaborated, etc.' (Neisser, 1967, p. 8). The term visual indicates that the information is transmitted to the perceiver by light energy or by differences in light energy and is received by the receptors in the retina of the eye.

The style of analysis and description in this study fits in with the information processing approach of perception and cognitive activities as used by Broadbent (1958), Sperling (1963), Neisser (1967), and Haber and Hershenson (1974), for example. The basic assumptions of this approach are: (a) perception and overt responding are not immediate outcomes of stimulation, but require a sequence of operations each of which requires a finite amount of time, and a number of stores in which the results of the operations can be maintained; (b) it is possible to devise experimental operations that allow us to investigate the nature and the time-course of the operations and the contents of the stores (see Haber and Hershenson, 1974, p. 158).

Within this approach, models and theories − sets of principles or hypotheses postulated to explain relationships in the data − are not only the ultimate goals, but also serve important functions as tools. First, models serve a summarizing function and make it possible to

1

communicate in an economic way about a variety of discrete observations. Second, they serve as guidelines for further observations and experiments. If sufficiently specific, implied consequences can be derived for situations not yet covered by the model. Investigation of such situations can then lead to the generalization, extension, or modification of a model.

In this study a number of visual information processing models and of more general information processing models applicable to visual information processing tasks are extensively discussed. Because in most visual tasks information is taken in during the fixation pauses of about 250 msec, between the saccadic eye movements, fixation pauses can be regarded as the functional time units in more complex visual information processing tasks such as reading. It is therefore especially investigated what hypotheses or principles are postulated in order to account for data obtained in situations simulating a single fixation. Also the experiments reported, except the one in chapter 1, are exclusively concerned with information processing within one fixation.

In this study the term 'processing' is generally used in a more strict sense than in the expression 'visual information processing'. Suppose a subject is presented with a brief flash consisting of many items (letters or digits for instance) and that he is instructed to name the items. In this task the subject has to derive the names or a representation of the names of the items (a name code) from an initial visual representation of the items (a visual code). The term processing in a strict sense will be used for this recoding from a visual code into a name code. Because this recoding implies identification or categorization (see Neisser, 1967, p. 49; Broadbent, 1971, p. 330), the terms identification and categorization can also be used for this process.

The task described in the previous paragraph is a 'whole report task'. A related type of task is the 'partial report task'. In a partial report task the items can be divided in a number of mutually exclusive subsets (for instance letters and digits, or red, green and blue items). By means of a coded instruction presented at or just after stimulus exposure the subjects are instructed to name the items of one of these subsets.

This study is mainly concerned with performance in whole report tasks in which the subjects are in addition required to reflect the spatial position of the item in responding, and with partial report tasks in which the relevant subset of items can be distinguished on the basis of an obvious physical characteristic that is unrelated to the items' identity. What we want to know about these tasks is whether there are capacity limitations in processing the items, where selective attention comes in and how selective attention operates.

Two classes of information processing models can be distinguished which are capable of providing answers to these questions: precategorical selection models and postcategorical selection models.

In precategorical selection models it is assumed that there is a limited capacity for processing or categorizing information. A selection mechanism is postulated that operates prior to the processing or categorizing of the items, that is, unidentified information is selected for identification. In postcategorical selection models it is assumed that there are no capacity limitations as far as the processing or categorization of the items is concerned. According to these models, capacity limitations are only met in later stages in the processing sequence, such as overt responding or storage in memory, and selective attention operates upon processed or categorized information.

Precategorical selection models have their origin in Broadbent's (1958) filter model, developed in the context of dichotic listening experiments. Broadbent (1970) summarizes his 1958 position as follows:

> When several simultaneous signals reach the senses, they are received first into a buffer store which can hold them in parallel, but can do so for only a limited time. During this time some of the information may proceed to a further processing mechanism, which is of limited capacity and operates serially. Thus part of the information from the buffer store will fail to pass this stage of serial processing before the time limit on the buffer store expires and those items which are lost in this way will have no further effect on behaviour. (Broadbent, 1970, p. 52)

A basic concept in this model is the filter that selects items in the buffer store for further processing. This filter operates by selecting those stimulus events which possess some common feature, such as coming from a certain spatial location, and passing on all other features of these events to the limited capacity portion for analysis.

Following Treisman (1960), Broadbent (1971) changes this model considerably. A second selection mechanism, response set, is introduced 'response set is the selection of certain classes of response . . . as having a high priority for occurrence even if the evidence in their favour is not especially high' (Broadbent, 1971, p. 177). In this new conceptualization filtering does not block but merely attenuates information from nonattended sources. 'Filtering is a hierarchical process, in which each stimulus event is first examined for the presence or absence of some key features: only if these features are present do all the other features have a normal probability of representation in the evidence' (Broadbent, 1971 p. xii). These modifications, however, have no consequence for Broadbent's interpretation of the tasks we are concerned with. From the results of a whole report experiment in which exposure duration was varied (Mackworth, 1963a), Broadbent concludes:

> We therefore have the evidence we wanted, that the selective process is limited in its rate of working rather than in the number of items it can pick off; that, just as we supposed in the auditory case, we have a buffer store lasting a fixed length of time, and a subsequent serial process which can extract one item after another from the buffer until the limit of time is exceeded. (Broadbent, 1971, p. 173)

In commenting upon the nature of this serial process, Broadbent remarks: 'The process in question is therefore the one we have named categorization, and must have occurred as soon as one can obtain a response to the stimulus' (1971, p. 330).

In the context of visual information processing tasks, similar or related precategorical selection models were proposed by, for example, Sperling (1963), Estes and Taylor (1964, 1966), Neisser (1967), Rumelhart (1970) and Coltheart (1972, 1975a).

Deutsch and Deutsch (1963) were the first to propose a postcategorical selection model as an alternative to Broadbent's filter model. They postulated a system containing a number of 'central structures', or 'classifying mechanisms'. 'A message will reach the same perceptual and discriminating mechanisms whether attention is paid to it or not; and such information is then grouped or segregated by these mechanisms' (Deutsch and Deutsch, 1963, p. 83). Each central structure also has a preset weighting of importance. Among the structures receiving an information input, the one with the highest weighting of importance will 'switch in further processes, such as motor output, memory storage, and whatever else it may be that leads to awareness' (Deutsch and Deutsch, 1963, p. 84).

In the context of visual information processing tasks similar or related postcategorical selection models were proposed by Morton (1969b), Shiffrin and Gardner (1972), Gardner (1973), Keele (1973), Shiffrin and Geisler (1973), Schneider and Shiffrin (1977) and Shiffrin and Schneider (1977) among others.

Up to now, precategorical selection models have dominated

theorizing about whole report and partial report tasks and these models have been very successful. There are detailed quantitative precategorical selection models that are capable of accounting for the results obtained with these tasks (see, for example, Rumelhart, 1970) while the postcategorical selection models are rather vague and general as far as these tasks are concerned (cf. for instance, Gardner, 1973, p. 132; Shiffrin and Schneider, 1977, p. 167). In a sense, whole report tasks and partial report tasks can be considered as bastions for the proponents of precategorical selection in visual information processing tasks and the defence of these bastions seems rather easy (see, for instance, the discussion between Holding, 1975, and Coltheart, 1975a).

In general, however, recent theorizing on selective attention in visual information processing research seems to show a gradual shift from precategorical selection models to postcategorical selection models. Other tasks than whole and partial report tasks often suggest that, except for acuity and masking effects, there are no limitations as far as the processing of visual information is concerned. Furthermore, in a number of tasks inadequacies in the functioning of the hypothetical precategorical filter are found. Some of this evidence led Posner (1973) to the conclusion:

> At this level of processing it is often more difficult to avoid the occurrence of a highly overlearned association than it is to achieve it. We have abundant evidence that the nervous system activates the name of visually presented words (e.g., Stroop effect) and frequent association . . . even when it is to subjects' interest to avoid doing so. These findings run directly counter to the views that subjects select from the stimulus distinctive features which control from the very start the way that stimulus is handled by the nervous system. Rather, he has great difficulty in avoiding the activation of habitual associations to a given item. (Posner, 1973, p. 38),

and,

> I think these results change the conception of the human nervous system which prevailed in the 1950's and 1960's. We must not think of a limited capacity system as restricting the range of associations which can be activated by input, provided that these associations are habitual. . . . Rather, we must understand the widespread parallel effects which a given item causes. The problem, then, becomes one of selection and coordination of these habitual

associations in guiding their use during the performance of tasks. (Posner, 1973, p. 41-2)

As stated, this study is mainly concerned with the problems of capacity limitations in processing visual information, the locus of selective attention and the mechanism of selective attention in whole report and partial report tasks. It is investigated whether the results obtained with these tasks have to be interpreted in terms of a precategorical selection model (as is strongly suggested in the literature) or whether an interpretation in terms of selection and co-ordination of habitual associations (i.e. postcategorical selection) is more adequate (this interpretation seems more in line with recent advances in visual information processing research).

Three parts can be distinguished in this study that are seemingly unrelated, but which together constitute the complete argument.

In the first part of this study (chapters 1, 2 and 3) we stay as close to the traditional interpretation of the results of whole report and partial report tasks as possible. In chapter 1 the results of a whole report task in which exposure duration was varied are reported. The mathematical description of the results of this experiment is easily interpreted in terms of Broadbent's filter model, but alternative interpretations as precategorical selection models as well as postcategorical selection models are possible. The interpretation most in line with Broadbent's model is taken as a preliminary starting point for further investigations and theorizing. In chapter 2 (on the processing of visual information) and in chapter 3 (on the selection of visual information), however, evidence is provided that indicates that this interpretation, and also the other interpretations in terms of precategorical selection, have to be put in serious doubt. So, at the end of the first part of this study we are left with the conviction that postcategorical selection offers the most parsimonious explanation for the results found with whole report and partial report tasks, and with a mathematical description of the results of a whole report task that can be interpreted as a postcategorical selection model in a number of ways. The remaining problem is how this description has to be interpreted as a postcategorical selection model.

In the second part of this study (chapters 4, 5 and 6) we change over to a rather different and apparently unrelated type of task (in fact it is a disguised form of partial report task). In this task, the subjects have to give only one response per trial, and from the literature we know (and the results of the experiments reported support this point of view) that this task shows the activities of a postcategorical selection mechanism. In chapters 4 and 5 the results of a number of experiments are reported in which this task is used. The conditions chosen are such that the properties of this mechanism can become apparent, possibly in a magnified form. In chapter 6 a postcategorical selection model is described that is capable of accounting for the results obtained in these experiments. This model is summarized in a mathematical description that specifies the duration of one selective operation as a function of the moment of initiation of this selective operation.

It will be clear that the third part of this study (chapter 7) is mainly devoted to a discussion about the relation between the mathematical description of whole report tasks presented in the first part of this study (this description reflects a series of selective operations) and the mathematical description of the postcategorical selection model presented in the second part of this study (this description specifies the duration of one selective operation as a function of the moment of initiation of the selective operation). It appears that a concatenation of selective operations as specified in the postcategorical selection model results in the same mathematical relation between the expected number of elements reported and the exposure time as was found in the whole report experiment reported in chapter 1. This result readily leads to an interpretation of the mathematical description of whole report tasks as a postcategorical selection model.

A word of explanation about the title of this study – short-term visual information forgetting – seems appropriate here. In a sense, this title reflects our ultimate conviction that selection in whole and partial report experiments is postcategorical selection. While proponents of precategorical selection models have to explain how the relevant information enters the system, proponents of postcategorical selection models have to explain how a system that takes in relevant and irrelevant information indiscriminately gets rid of the irrelevant information. In relation to an auditory information processing task, Broadbent remarks 'it is hard to understand why rejected items, once fully analysed, are so completely lost that no saving occurs in subsequent learning of material which has struck the ear but not received attention' (Broadbent, 1970, p. 53). This problem is hardly ever mentioned in the literature. Of course, it is easy to postulate that irrelevant information is simply forgotten in one or another way, and this is one of the main claims of the present study, which is reflected in the title. During the time that the irrelevant information is in the system, however, effects on, or interference with, other ongoing processing activities are to be expected. One way in which irrelevant information can hamper performance before it is forgotten is worked out in detail in chapters 6 and 7.

1 Whole report as a function of exposure duration

Summary

In this chapter it is investigated whether processing time or short-term memory (STM) capacity sets a limit in a task in which observers look at a briefly exposed array of numbers and try to write down as many of these numbers as possible.

Mackworth (1962, 1963a) reported results obtained in a similar type of experiment and showed that processing time is a crucial variable: the number of elements reported showed a linear increase with exposure duration. Broadbent (1971) makes this observation one of the cornerstones on which his filter notion in visual information processing rests:

> We therefore have the evidence we wanted, that the selective process
> is limited in its rate of working rather than in the number of items
> it can pick off; that . . . we have a buffer store lasting a fixed length
> of time, and a subsequent serial process which can extract one item
> after another from the buffer until the limit of time is exceeded.
> (Broadbent, 1971, p. 173)

Sperling (1960) reports the results of a similar experiment and shows that the exposure duration has a negligible effect on the number of elements reported.

The results of the experiment reported in this chapter showed an increase, but not a linear increase in the number of elements reported with exposure duration. A search of the literature showed that often a non-linear relation between number of elements reported and exposure duration is found.

The results of the experiment reported and of other results reported in the literature can be described with a simple equation. Contrary to the linear function fitted by Mackworth, the non-linear function derived from the equation gives estimates of the buffer duration that are in accord with independent estimates of buffer duration in the visual case.

The equation suggests a two-process model for this type of task: on the one hand, the elements on the stimulus card are processed at a rate of 'b' elements per unit of time, and on the other hand, during each unit of time a proportion of the elements already identified disappear from STM, or cannot be retrieved.

Besides a number of advantages that this interpretation has in common with other interpretations of the equation, it also seemed to have two specific advantages. First, it presents only a minor deviation from Broadbent's (1971) point of view. It remains possible to interpret parameter b as reflecting the serial extracting of items from the buffer. The only new feature added is the forgetting of elements already extracted and identified. Second, this interpretation applies to the whole range of exposure durations, that is, there is no need for postulating different processes for different ranges of exposure durations.

This interpretation was taken as a background for further theorizing in chapters 2 and 3.

One problem with this interpretation is that it leads to STM notions that appear rather obsolete in the light of recent advances in STM research. In an appendix a number of alternative interpretations are given that are possibly more compatible with recent theories on STM, and that at least cannot be ruled out given the evidence presented in this chapter.

Introduction

In a visual whole report experiment, an observer is shown a display containing a number of elements, for example, digits or letters, and is asked to name or write down as many of the elements as possible after the exposure. When the exposure duration is such that only a single glance is possible (that is, no shift in fixation is possible during the exposure), only a limited number of elements presented are reported by the observer. Woodworth and Schlosberg (1954) and Neisser (1967) mention an average of between four and seven elements.

This limit on the number of items reported after a brief exposure can be seen as just another manifestation of a general limitation of human memory, 'the span of immediate memory', and is then called 'the span of attention', 'the span of apprehension' (cf. Miller, 1956; Neisser, 1967) or 'the span of immediate memory' (Sperling, 1960, 1963). With this interpretation, the upper limit on the number of elements reported after a brief exposure only depends on the capacity of a memory that has to hold the results of processing the display, until written or oral reporting takes place. This explanation will be called the 'span hypothesis'. Proponents of this explanation regard exposure duration as a variable of minor importance. Only if the time that the visual information is available for processing is artificially reduced to times much shorter than the duration of a fixation, an effect of exposure duration is to be expected.

Another explanation of the limit on the number of elements reported with brief exposures may be called the 'processing time hypothesis'. This states that with brief exposures there is not enough time to transfer information about the elements to a postcategorical level. The number of elements reported only depends on the time for which the visual information is present and the rate of processing the information. Only in the case of extended exposures do the capacity limitations of the memory that has to hold the names of the elements have an effect on the number of elements reported.

In the early 1960s, two independent attempts were made to incorporate the 'whole report' data in more general information processing models. Both explanations were maintained and investigated with rather different results. Sperling (Sperling, 1960, 1963; Averbach and Sperling, 1961) was the prime advocate of the 'span hypothesis' and gathered much evidence in favour of this explanation, whilst Mackworth (Mackworth, 1962, 1963a) advocated the 'processing time hypothesis' and carried out a number of experiments that firmly supported this point of view. (Later on, both investigators (Sperling, 1967, 1970; Mackworth, 1972) changed some of their interpretations of their data. For ease of exposition and as we are mainly concerned with the results of their experiments we will confine ourselves to the data and interpretations mentioned in the earlier papers.)

There are three points both investigators agreed upon.
1 Visual information from brief exposures is not only available for processing during the exposure, but persists for some time after the exposure as a 'rapidly fading visual image of the stimulus' (Sperling, 1960, p. 26), or as a 'visual image' (Mackworth, 1962, 1963a). Upon arrival, visual information is stored in VIS (visual information storage), which 'acts as a buffer which quickly attains and holds much information to permit its slow utilization later' (Sperling, 1963, p. 22). Subsequently, Neisser (1967) gave the term 'iconic memory' or 'icon' to this rapidly decaying visual persistence from which a subject could read information as if the stimulus was still present.

11

2 During stimulus exposure and icon, items are 'read' or processed one after another and transferred to a more endurable memory. This memory was named 'immediate memory' (Sperling, 1960), 'Auditory Information Store' or 'AIS' (Sperling, 1963), 'the memory trace' (Mackworth, 1962), and 'post-perceptual immediate-memory' (Mackworth, 1963a).

3 Only during the first interval of time that the stimulus information is available for processing is the rate of increase of the number of elements in the more endurable memory constant. After that interval, the processing rate decreases (Sperling, 1963) or a reduction in the efficiency of information intake in that memory will take place (Mackworth, 1962, 1963a).

To conclude, there is a general agreement on the outline of a model for visual information processing in whole report tasks. Visual information is stored in a buffer memory and outlasts objective exposure. Information about the elements in the display is serially transferred to a more durable memory.

There is, however, a remarkable disagreement between the two investigators about the parameters of this model, namely, the duration of the icon, the rate of processing the elements, and the interval of time that the processing rate is constant. These parameters, except Sperling's estimate of icon duration, are derived from whole report experiments in which the relation between number of elements reported and exposure time is investigated. (Sperling's estimate of icon duration is based upon the results of his well-known partial report experiments. Recent evaluations of this method are given by Dick (1974) and Coltheart (1975a). Mackworth (1963b) gives additional estimates of icon duration using methods other than whole report.) Of course, this type of experiment provides the most direct way for deciding between the 'span hypothesis' and the 'processing time hypothesis'.

Two types of whole report experiments with varying exposure duration were used. Mackworth (1962) (and also Mackworth, 1963a, exp. 3, and Sperling, 1960, exp. 2) had the display followed by a homogeneous post-exposure field. Sperling (1963, p. 25) (see also Sperling, 1960, p. 24) and Averbach and Sperling (1961, p. 202) presented data obtained from an experiment in which the display was followed by a patterned post-exposure field, consisting of densely scattered pieces of letters. In Sperling's opinion, such a 'noise' field erases the icon, leaving only visual information storage during exposure.

With both procedures it was found that the first part of the function relating the number of elements reported to the exposure time, was linear, or, could be characterized by

$X = aT + b$,

where X equals the number of elements reported, and T equals the objective exposure time.

Mackworth, as well as Sperling, assumes that for the range of exposure durations for which this linear relation holds, the processing rate is constant. Sperling's (1963) results with the pattern mask show that this relation holds for the first 50 msec of exposure duration. Mackworth (1962) presents results, obtained with the homogeneous post-exposure field, which show that the linear relation holds for all exposure durations shorter than one second (see also Mackworth, 1963a, exp. 3, for similar results). Sperling concludes that the processing rate has to be derived from the relation between the number of elements reported and the exposure times when these range between 0 and 50 msec. Mackworth concludes that this parameter can be estimated from this relation for exposure times between 0 and 1 second.

Mackworth assumes that for homogeneous post-exposure fields and for the range of exposure times mentioned, parameter a in equation $X = aT + b$ reflects the processing rate. For digits, Mackworth (1962) finds 'a' values of 2.98 and 2.70 (T in sec), or, processing times of 336 msec and 370 msec per digit. Similar results are found by Mackworth (1963a). So in both experiments a strong dependence of number of elements reported on exposure time is found. In a similar experiment, Sperling (1960), however, finds no effect of exposure duration and he concludes that exposure duration, even over a wide range, is an unimportant parameter! (1960, p. 6).

Sperling (1963) assumes that for patterned post-exposure fields and for exposure times up to 50 msec, parameter 'a' reflects the processing rate. The 'a' value found for this range of exposure durations equals about 80 (T in sec). Sperling (1963, p. 25) concludes that elements of good contrast are scanned or processed at a rate of about one letter within 10 to 15 msec. With exposure times greater than 50 msec no substantial further increase in number of elements reported was found. So from these results it can be concluded that exposure time is only an important variable in a range of times appreciably below the duration of a normal fixation.

The value of b in the equation $X = aT + b$ is a constant, independent of the exposure time. It can be interpreted as reflecting the number of elements processed independent of objective exposure time, or processed from the icon after stimulus exposure. Mackworth (1962) gives

13

b-values of 3.85 and 3.4 (Mackworth, 1963a, exp. 3, and Sperling, 1960, exp. 2, show roughly comparable figures). Mackworth derives estimates of icon duration by multiplying these values by the processing time per element (or by extrapolating the linear function to X = 0, which is a graphical solution for T in the equation 0 = aT + b). The icon duration found in this way lies between 1 and 2 seconds. Sperling's (1963) data obtained with the patterned post-exposure field show a b-value of approximately 0. This may be taken as evidence that the patterned 'noise' mask was effective in erasing the icon from the visual information store; no elements are processed independent of objective exposure time. As already mentioned, Sperling derived his estimates of icon duration from partial report experiments. When, with these partial report experiments, pre- and post-exposure conditions are comparable with those in Mackworth's whole report experiments, values of about 300 to 400 msec are found (Sperling, 1960, 1963; Averbach and Sperling, 1961).

Since the general procedure used to estimate the parameters, that is, the fitting of the linear function and the interpretation of the parameters, seems adequate, additional evidence is necessary to break the tie.

Two pieces of information are especially relevant.

First, nearly all research on icon duration shows estimated durations of less than 1 second, with a modal value between 200 and 400 msec (see Haber and Hershenson, 1974; Dick, 1974). Therefore it seems profitable to have a closer look at Mackworth's (1962) data in order to find out whether there are methodological flaws that influence the 'a' and 'b' values. It then appears that she used a rather peculiar way of scoring the data. 'Digits were recorded as correct if they appeared in the correct position in the sequence. Half a mark was allotted to a digit which was misplaced by one position in the sequence either vertically or horizontally.' (Mackworth, 1963a, gives no detailed information about the way of scoring the data.) This, however, is a 'negative' correction for guessing, that probably inflates the score considerably, especially when only a small number of elements are really processed. (Of course, there is some value in the argument that subjects sometimes remember the identity of some elements but have forgotten their positions. There is, however, as much value in the argument that subjects sometimes correctly guess identity and location or identity and approximate location of elements they have not processed. One might as well assume that both effects cancel each other out. The number of items correct, and in the correct position, is then the best estimate of the number of elements processed.)

If Mackworth's (1962) way of scoring the data overestimates the number of elements processed, and if the amount of overestimation is a decreasing linear function of the number of elements really processed, the value of b in $X = aT + b$, will be too large, and the value of a will be too small. Because icon duration is derived from b/a, this procedure overestimates icon duration.

Second, recent investigation on the effect of a patterned post-exposure field as used by Sperling (1963), indicates that such a field does not immediately erase the icon. Since Sperling introduced this technique, there has been much debate about the effects of such a masking field. There were two opposite points of view. One group of investigators maintained that two stimuli that follow one another in rapid succession are simultaneously available for processing as a composite picture. In the second point of view it is assumed that the display is only processed prior to the exposition of the masking stimulus. The patterned masking stimulus immediately terminates the processing of the stimulus (see Kahneman, 1968; Liss, 1968; Neisser, 1967; Van der Heijden, 1971; Schulz and Eriksen, 1977).

Both Scheerer (1973), from a review of the literature, and Turvey (1973), from a series of experiments, concluded that for short intervals (less than about 100 msec) between stimulus onset and mask onset the two fields seem to fuse, whilst with longer intervals the mask field interrupts the processing of the stimulus. This means that for stimulus durations up to 100 msec the number of the elements processed cannot legitimately be related to objective exposure time because there is not enough evidence concerning the exact effect of the patterned post-exposure field on the processing rate. Turvey (1973) suggests that with longer stimulus exposures there is a gradual replacement of stimulus features in central storage units by post-exposure field features. At what time after masking field onset the stimulus features have disappeared is not clear.

Beside the use of different post-exposure fields, there are, of course, several other differences between the experiments considered before, such as stimulus material, exposure condition, and subjects. Therefore it seems worthwhile to further investigate whether the 'span hypothesis' or the 'processing time hypothesis' applies in an experiment in which both types of whole report tasks are given to the same subjects under comparable conditions. In order to circumvent the problems connected with the use of a patterned post-exposure field, only exposure times of 100 msec or more were used.

15

The number of elements correct and in the correct position was taken as an estimate of the number of elements processed.

The planned strategy was to fit linear functions, $X = aT + b$, over the initial range of exposure durations where this relation holds, and to derive estimates of processing rate, 'a', and the number of elements processed independently of time 'b'. From these two parameters the icon duration can be estimated if it is assumed that the rate of processing after stimulus exposure, that is, the rate of processing from the icon, equals the rate of processing during stimulus exposure (icon duration then equals b/a). This estimated icon duration can be used to check the validity of the procedure. From other investigations (see, for example, Dick, 1974) we know that with the homogeneous post-exposure field, an icon duration of about 250 msec is to be expected. With the patterned post-exposure field no icon or a much shorter one is to be expected.

Method

Material

Forty slides were prepared containing 3 x 3 matrices of digits. The digits were drawn with replacement from the set 0 to 9. One degree in visual angle separated the outer digits from a fixation point that was located on the projection screen. The height of the digits was about .20° in visual angle. For the patterned post-exposure field, a slide was used containing a random pattern of pieces of the same type of digits used for the stimulus slides. This pattern completely covered the area of the 3 x 3 matrix. About 40 per cent of this area contained parts of digits. No slide was used for the homogeneous post-exposure field condition. The stimuli and the post-exposure field were first prepared with Letraset letters on white cards, and photographed afterwards.

Design

Eight exposure durations were chosen: 100, 300, 500, 700, 900, 1100, 1300 and 1500 msec. Either an increasing or a decreasing order of exposure durations was used. This order of exposure duration was factorially combined with the order of post-exposure field condition. (So, one group of subjects first received stimuli in the homogeneous post-exposure field condition with increasing exposure durations, and then stimuli in the patterned post-exposure field condition with decreasing exposure durations.) Each subject was thus tested under sixteen different treatment-exposure duration combinations. Each combination was replicated with ten different stimuli. The forty slides were divided into four groups of ten different stimuli and assigned to the treatment-exposure duration conditions in such a way that each group appeared in each condition an equal number of times.

Apparatus

The slides were projected by a home-made projection tachistoscope. This tachistoscope consisted of two random access slide projectors. Electronically controlled shutters were placed in front of the projection lenses.

Subjects

Twelve staff members and assistants of the Psychological Institute of the University of Leiden served as volunteer subjects. All had normal or corrected to normal vision.

Procedure

Subjects were run in groups of three in a moderately illuminated room. In the patterned post-exposure field condition, the stimulus was immediately followed by this post-exposure field. This field lasted for three seconds. In the homogeneous post-exposure field condition the projection screen remained dark after exposure. Ss were instructed to write their answers on 3 x 3 matrices provided at the beginning of the experiment. They were told that an item was only correct when it was located in its correct position. Subjects were instructed to fill in the complete matrix.

Before the experiment, twenty practice trials were given at various exposure durations to acquaint the subjects with the procedure and to allow time for adaptation to the illumination level of the room.

Results

Table 1.1 shows the mean number of elements correct and in the correct position over the twelve subjects for the two types of post-exposure field and for the eight exposure durations. An analysis of variance over the mean number of elements correct per subject, post-exposure field, and exposure duration revealed significant effects for post-exposure field ($F(1,165) = 20.55$, $p<.01$), exposure duration ($F(7,165) = 91.84$, $p<.01$), and for the interaction between post-exposure field and exposure duration ($F(7,165) = 3.40$, $p<.01$). Separate trend analyses over exposure durations within each post-exposure field condition were performed. For the patterned post-exposure field and for the homogeneous post-exposure field, both the linear components ($F(1,77) = 330.11$, $p<.01$ and $F(1,77) = 197.50$, $p<.01$, respectively) and the quadratic components ($F(1,77) = 73.55$, $p<.01$ and $F(1,77) = 45.27$, $p<.01$, respectively) appeared to be significant. No significant higher order components were found.

Table 1.1 *Mean number of elements correct and in the correct position over twelve subjects for the two types of post-exposure field and eight exposure durations*

Post-exposure field	Exposure duration (msec)							
	100	300	500	700	900	1100	1300	1500
Patterned	2.88	4.45	5.27	5.83	6.34	6.49	6.53	6.56
Homogeneous	4.08	5.30	5.48	6.13	6.60	6.52	6.63	6.57

For both post-exposure field conditions, Table 1.1 shows that there is no initial range of exposure durations where the number of elements reported can adequately be characterized by the linear relation $X = aT + b$. This is more readily apparent from Table 1.2, where the increase in the number of elements reported, ΔX, for each 200 msec increase in exposure duration, ΔT, is shown. For a linear relation, ΔX has to be constant. Table 1.2 shows that there is no initial range of exposure durations for which ΔX is constant.

Further investigations of the data showed that there was a strong linear relation between X and ΔX as previously defined:

$$\Delta X = -aX + b \tag{1}$$

which can be written as

$$X_{i+1} = (1-a)X_i + b. \tag{2}$$

For the patterned post-exposure field condition, the functional relation

$$\Delta X = -.4025X + 2.6988 \tag{1a}$$

18

explained 99.8 per cent of the variance. For the homogeneous post-exposure field condition the functional relation

$$\Delta X = -.4190X + 2.7945 \qquad (1b)$$

explained 97.1 per cent of the variance. These functional relations were identified by minimizing the sum of the squared distances from the observation points to the line.

Table 1.2 *Number of elements reported (X) and increase in the number of elements reported (ΔX) for each 200 msec increase in exposure duration for both types of post-exposure field*

| Exposure duration (msec) | Post-exposure field | | | |
| | Patterned | | Homogeneous | |
	X	ΔX	X	ΔX
100	2.88	1.57	4.08	1.22
300	4.45	.82	5.30	.18
500	5.27	.56	5.48	.65
700	5.83	.51	6.13	.47
900	6.34	.15	6.60	−.08
1100	6.49	.04	6.52	.11
1300	6.53	.03	6.63	−.06
1500	6.56		6.57	

Equation (1) is a linear difference equation with solution

$$X = \frac{b}{a} - q(1-a)^t. \qquad (3)$$

In Appendix A it is shown that this equation can be rewritten as

$$X = \frac{b}{a}(1 - e^{-\alpha(t + c)}) \qquad (4)$$

with $\alpha = -\ln(1-a)$ and $C = (\ln \frac{aq}{b})/\ln(1-a)$. Parameter q can be estimated from the relation

$$\ln(\frac{b}{a} - X) = \ln q + t \ln(1-a), \qquad (5)$$

derived from equation (3).

For the patterned post-exposure field condition, parameter q equals 4.8525, and therefore C in equation (4) equals .6278. The parameters α and b/a of equation (4) can be derived from equation (1a). By

19

substituting these parameters in equation (4) the function relating X to t for the patterned post-exposure field condition,

$$X = 6.7046\,(1-e^{-.5150(t + .6278)}) \tag{4a}$$

is obtained (t and C in units of 200 msec).

For the homogeneous post-exposure field condition, parameter q equals 2.7377, and therefore C in equation (4) equals 1.6398. The parameters α and b/a of equation (4) can be derived from equation (1b). By substituting these parameters in equation (4) the function relating X to t for the homogeneous post-exposure field condition,

$$X = 6.6689\,(1-e^{-.5430(t + 1.6398)}) \tag{4b}$$

is obtained (t and C in units of 200 msec).

Figure 1.1 represents these two functions, together with the observed values of X for the two conditions.

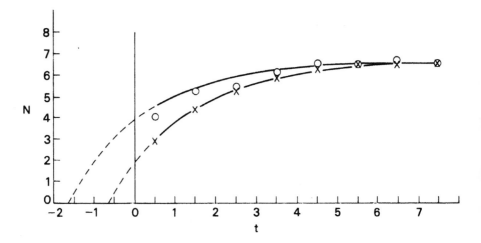

Figure 1.1 *Mean number of elements reported (N) per exposure duration and kind of post-exposure field. Exposure duration is in units of 200 msec. The open circles represent a homogeneous post-exposure field; the crosses a patterned post-exposure field. Fitted functions are*

$X = 6.7046\,(1-e^{-.5150\,(t + .6278)})$ *for the patterned post-exposure field and*

$X = 6.6689\,(1-e^{-.5430\,(t + 1.6398)})$ *for the homogeneous post-exposure field. The dashed part of the curve is extrapolated to* $t + c = 0$

Because it was thought that, especially in the patterned post-exposure field condition, the data might be strongly influenced by guessing,

20

taking into account that subjects were forced to fill in the complete matrix, a correction for guessing was applied to the data of this condition. This correction was derived from the assumption that the number of elements correct and in the correct position, X, equals the number of elements of which the subject knows the identity and the position, Y, plus a proportion, P, of the number of cells the subject has filled in without knowing the identity and position, that is,

$$X = Y + P(N - Y),$$

and

$$Y = \frac{X - NP}{1 - P}.$$

With p = .1 the functional relation for the patterned post-exposure field condition becomes

$$\Delta Y = -.4025Y + 2.5961. \tag{1c}$$

Parameter q obtained with equation (5) equals 5.4710, and therefore C in equation (4) equals .3196. The parameters α and b/a of equation (4) can be derived from equation (1c). By substituting these parameters in equation (4) the function relating Y to t for the patterned post-exposure field condition, corrected for guessing,

$$Y = 6.4499 \left(1 - e^{-.5150 (t + .3196)}\right) \tag{4c}$$

is obtained (t and C in units of 200 msec).

Discussion

In the section on 'results' it was shown, that in the present experiment no initial range of exposure durations was found where a linear relation between the exposure duration and the amount of elements reported holds. For the whole range of exposure durations, however, it was found that the relation

$$X = \frac{b}{a} (1 - e^{-\alpha (t + c)}) \tag{4}$$

gave an adequate description of the data. From this equation it follows that X = 0 for t + C = 0, or −t = C. This value for C can be interpreted as the amount of time beyond objective exposure duration during which the subjects can process information, that is, as the duration of the icon. In the homogeneous post-exposure field condition, this value for C equalled 1.64 (328 msec), a value well in line with other estimates of icon duration under comparable conditions (cf. Dick, 1974, and Haber and Hershenson, 1974). In the patterned post-exposure field condition, respective values of .63 (126 msec) and .32 (64 msec) for raw data and data corrected for guessing were found. These values are considerably lower than the value obtained with the homogeneous post-exposure field, and so these values can also be legitimately interpreted as the amount of time after objective exposure during which subjects can process information when a patterned post-exposure field is presented. As stated already, some investigators assume that processing of the icon immediately stops on the appearance of a patterned post-exposure field. It is possible that the values derived from the present experiment somewhat overestimate the interval of time during which the subjects can continue processing elements despite the presence of a patterned post-exposure field, this as a result of the exposure conditions (possibly a more effective patterned field can be made), or the subjects' guessing strategies (possibly another correction has to be used). However, recent evidence shows that over short intervals of time (up to 100 msec), integration of stimulus and patterned field is to be expected. Furthermore, direct subjective estimates of the duration of a stimulus, masked with a patterned post-exposure field, somewhat exceed objective exposure duration (see Sperling, 1967, fig. 3a). So it seems that C can reasonably be interpreted as the duration of the icon. The fact that the icon durations found agree well with icon durations found with other methods, suggests that equation (4) not only provides a good description of the data over the range of exposure durations used in the present experiment, but also of what happens immediately after the exposure of the stimulus.

In order to show that equation (4) can also be used to describe the results of other whole report experiments, two sets of functions are presented in Figure 1.2. The starting point for generating these functions was equation (6) in Appendix A, which, given that X = 0 if t = 0, has the solution

$$X = \frac{\beta}{\alpha}(1 - e^{-\alpha t}).$$

For ease of comparison, values of 5 and 10 for β/α were chosen for the two sets. In the first set, the (β, α) pairs chosen were (10,2), (5,1), (2.5, .5), (1.25, .25) and (.625, .125). For the second set the values were (10, 1), (5, .5), (2.5, .25), (1.25, .125) and (.625, .0625). The first set is drawn with solid lines, the second with dashed lines. For each set the topcurves represent the functions with the highest value for β, and the lowest curves represent the functions with the smallest value for β. These functions give some idea about: (1) the effects of covarying β

and α while keeping the ratio, β/α, constant (thus the effects in set 1 or in set 2); (2) the effect of a change in α when β is fixed, that is, [(10, 1) and (10, 2)], [(5, .5) and (5, 1)], and so on, or, the upper dashed curve and the upper solid curve, the second dashed curve and the second solid curve, and so on; and finally (3) the effect of a change in β when α is fixed, that is, [(10, 1) and (5, 1)], [(5, .5) and (2.5, .5)] and so on, or, the upper dashed curve and the second solid curve, and the second dashed and the third solid curve. The value of t in Figure 1.2 is given in units of 100 msec. The X axis is numbered twice. The first numbering, 0 to 15, is the time scale for whole report experiments with patterned post-exposure fields. The t values represent exposure time prior to the occurrence of the patterned post-exposure field, and it is assumed that this field immediately stops processing the stimulus. The second numbering, 0 to 12, is for whole report experiments with homogeneous post-exposure fields, where processing from the icon contributes to the number of elements processed. The icon duration is arbitrarily fixed at 300 msec.

It is interesting to compare this figure with a number of results from whole report experiments in the literature: Sperling (1960), fig. 4; Mackworth (1963a), fig. 2 (also reproduced in Broadbent, 1971, p. 173); Sperling (1963), fig. 5; Raymond and Glanzer (1967), fig. 1; Sperling (1967), fig. 3b; Allport (1968), fig. 1; Mewhort et al. (1969), fig. 1; Coltheart (1972), fig. 3; and Merikle and Glick (1976), fig. 3. Such a comparison suggests that if suitable parameters are chosen equation 4 is capable of describing the results. In Appendix B it is furthermore illustrated how equations (1) and (4) can be used for describing the increase in probability of letters reported correctly as a function of exposure duration for the individual locations in a display.

Equation (4) was based on the observation that

$$\Delta X = -aX + b. \tag{1}$$

The values of 'a' (.4025, .4025 and .4190) and the values of 'b' (2.699, 2.596, and 2.795) for the patterned post-exposure field, uncorrected and corrected for guessing and for the homogeneous post-exposure field respectively, appeared to be nearly identical. These values can be considered estimates of the parameters of a process that is identical for the two exposure conditions. An obvious interpretation of (1) is that during each interval of time, ΔT, b elements are processed, while during the same interval of time a number of elements already identified, aX, cannot be retrieved from memory. As far as equation (1) is concerned, such a disappearance from memory can be conceptualized in at least two ways: (1) as decay of elements in memory, and (2) as displacement

23

of elements in memory by newly arriving elements.

In the first interpretation, aX indicates that in each interval of time, ΔT, all elements already in memory have a probability 'a' of disappearing. This is a 'geometric' decay function with parameter a. In the continuous representation, that is for $\lim_{\Delta T \to 0}$, this becomes an 'exponential' decay function.

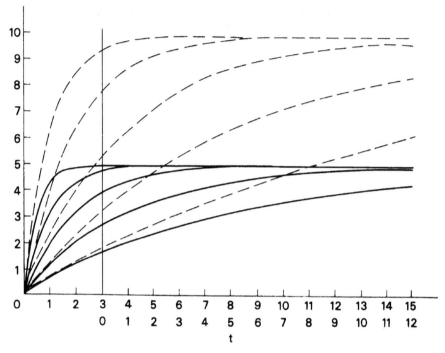

Figure 1.2 *Two sets of functions of the type $X = \beta/\alpha\,(1 - e^{-\alpha t})$. Broken lines approach the limit $\beta/\alpha = 10$; solid lines approach the limit $\beta/\alpha = 5$. t is in units of 100 msec. Upper time-scale for whole report experiments with patterned post-exposure fields; lower time-scale for homogeneous post-exposure fields (for further explanation see text)*

With the second interpretation, a memory with a limited number of places or slots is postulated. The processed elements apply for one of the slots, chosen at random. Should that place be empty, the element is placed in memory. If that place is already occupied by an element processed earlier, the new element replaces the old. If there are N places in memory, and no elements are stored, the probability that an element will enter equals N/N and the expected increase equals N/N x 1. When one element is in store, the probability that an element will enter without replacing an element already in store, equals $^{N-1}/N$, and the

24

expected increase is $N-1/N$. When two elements are in store, the expected increase is $N-2/N$ and so on. Making ΔT equal the processing time of one element, the relation between X and ΔX (X and ΔX as defined earlier) is given by

$$\Delta X = -\frac{1}{N} X + 1$$

and this is equation (1).

Of course, it is not necessary to assume that newly arriving elements displace old ones (A). The same relation is obtained if it is assumed that elements already in store prevent newly arriving elements, applying for the same place, from entering (B). Also a mixture of mechanisms, A and B, results in the same equation.

These two interpretations strongly remind one of two theories on forgetting in short-term memory. The first interpretation is reminiscent of the decay theory of forgetting in short-term memory (STM) (Brown, 1958, 1964). The second is in accord with a displacement theory (Waugh and Norman, 1965). For a review see Kintsch (1970).

The value b/a can be interpreted as the limit of the capacity of the memory in which the processed elements are stored. In the decay interpretation, this limit depends upon the rate of processing the elements, b, and on the rate of forgetting, a. With the 'place' interpretation, the value of b/a is an estimate of the number of slots in this memory. The values obtained were respectively 6.7046 and 6.4499 for the patterned post-exposure field, for uncorrected and corrected data, and 6.6689 for the homogeneous post-exposure field. These values also remind one strongly of Miller's (1956) estimate of the span of immediate memory: 7 plus or minus 2.

A problem with these interpretations is, that recent developments in research on STM have rendered a 'slot-notion', operating on either decay or displacement, very unlikely. The traditional types of tests on STM appear to be much more liable to associative interference than was originally anticipated. Moreover, the STM capacity is very dependent on the content of the presented material which cannot be accounted for by any slot model (Sanders, 1975). Yet, an associative STM theory arrives at the same predictions with respect to the rate of increase and the limits of the memory span, at least when the presented material belongs to a homogeneous class (as was always the case throughout our discussion).

As already stated, in this interpretation of equation (1) parameter b reflects the processing of the elements. Chapter 2 is devoted to a discussion of how this parameter has to be interpreted given that it indeed reflects the processing of the elements. For the moment we assume that the elements are processed at a constant rate of b elements per unit time.

One advantage of the interpretation forwarded here seems to be that it presents only a minor change in the usual interpretation of the results of whole report experiments. The important assumption of a linear increase in number of elements processed with increasing processing times (cf. for example Broadbent, 1971, p. 173) is maintained. The new feature added in this interpretation is that 'forgetting' is assumed to occur during the whole range of exposure durations.

In summary, we propose the following tentative model.

1 During exposure and for a short time after exposure of the stimulus, the elements on the stimulus card are processed at a constant rate of b elements per unit of time. (The value, b, will vary between experiments because of the exposure conditions, the kinds of elements used, and so on.)

2 During the processing of the elements, in each unit of time, a constant proportion (a) of the elements already processed (X), disappears from, or cannot be retrieved from memory.

3 This memory is tentatively identified as 'short-term memory'. As already stated, STM conceptualizations are rapidly changing as a result of recent research and a strict definition cannot be given at the present moment. As a preliminary starting point, we take Sperling's (1970) point of view with regard to STM: 'There is now fairly widespread agreement ... that short-term memory is short-term not because its neurons remember poorly (although that is probably a factor) but because every new stimulus overwrites its predecessor or at least pushes it away from the fore of memory' (Sperling, 1970, p. 201).

This model will be taken as a preliminary starting point for further investigations of visual information processing in chapters 2 and 3. (In Appendix C a number of alternative interpretations of equation (1) is given that at least cannot be ruled out given the evidence presented in this chapter.)

A point in favour of the model proposed here is, that it is more parsimonious than most other models proposed up to now (Sperling, 1963, 1967; Mackworth, 1962; Coltheart, 1972). First, this model applies equally well for whole report experiments with patterned post-exposure fields (where masking with visual 'noise' takes place), and whole report experiments with homogeneous post-exposure fields. Second, this model can apply to the whole range of exposure durations. (This means that there is no need for postulating different processes for different sets of exposure durations.) Of course, it was known for a long time that information is forgotten in whole report tasks. Sperling (1960) invented the 'partial report' method to circumvent memory limitations. However, he subsequently interpreted the loss of information as the decay of the icon. In order to circumvent memory limitations, Estes and Taylor (1964, 1966) developed a 'detection method' for estimating the amount of information a subject has processed. They found that for a 50 msec exposure duration the estimated number of elements processed was about twice the number of elements reported under comparable conditions in whole report experiments. This method will be further discussed in chapter 2.

Returning to the 'span hypothesis' and the 'processing time hypothesis', the data of the present experiment show that both hypotheses apply. With sufficient exposure time the short-term memory limit is reached and the 'span hypothesis' applies. From the literature it appears that this limit is not a fixed value. Mackworth (1963a), for instance, shows that the limit depends upon the kind of material used: digits, letters, colours or forms. Mewhort et al. (1969) show that the degree of familiarity of letter sequences has a strong influence on the limit ultimately reached. With shorter exposure times, the balance between processing and forgetting is not yet reached and the number of elements reported depends upon the exposure time, that is, the 'processing time hypothesis' applies. (The invariance of number of elements reported with varied exposure times as found by Sperling (1960) probably resulted from the small number of elements presented and from a sequence of exposure durations that did not encourage fixation shifts.)

The most important implication of the interpretation of the present experiment, however, concerns the selection of information for report. Most current models of short-term visual information processing postulate only a processing mechanism. This leaves, of course, only one selection mechanism: selective processing. The model here proposed contains both processing and forgetting. In principle, this results in two possible selection mechanisms: selective processing and selective forgetting or remembering. From this point of view it is therefore worthwhile to have a closer look at the parameters, a and b, from $\Delta X = -aX + b$.

27

Appendix A

The function relating X to t

The linear difference equation

$$\Delta X = -aX + b \tag{1}$$

can be rewritten as

$$X_{i+1} = (1-a)X_i + b. \tag{2}$$

The general solution for this equation is

$$X = \frac{b}{a} - q(1-a)^t \tag{3}$$

$$= \frac{b}{a}\left(1 - \left(\frac{aq}{b}\right)(1-a)^t\right)$$

$$= \frac{b}{a}\left(1 - e^{t.\ln(1-a) + \ln aq - \ln b}\right)$$

$$= \frac{b}{a}\left(1 - e^{\ln(1-a)(t + (\ln aq - \ln b)/\ln(1-a))}\right)$$

which could be written as

$$X = \frac{b}{a}\left(1 - e^{-\alpha(t+c)}\right) \tag{4}$$

with $-\alpha = \ln(1-a)$

$$C = (\ln \frac{aq}{b})/\ln(1-a).$$

For small values of a, equation (1) can be solved as the differential equation

$$\frac{dx}{dt} = -aX + b. \tag{6}$$

This differential equation has the solution

$$X = \frac{b}{a}(e^{-a(t+c)}) \tag{7}$$

given that $X = 0$ for $t + C = 0$.

A comparison of equations (4) and (7) shows, that the latter procedure is justified only if $-a \approx -\alpha = \ln(1-a)$, and this is true only if a is very small.

Appendix B

The increase in probability of letters reported correctly as a function of exposure duration for the individual locations in a display

Here we will show that equations (1) and (4) can also be used for describing the increase in probability of letters reported correctly as a function of exposure duration for each location in the display separately.

For each location in the display we can represent the increase in probability of being in the state 'processed' or in the state 'retrievable from STM' for the element in that location (ΔP_i) per unit of time (Δt) with

$$\frac{\Delta P_i}{\Delta T} = -a_i P_i + b_i; \, b_i \leqslant a_i.$$

In this equation b_i reflects the probability of finishing processing during Δt for the element in location i, and a_i the probability for that element of returning to the state 'unprocessed' or 'irretrievable from STM'.

From the assumption that all elements are ultimately processed, that is,

$$\lim_{t \to \infty} \Delta P_i = 0 \text{ and } \lim_{t \to \infty} P_i = 1$$

it follows that $a_i = b_i$.

From the continuous representation

$$\frac{dP_i}{dt} = -\beta_i P_i + \beta_i$$

follows, given $P_i = 0$ for $t = 0$

$$P_i = (1 - e^{-\beta_i t}).$$

Figure 1.3 gives a set of five 'growth curves' for individual locations with β parameters respectively $1; .3; .1; .05; .03$. These curves can be compared with the curves in Figure 3c from Sperling (1967). (Cf. also Sperling, 1970, p. 206, Fig. 3c.)

From a set of curves like those in Figure 1.3, Sperling (1967) concluded: 'The observation that all locations begin to be reported at better than chance levels even at the briefest exposures, may be interpreted as evidence of an essentially parallel process for letter recognition.' To this issue of parallel vs serial processing we will return in chapter 2. In chapter 7 we will return to Sperling's interpretation of this pattern of increase in accuracy of report for individual locations.

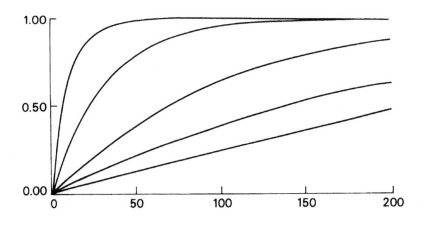

Figure 1.3 *Predicted probability of being correctly reported for individual locations: predictions generated from $P_i = (1 - e^{-\beta_i t})$ for β values 1, .3, .1, .05, and .03 (for further explanation see text)*

Appendix C

Alternative interpretations

I A number of alternative interpretations easily follows if equation (1) is rewritten. Three possibilities will be considered.

(a)

$$\frac{\Delta X}{\Delta T} = -aX + b \tag{1}$$

$$= -aX + (a\delta + b') \; ; X \geqslant \delta$$
$$= -a(X - \delta) + b' \; ; X \geqslant \delta \tag{8}$$

The interpretation of this equation is the same as the interpretation forwarded for equation (1), except that this equation states that a number of elements already identified, δ, for instance the first δ elements identified or the last δ elements identified, is not subject to forgetting.

(b)

$$\frac{\Delta X}{\Delta T} = -aX + b \tag{1}$$

$$= \frac{a}{a}(-aX + b)$$

30

$$= a \left(\frac{b}{a} - X\right)$$

$$= a (L - X) \tag{9}$$

This equation suggests a completely different information processing model. X equals again the number of elements already identified. L can be conceived of as the limit of the memory that has to hold the names of the identified elements. In this equation 'a' is the processing parameter. According to this interpretation, the rate of processing the elements depends on the number of elements already identified and on the capacity of the memory, and decreases if the number of elements identified increases. With this interpretation no forgetting of identified information is assumed to occur.

(c) Also a combination of the interpretations given under (a) and (b) is possible. It is conceivable that for information processing within a fixation the interpretation given under b gives an adequate account of what happens, while over a series of fixations the interpretation given under (a) is more adequate. In other words, it is conceivable that no forgetting takes place of the elements identified during the last fixation, while elements identified during previous fixations are subject to forgetting. With this interpretation equation (8) reduces to equation (1), (that is, $\delta = 0$) if ΔT equals the duration of a fixation. For arbitrarily fixed values of $\Delta T, \delta \neq 0$.

II A reformulation of the interpretations given leads to a completely different group of interpretations. Up to now the parameters b, b' and a in equations 1, 8 and 9 respectively, were interpreted as 'processing' parameters, i.e. parameters reflecting the rate of identifying the elements. This interpretation is in line with Broadbent's (1958, 1971) filter concept (cf., for example, Broadbent, 1971, p. 173). More in line with Deutsch and Deutsch's (1963) position, these parameters can also be interpreted as reflecting the selection of already identified information for storage in a more endurable memory. Recently, Schneider and Shiffrin (1977) and Shiffrin and Schneider (1977) made a strong case for this kind of interpretation.

2 The processing of multi-element visual displays

Summary

In this chapter it is investigated whether parameter b in the two process model discussed in chapter 1 has to be interpreted as reflecting 'a subsequent serial process which can extract one item after another from the buffer' (Broadbent, 1971, p. 173). In other words, the capacity of a 'processor' engaged in identifying the elements is investigated. This capacity issue is of great theoretical importance. If the processor has a limited capacity (LC), then it is worthwhile to look for mechanisms that try to ensure that this capacity is used in an optimal way (Broadbent's position). If the processor has an unlimited capacity (UC), then there is no need for such mechanisms. It is then more worthwhile to investigate how from among the identified information relevant information is selected for further activities (Deutsch and Deutsch's position).

The first topic discussed concerns the identifiability of serial vs parallel and LC vs UC processing systems. It is argued that special tasks have to be used and that a number of precautions have to be taken in order to give the processor a fair opportunity to show his capabilities. An experiment, intended to provide these opportunities, is described. The results seem equivocal with regard to the LC vs UC issue: one subset of the data indicates UC processing, another subset LC processing. It is, however, likely that this appearance of LC processing is caused by response competition in a processing stage after the identification of the elements. It is therefore tentatively concluded that this task shows the activities of a UC processor.

As stated, only special tasks can be used for investigating the activities of the processor. Therefore, the problem remains whether the processor performs the same job in these tasks and in other visual information processing tasks such as whole report tasks. No firm conclusion can be reached, but recent evidence indicates that also in the latter type of tasks there are no limitations as far as the identification of visual information is concerned, and that, given adequate exposure conditions, the identification of visual information cannot be prevented.

Two tentative conclusions, both in line with Deutsch and Deutsch's position, are given:

(a) there is a real possibility that in experiments intended to show the temporal characteristics of the processing mechanism, subsequent operations performed upon already identified information are mistakenly taken as time consuming operations of the processor.

(b) There is growing and converging evidence that the processing mechanism operates in parallel over all elements presented and that it has unlimited processing capacity.

Because it is likely that there are no capacity limitations as far as the identification of visual information is concerned, there seems no need for 'early selection' or 'precategorical selection' within one fixation. Chapter 3 will be devoted to a critical discussion of some evidence generally put forward in favour of precategorical selection.

In whole report experiments, the increase in the number of elements reported (ΔX) per unit exposure time (ΔT) can be described with

$$\frac{\Delta X}{\Delta T} = -aX + b.$$

This equation can be considered a model for visual information processing in this type of task. The parameter 'a' can be interpreted as a 'forgetting parameter' and 'b' as a 'processing parameter'. Interpreted in this way, the equation also suggests two possible mechanisms for selecting information:

1 early selection, precategorical selection or selection of unidentified information for identification (connected with parameter 'b').

2 Late selection, postcategorical selection, selective remembering or selection of identified information for further activities (connected with parameter 'a').

In the recent literature these two types of selection have been strongly connected with certain assumptions about the way in which visual information is processed. In order to introduce this topic, we first assume that somewhere in the chain of activities between stimulus registration and response execution, there is a subsystem, the processor, engaged in identifying the elements. As the unit of analysis for the processor we take the element (that is, a letter, a digit, etc.), and not the features of the elements (cf., for example, Neisser (1967), Rumelhart (1970) and Townsend (1972) for models incorporating both the processing of features and of the elements).

Now the general problem of how a number of discrete elements, presented during a brief exposure, are processed, can be subdivided by asking a number of independent specific questions. (See Townsend, 1974, for an insightful discussion.) In connection with the problem of the locus of the selective mechanism, the most important issue is limited capacity (LC) vs unlimited capacity (UC) processing. The processor might either be limited in the number of elements it can handle per unit of time or it may have sufficient independent processing channels so that all elements presented are processed simultaneously without delays or interference. With LC processing, a further question is that of serial vs parallel processing, that is, the problem whether the processor works on one element at a time in sequence, devoting its full capacity to that particular element, or whether it starts processing on all elements together, spreading its capacity over the elements not yet processed (the elements possibly finishing processing at different times).

Early selection, or processing restricted to stimulus elements that appear relevant as revealed by some kind of preliminary analysis, is strongly connected with LC processing, and is indeed the most efficient strategy for a system with LC (cf. Broadbent, 1971, p. 9). In particular, one special case of LC processing, serial processing, has been strongly connected with early selection. Two quotations will make this clear: 'Selective attention may be conceived as the programming by the O (observer) of which stimuli will be processed or encoded and in what order this will occur' (Eriksen and Hoffman, 1972b, p. 169), and 'It is reasonable that a serial system can predetermine processing order ... but the order of processing evolves by chance in probabilistic parallel systems' (Townsend, 1974, p. 145). Also Broadbent's (1958, 1971), Sperling's (1963) and Neisser's (1967) information processing models are characterized by serial processing and early selection. However, LC parallel processing models combined with early selection have been proposed also. In these models, 'a changing rate of acquisition at different locations', some kind of 'zooming in', or 'narrowing of attention' is assumed (cf., for example, Sperling, 1967; Eriksen and Spencer, 1969; Rumelhart, 1970).

Late selection theories have generally assumed UC processing up to the level of identification. Only a system with UC processing can afford, without loss of efficiency, to process also irrelevant stimulus elements and select information for further activities after complete identification. Deutsch and Deutsch (1963) and Norman (1968) proposed general information processing models having this characteristic. Gardner (1973) among others proposes such a model for visual information processing tasks. In his model, each element presented is processed in a separate channel. In his opinion, the operation of the whole system often gives the appearance of LC processing because of inadequately controlled experimental factors and because of errors made by the Ss. Indeed, Gardner (1973) and Estes (1974) have convincingly shown, that if LC processing is found, it is necessary to further investigate whether artefacts have given rise to it. To this issue we will return on page 37.

Given this connection between processing capacity and locus of the selective mechanism, it seems worthwhile to further investigate the processing mechanism in order to assess its spatio-temporal characteristics.

Now we can start our investigation of the processing mechanism by decomposing

$$\frac{\Delta X}{\Delta T} = -aX + b.$$

From our interpretation of this equation it follows that the increase in the number of elements processed (ΔY) per unit of exposure time (ΔT) is constant, that is,

$$\frac{\Delta Y}{\Delta T} = b$$

where b can be interpreted as the capacity of the processing system per unit of time. From the continuous case follows the differential equation

$$\frac{dy}{dt} = \beta$$

which has as solution, given $Y = 0$ for $t + c = 0$;

$$Y = \beta (t + c)$$

where $t + c$ is the effective processing time, that is, exposure duration (t) plus icon duration (c). The last equation states that the number of elements processed, Y, is a linear increasing function of effective processing time, with a constant rate of increase, β.

In the recent past, such a linear relation was typically taken as evidence for serial processing (cf., for example, Sperling, 1963; Mackworth, 1962; Broadbent, 1971, p. 183). This linear relation, or the constant rate of change, is, however, consistent with a great number of LC probabilistic information processing models, the three most interesting being (1) a serial model, (2) a parallel model, and (3) a mixed model with partly serial and partly parallel processing. (Also, Rumelhart's (1970) LC processing model is capable of acting in these ways.)

In all these probabilistic information processing models, it is assumed that during any small time interval $\Delta t = h$ each element in the processor has a probability of $\frac{ph}{S}$ of finishing processing where S is the number of elements in the processor, while h is furthermore sufficiently small that it is reasonable to assume that there will be either one or no element that ends processing during h. The rate of change then equals the probability of finishing processing, $\frac{ph}{S}$, times the number of elements in the processor, S. So the rate of change equals $\frac{ph}{S}$. S = ph, and is constant and independent of the number of elements in the processor.

(a) LC serial processing. $S = 1$. The probability of finishing processing equals ph. The rate of change equals ph. This model can be thought of as if the total processing capacity of the processor is devoted to the one element in the processor, giving a probability ph of finishing processing.

(b) LC parallel processing. $S = N - X$, $X = 0, 1, 2, \ldots N$; where N is the total number of elements presented, X the number of elements already processed. The probability of finishing processing for each element in the processor equals $\frac{ph}{(N-X)}$. The rate of change equals $(N-X) \frac{ph}{(N-X)} = ph$. This system can be conceived of as dividing its total processing capacity over the elements not yet processed, $(N-X)$, the processing capacity being redistributed each time an element finishes processing, resulting in a probability of finishing processing of $\frac{ph}{(N-X)}$. This LC parallel processing model was first suggested by Atkinson et al. (1969). Townsend (1972) has worked out the precise conditions under which this model completely 'mimics' the LC Serial processing model in all parameters.

(c) LC mixed models. $S = S_1, S_2, \ldots S_i \subset N - X$. For S_1 the probability for each element in the processor of finishing processing equals $\frac{ph}{(S_1-X)}$; the rate of change equals $\frac{ph}{(S_1-X)} (S_1-X) = ph$. For S_2 the probability of finishing processing equals $\frac{ph}{S_2-(X-S_1)}$; the rate of change $\frac{ph}{S_2-(X-S_1)} S_2-(X-S_1) = ph$, etc.

This system can be thought of as dividing its processing capacity over a subset of the elements, and, after finishing processing this subset, over a second subset, etc. Processing of the subsets takes place as in the parallel processing model. When the subsets contain only 1 element, and when $S_1 = N$, this model reduces to the serial and the parallel processing model respectively. This model is particularly interesting because with extended exposures, the eyes jump to different positions of the visual scene a number of times each second. It can be thought that with each fixation a fresh batch of unprocessed elements is delivered to the processor. Only with very brief exposures (less than

200 msec) are these fixation shifts precluded.

So, a linear relation between the number of elements processed and the effective processing time (or between the number of elements to be processed and the processing time as found by Neisser, 1964; Atkinson et al., 1969; and Sternberg, 1967) cannot be used to decide between parallel, serial or mixed LC models. But the situation is even worse. A linear relation cannot even be used to choose between LC processing (parallel, serial or mixed) on the one hand, and UC processing on the other hand.

The essential characteristic of UC processing is that there are sufficient, independent (that is, not sharing a common capacity pool) parallel processing channels, and each element to be processed can, in principle, be allotted to a separate processing channel. It is, however, possible, as Gardner (1973) suggests, that in most experiments the UC processor appears as a LC processor, this as a result of factors having nothing to do with a limited and shared capacity of the processor. We will consider some of these factors in turn.

First, with brief exposures, excluding fixation shifts, factors such as (1) the differential visual acuity for the different points on the retina, and (2) the differential effects of lateral masking or mutual interference for different points on the retina, can make an UC processor appear as a LC processor (cf. Eriksen and Spencer, 1969; Estes, 1972; Gardner, 1973; Van der Heijden and Menckenberg, 1974).

Second, with extended exposures, the saccadic eye movements and the fixation pauses introduce a serial component, resulting in an impression of LC processing (cf. Sperling et al., 1971).

Furthermore, it is possible that in whole report tasks, the elements are identified in independent parallel channels, but that the results of this processing enter short-term memory serially (see Wolford et al., 1968, p. 144, and Gardner, 1973, p. 132, for this suggestion). We have already introduced this point of view in chapter 1, Appendix C, under II.

These considerations, and the fact that the processing parameter b can be isolated from $\frac{\Delta X}{\Delta T} = -aX + b$ only in theory, make it clear that whole report tasks are not suited for investigating the spatio-temporal characteristics of the processor.

What is needed is a paradigm that (1) allows a pure look at processing of visual information, uncontaminated by forgetting of processed elements; (2) does not involve a serial loading of items in short-term memory; (3) allows for a sufficient control of visual acuity and lateral masking effects; (4) is restricted to a single fixation. A promising paradigm is the 'detection paradigm' or 'detection-type visual span of apprehension experiment', that was developed by Estes and Taylor (1964, 1966), in order to determine the number of elements that can be processed in a brief tachistoscopic exposure.

On a trial, the subject is briefly shown in a tachistoscope a display containing a matrix of letters. Two letters are designated as 'critical elements' (B and F for instance) the other letters as 'noise'. Each display contains exactly one of the critical elements. The task for the subject is to indicate, that is, to make a forced choice, which of the two critical elements was present. The number of elements processed can be estimated from the proportion of correct choices, corrected for guessing. Estes and Wessel (1966) extended the paradigm by introducing reaction time (RT) as a second dependent variable, beside the proportion of correct responses. The basic assumption underlying the use of RT as a dependent variable is that under carefully selected conditions RT reflects the temporal characteristics of the processor (see, for example, Sternberg, 1969).

However, if the chosen experimental conditions result in a high proportion of errors (8, 12 and 16 elements during 50 msec and 1, 4 and 8 elements during 1 msec (Estes and Wessel, 1966); 16 and 25 elements during 50 msec (Wolford et al., 1968)), the interpretation of RT becomes very difficult. The latencies have to be corrected in order to estimate latencies on true detection trials and definite conclusions about processing times are impossible.

This was the prime reason for Atkinson et al. (1969) to modify the detection paradigm in what may be called a 'high accuracy brief visual display search task'. Linear arrays from one to five letters were presented to the subjects during 400 msec. Before the stimulus exposure a target letter was shown. 50 per cent of the arrays contained the target, 50 per cent did not. Subjects had to indicate as rapidly as possible whether or not a target was present without making errors, that is, the forced choice detection task was changed to a yes-no detection task allowing comparison between positive and negative responses.

For positive (target present) and negative (target absent) responses, linear relations between RT and the number of elements presented, with about the same slope, were found. Atkinson et al. (1969) concluded that a serial exhaustive and a parallel exhaustive processing model could account for these results. In fact, these are the same serial and parallel processing models as described earlier under (a) and (b). (The issue of self-terminating vs exhaustive processing will not be further dealt with. For the tasks discussed in this chapter, it seems reasonable to assume that processing is self-terminating, or, that subjects initiate a response on the moment that sufficient elements for an adequate response have been processed (cf., for example, Kinsbourne and Innis, 1972; Townsend, 1974; Van der Heijden and Menckenberg, 1974; Holmgren et al., 1974; Van der Heijden, 1975, for further information on this issue).) The Atkinson et al. (1969) experiment was replicated by Townsend and Roos (1973) with essentially the same results.

On three points these experiments do not fulfil the requirements for UC processing to show up.

First, with exposure durations of 400 msec, fixation shifts are possible. Probably this factor was of minor importance, because array sizes were small, and therefore fixation shifts were not necessary. Furthermore, Atkinson et al. (1969) show data of a comparable experiment in which a 150 msec exposure duration was used. These data showed the same linear increase. However, only with exposure times less than 200 msec can no refixations occur.

Second, when the display size of linear arrays is varied from one to five, the overall visual angle increases. The elements of large display sizes then fall on retinal locations that are on the average less sensitive than the locations stimulated by small arrays. This probably results in increased processing times with an increasing number of elements (cf., for example, Van der Heijden and Menckenberg, 1974). With circular arrangements of the elements the distance from the fovea can be kept constant with varying number of elements presented.

Third, the letters in the array were closely spaced. Bouma (1970) showed that recognition of letters is impaired when there are adjacent letters, this effect increasing with the distance from the fovea. He concludes: 'For complete visual isolation of a letter presented at an eccentricity of $\gamma°$, it follows that no other letters should be present within $0.5\gamma°$ distance' (p. 178). This decrease in identifiability is probably accompanied by an increase in processing time (see Van der Heijden and Menckenberg, 1974). (For further evidence on mutual interference see among others, Townsend et al., 1971; Estes and Wolford, 1971; Banks et al., 1977.)

In order to investigate the LC vs UC issue and the parallel vs serial processing issue, an experiment was carried out in which a modified and simplified 'high accuracy brief visual display search task' was used.*

* This experiment was earlier reported in 'Acta Psychologica', 1975, 39, 21-42, under the title Some evidence for a limited capacity parallel selfterminating process in simple visual search tasks. For further details the reader is referred to this article.

In the experiment the letters E and F were used. 'E' was defined as the target, or 'signal', 'F' as noise. Stimuli with one, two, or three letters were used. The number of signals for a display of given size varied from 'all signals' to 'no signals'. (The different types of stimulus cards will be represented with (x, y), where x denotes the number of signals on the card, and y the total number of letters.) Subjects had to respond 'yes' as fast as possible when one or more signals were in the display, 'no' otherwise. Because of the small memory load imposed with this task, retention loss can only be a factor of minor importance. The letters were placed on the circumference of an imaginary circle, so that with varying numbers of elements presented, the distance of each element from the fixation point remained constant.

The elements were sufficiently spaced to exclude mutual interference or lateral masking (see Bouma, 1970).

To exclude eye movements during a stimulus presentation an exposure duration of 150 msec was used.

We attempted to ensure high accuracy of responding by creating conditions in which errorless performance was possible (maximal three elements presented, high contrast between letters and background, circular arrangements around the fixation point, 150 msec exposure duration). A pilot experiment showed that all Ss could name the elements under these conditions. If the processor has UC and sufficient parallel independent processing channels, but appears in most experiments as a LC parallel processor or as a serial processor as a result of artefacts, the conditions of this experiment should be adequate for UC parallel processing to show up.

The specific predictions for LC and UC processing will be derived, assuming exponentially distributed processing times. (Other distributions possessing non-zero variance lead to comparable predictions (see Townsend, 1972, p. 174, for reasons using exponentially distributed processing times).) Because under LC processing, parallel and serial processing models predict the same results under a fairly wide range of conditions (see Townsend, 1972), we can derive predictions for LC processing from a serial processing model. It is assumed that the mean processing time for each element equals the mean of an exponentially distributed random variable with parameter α

$$E(t_1) = {}_0\!\int^\infty t\, f\,(t)\, dt = {}_0\!\int^\infty t\alpha e^{-\alpha t}\, dt = \frac{1}{\alpha}.$$

The predictions for serial processing (LC processing) can be contrasted with predictions for UC processing, derived from an independent channels parallel processing model. In this model it is assumed that all elements are processed in separate and independent channels and that the processing times for the channels are identical, exponentially distributed, random variables, with parameter β. The mean processing time per channel so equals $1/\beta$. The mean processing time of the fastest of two simultaneously processed elements equals

$$E(t_2) = 2\int_0^\infty tf(t)\,[1-F(t)]\ dt = \int_0^\infty 2\beta te^{-\beta t}[e^{-\beta t}]\ dt = 1/2\beta.$$

The mean processing time of the fastest of three simultaneously processed elements equals

$$E(t_3) = 3\int_0^\infty tf(t)\,[1-F(t)]^2 dt = \int_0^\infty 3\beta te^{-\beta t}\,[e^{-\beta t}]^2\ dt = 1/3\beta.$$

The most important comparison is between conditions $(1, 1)$, $(2, 2)$, and $(3, 3)$, i.e., the conditions restricted to signals only (E, EE, EEE).

For LC processing, the expected processing times equal the time to process one element under serial processing, that is, $1/\alpha$, $1/\alpha$, $1/\alpha$. For UC processing, the expected processing times equal the mean processing time, the shortest of two, and the shortest of three, respectively, that is, $1/\beta$, $1/2\beta$, $1/3\beta$. So, with LC processing, constant mean RTs, with UC processing, decreasing mean RTs, for these three conditions are predicted.

A second comparison of interest is between $(1, 1)$, $(1, 2)$ and $(1, 3)$, (the stimuli E, EF and EFF).

For LC processing, the expected mean processing times equal the time to process 1, 1.5 and 2 elements under serial processing. This results in mean processing times $1/\alpha$, $3/2\alpha$, $2/\alpha$. For UC processing, the mean processing time equals the mean of the random variable under all three conditions, that is, $1/\beta$, $1/\beta$, $1/\beta$. So with LC processing, increasing mean RTs, with UC processing, constant mean RTs, are predicted.

Method

Apparatus

A Scientific-Prototype two-channel tachistoscope model 800-F-1 was used to present the stimuli. The S was provided with a remote control switch to initiate stimulus exposure himself. The tachistoscope was connected to an electronic timer. The timer started counting when the stimulus appeared, and stopped when the S spoke his response in a voice key. Latencies were recorded, accurate to 1 msec.

Stimulus materials

9½ x 12½ cm stimulus cards were prepared, containing letters in a circular array. Letters were drawn in indian ink. The height of the letters was 0.30° in visual angle. The pre-exposure field consisted of a blank card, containing a fixation point in the centre. The stimulus cards and the blank card appeared at a luminescence of approximately 51 cd/m².

The letters E and F were used as stimulus elements. They were placed on an imaginary circle, 1.5 degrees in visual angle from the fixation point. Six sets of eighteen stimulus cards were prepared. The cards in the first two sets contained an E or an F, each letter appearing on each of three possible places an equal number of times. Cards in the second two sets contained two elements; 50 per cent of these cards contained 2 Fs, 33 per cent an E and an F, 17 per cent 2 Es. Within these three groups all possible combinations of places and elements appeared an equal number of times. Cards in the third two sets contained three elements. 50 per cent of these cards contained zero Es, 17 per cent one E, 17 per cent two Es, and 17 per cent three Es, the Es appearing in all positions and combinations of positions. The remaining places were filled with Fs. The six sets of cards were mixed and presented to each S each day in a different random order. Ss were instructed to respond 'yes' when one or more Es were presented, 'no' when there were only Fs.

Subjects

Three adult staff members of the Psychological Institute at the University of Leiden served as volunteer Ss in the experiment. They all had normal vision or corrected-to-normal vision. All three had previously participated in experiments using the same kind of task and different letters. The Ss were tested over a period of nine days. Each day they were presented with the six sets of stimulus cards.

Procedure

Ss were run individually in a moderately illuminated room. They were instructed to look into the tachistoscope until they saw the fixation point clearly. Then they had to press the remote control switch, whereupon the stimulus card appeared for 150 msec. After the presentation of the stimulus, a dark post-exposure field appeared, lasting 3 sec and then the pre-exposure field containing the fixation point reappeared. Ss were instructed to respond verbally as quickly as possible while maintaining accuracy.

When an error was made, the stimulus was presented again later in the session. The number of errors was counted. Starting with the fourth experimental day also latencies of errors were recorded.

Before each session between ten and twenty practice trials were given. This practice continued until S felt ready for the experimental trials. Each session lasted about 45 minutes.

Results

Figure 2.1 shows the mean RTs over the three Ss per block of three days. In this figure, the line labels 0, 1, 2 and 3, indicate the number of signals per display. The values on the X axes represent the total number of elements presented.

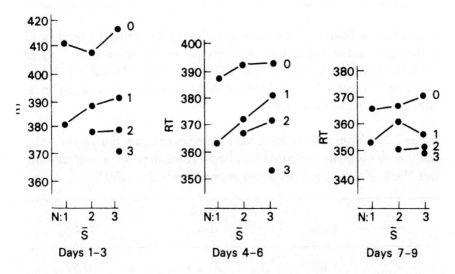

Figure 2.1 *Mean latencies (msec) per block of three days as a function of the number of elements presented. Lines and points are labelled with 0, 1, 2, and 3 to indicate the number of signal elements presented. The numbers 1, 2, and 3 on the x-axes represent the total number of elements presented*

Figure 2.1 shows that when only signal elements are presented, the mean RTs generally decrease when the number of signals increases:

RT(3, 3) < RT(2, 2) < RT(1, 1). (The means are represented by the points furthest left on the lines labelled 1, 2 and 3.) Table 2.1 gives per S and over the three Ss per block of three days the slopes of the linear functions fitted to these points.

Table 2.1 *Slopes for mean correct latencies as a function of the number of elements presented for stimuli containing only signal elements (E, EE, EEE) per block of three days, per S and averaged over Ss ($\bar{S}$)*

| | Days | | |
	1–3	4–6	7–9
S_1	−6.78	1.645	2.46
S_2	−2.66	−7.95	−2.23
S_3	−5.92	−9.31	−5.23
$\bar{S}$	−5.12	−5.18	−1.66

Inspection of Figure 2.1 also shows that mean RTs generally increase as a function of the number of elements presented, when only 1 signal element is presented: RT(1, 1) < RT(1, 2) < RT(1, 3). Table 2.2 gives per S and over the 3 Ss per block of three days, the slopes of the linear functions fitted to these points.

Table 2.2 *Slopes for mean correct latencies as a function of the number of elements presented for stimuli containing one signal element per block of three days, per S and averaged over three Ss ($\bar{S}$)*

| | Days | | |
	1–3	4–6	7–9
S_1	9.00	11.26	−0.57
S_2	1.01	1.66	1.83
S_3	5.42	13.05	3.84
$\bar{S}$	5.14	8.68	1.32

Table 2.3 gives the proportions of errors per condition and per block of three days. Table 2.4 gives the mean latencies for the incorrect responses for the last two blocks of three days. Overall mean correct

and incorrect RTs over conditions equal 375 and 371 msec for days 4–6, and 358 and 358 msec for days 7–9, respectively.

Table 2.3 *Proportion errors over three Ss per block of three days for the nine conditions. The conditions are represented with (x, y) where x denotes the number of signals, y the total number of elements presented. Proportions are in relation to the number of cards per condition*

	Conditions									
Days	(0,1)	(1,1)	(0,2)	(1,2)	(2,2)	(0,3)	(1,3)	(2,3)	(3,3)	total
1–3	.074	.019	.086	.148	.000	.099	.314	.000	.019	.081
4–6	.074	.056	.080	.139	.019	.105	.203	.019	.000	.081
7–9	.117	.062	.062	.213	.019	.148	.240	.093	.019	.109
1–9	.088	.045	.076	.166	.012	.117	.253	.037	.012	

Table 2.4 *Mean RTs for incorrect responses for days 4–6 and 7–9*

	Conditions								
Days	(0,1)	(1,1)	(0,2)	(1,2)	(2,2)	(0,3)	(1,3)	(2,3)	(3,3)
4–6	397	391	365	365	355	377	382	340	—
7–9	351	350	380	357	364	363	371	373	317

Table 2.3 also shows that the proportions of errors (E) follow approximately the same trends as the RTs, that is, $E(3, 3) < E(2, 2) < E(1, 1)$ and $E(1, 1) < E(1, 2) < E(1, 3)$.

Discussion

Contrary to the expectations, this 'high accuracy brief visual display search task' resulted, for some conditions, in an appreciable number of errors. Furthermore, the proportions of errors increase if mean RT increases. Also, the mean error RTs for 'signal only' stimuli decrease with decreasing correct RTs. (Mean error RTs for (1, 1), (2, 2) and (3, 3) are respectively 369, 360 and 317 msec.) First, a consistent interpretation of this pattern of results will be given.

The error data are consistent with 'pure guessing', that is, responding before enough information from the stimulus is obtained. Assume that Ss have a constant or increasing tendency to emit a pure guessing response up to the moment the stimulus is completely processed. Then, in the conditions in which sufficient information for a response can be obtained quickly, there are opportunities for pure guessing during a smaller interval of time than in the conditions with longer mean processing times, resulting in a smaller proportion of guesses. These pure guesses also have to be made earlier, and smaller mean RTs result. Therefore, proportions of errors and mean RTs for incorrect responses as found in the present experiment, can be interpreted as supporting the trends found in mean correct RTs. (A correction for guessing to obtain estimated latencies on true detection trials as suggested by Estes and Wessel (1966, p. 372) resulted only in minor changes in mean RTs, leaving the relation between the RTs for the different conditions essentially the same.)

This interpretation of the error data is at variance with Gardner's (1973) suggestion. In his 'Independent-Channels-Confusion Model' (ICC) an increase in proportion of errors with increasing number of elements presented for the 1 signal condition (in the experiment here reported the error proportions $E(1, 1)$, $E(1, 2)$ and $E(1, 3)$ were, respectively, .045, .166 and .253) is explained by 'noise item — critical alternative confusions plus the decisional structure of the detection task' (p. 146). (See also Eriksen and Spencer, 1969, p. 9; Estes, 1974, for comparable interpretations of error data.)

Therefore, Van der Heijden (1975) fitted Gardner's 'confusion error model' and an 'anticipation error model' (that is, a pure guess model) to the error data of Table 2.3, and showed that the latter model handled the data more adequately. (It also appeared that from the parameters estimated with the 'anticipation error model' the overall pattern of correct RTs for the different conditions and the three blocks of three days could be reconstructed. This at least indicated that this interpretation of the error data is consistent with the pattern of RTs for correct responses obtained in the experiment. For details, see Van der Heijden, 1975, pp. 33-41.)

Probably, the prime reason for this difference in kind of response errors as found by Gardner (1973) and Estes (1974), on the one hand, and those in the experiment here reported, on the other hand, results from the exposure conditions used. As already mentioned, the conditions of the present experiment were such that high accuracy should have been possible. Errors then probably result from Ss response strategies. Gardner (1973), however, starts his experiment with stimulus durations resulting in 80 per cent detection accuracy (the average exposure durations used were about 10 msec). Estes (1974) used linear arrays and an exposure duration of 100 msec. The stimulus was preceded and followed by a mask. It is conceivable that under these conditions 'imperfect perceptual samples' or 'degraded inputs' are available to the processor, and that elements sharing features with a critical element are easily confused with the critical element. (See Egeth et al. (1972, 1973) and Schneider and Shiffrin (1977) for other experiments run under high accuracy conditions in which no apparent effect of confusion errors was found.)

So, it seems that the increasing proportions of errors for E(1, 1), E(1, 2), E(1, 3), and E(3, 3), E(2, 2), and E(1, 1) have to be interpreted as an increasing proportion of anticipations under conditions with increasing mean processing times. Now we can evaluate the predictions concerning UC and LC processing.

According to the processing models outlined previously, the relation RT(3, 3) < RT(2, 2) < RT(1, 1) indicates UC parallel processing. Of course, a LC processing model that increases its speed of processing if the number of elements to be processed is increased, is conceivable, but we agree with Townsend (1972): 'Although this is mathematically unassailable, we do not expect, on the basis of general knowledge of biological and psychological processes, to often discover mechanisms that function in such a manner' (p. 196). So this relation adds to the '... mounting credibility of parallel processing ability in "detection-type visual span of apprehension experiments"' (Townsend, 1972, pp. 195-7; cf. also Egeth et al., 1972, 1973; Gardner, 1973; Estes, 1974; Schneider and Shiffrin, 1977; Shiffrin and Schneider, 1977; Logan, 1976, 1978).

However, this mounting evidence primarily consists of the finding that under suitable chosen experimental conditions RT is invariant with the number of elements presented (N) for displays containing one signal element (Egeth et al., 1972, 1973; Estes, 1972). This is exactly the relation we predicted for the UC parallel processing model: RT(1, 1) = RT(1, 2) = RT(1, 3). Again, a serial system, and therefore a system with LC capable of producing this result, must increase its speed of processing if N increases, and this seems psychologically implausible. In the present experiment, however, the relation RT(1, 1) < RT(1, 2) < RT(1, 3), accompanied by the relation E(1, 1) < E(1, 2) < E(1, 3) was obtained. These relations indicate LC processing, whether serial or parallel.

So, the two relations lead to opposite conclusions. It is therefore necessary to consider whether the appearance of LC processing stems from real capacity limitations in the processor (see Rumelhart, 1970; Kahneman, 1973) or whether this appearance might be due to artefacts. There are at least two possible factors that can have made a UC processor appear as an LC processor in the present experiment.

(a) Although a number of precautions were taken, it remains possible that such an effect is caused by peripheral perceptual limitations resulting from inadequately controlled factors in the present experiment. An explanation of this type can possibly be found in the fact that Bouma's (1970) rule — for complete visual isolation of a letter presented at an eccentricity of γ° no other letters should be present within $0.5\gamma^{\circ}$ distance — applies to identification probabilities. It is possible that processing times keep decreasing over distances greater than $0.5\gamma^{\circ}$. Furthermore, it is possible that the amount of lateral interference and the distance over which it obtains, as reflected in RTs, depends upon the number of features the noise elements share with the targets. Estes (1972) proposed such a model, in which inputs to feature detectors undergo this type of inhibitory interactions, resulting in lower detection probabilities and longer mean RTs (the Interactive Channels Model). Estes (1974) states:

> It is quite possible, and in fact is an assumption of the interactive
> channels model, that lateral inhibitory effects decrease with the
> distance between the letters. Consequently, it is to be expected
> that at sufficiently wide separations of the letters of a display,
> interactive effects would become negligible and performance
> might conform closely to that predicted from independent channels.
> (cf. p. 58)

Bjork and Murray (1977) and Krumhansl (1977) provide further evidence for feature-specific peripheral interference.

(b) It is also possible that the increasing RTs result from interference on a much higher level of processing, that is, the stage of response selection or response programming. In the present experiment the element 'E' is connected with the response 'yes', the element 'F' is, in some way, connected with the response 'no'. If 'Es' and 'Fs' are presented simultaneously and if processing is parallel with UC, the noise letters may increase RTs due to eliciting competing incompatible responses. In most of the experiments in which RT was found invariant with the number of elements presented (Egeth et al., 1972, 1973;

Estes, 1972) there were no responses connected with noise elements. Ss had to indicate which signal was present on a trial (Estes, 1972) or had to respond only if a signal was present (Egeth et al., 1972, 1973). In chapters 3, 4 and 5 substantial evidence for this kind of interference is presented.

This last consideration especially brings us to the conclusion that it is likely that also in the present experiment a UC processor (as indicated by the first relation investigated) appeared as an LC processor (as indicated by the second relation investigated) only as a result of experimental artefacts. We therefore tentatively conclude that the data of this experiment can be accounted for by a UC parallel processing model. (Recently, Eriksen and Schulz, 1979, presented an analysis that strongly supports this conclusion.)

A problem of considerable importance is whether the processing of an element in a detection paradigm in order to classify it as 'signal' or 'noise' is equivalent to processing an element in whole report tasks, in which Ss must identify a character in the sense of being able to name it. Especially in a simple detection task as here reported, it is conceivable that Ss do not process the elements in order to see whether it is an E or an F. Various points of view have been propagated in the recent past. Neisser (1967) suggests, that 'Through prolonged practice, the subjects develop preattentive recognition systems, sensitive to features of the display as a whole, which can signal the presence of a target' (p. 100). According to Neisser's view, real identification of letters requires 'focal attention', synthesizing the letters one at a time. It is also possible that in detection tasks, Ss can effectively turn off analysers which are irrelevant for performance in such a task, but necessary when full identification is required (see Treisman, 1969, for this suggestion). Furthermore, it is conceivable that processing for adequate responding in the detection experiment and processing necessary for full identification occur in parallel, but that the detection response does not reflect processing necessary for full identification. It may be assumed that processing for identification, having nothing to do with the processing for the detection response, is so highly overlearned that it cannot be turned off (see Nickerson, 1972, for this suggestion). It is also possible that in both tasks the same processing takes place, but that this processing can terminate at an earlier stage in the detection task than in a task requiring full identification (cf. Rumelhart, 1970). And finally, it is of course also conceivable that in 'detection type visual span of apprehension tasks', no matter how simple, processing is identical with processing in tasks requiring full identification; Estes and Taylor (1964) developed the detection paradigm on this assumption (see also Wolford et al., 1968; Sperling, 1970; Sperling et al., 1971; Gardner, 1973; Graves, 1976, for this point of view). In his Independent Channels Confusion Model, Gardner (1973), for instance, explicitly states: 'It is assumed that each channel registers its estimate of the identity of the item it is processing by taking on one of ξ different endstates, where ξ is the size of the vocabulary of stimulus items used' (Gardner, 1973, p. 138).

Up to very recently, firm evidence in favour of the point of view that the elements are completely identified in search and detection tasks was sparse, however. Substantial evidence was provided by Graves (1976) in two important experiments. In the first he showed that if, in the detection paradigm, the pair of critical letters was read aloud to the subjects 600 msec after stimulus exposure, the results were about the same as in the standard condition in which the pair was read prior to stimulus exposure. Under both conditions the estimated number of items processed was about twice the full report span. This indicates that in the Estes and Taylor (1964) detection paradigm Ss really identify the elements and that the results of this processing are retained in memory. Graves suggests that the results of processing are retained in visual STM: 'Since identification processing must involve the production of some analyzed-form representation, and since visual STM may be such a representation, the type of hypothesis in which identification processing provides a memory trace, is both plausible and parsimonious' (p. 211).

In the second experiment, Ss had to indicate as well in what position in the display the critical element had been presented. If the two alternatives were read after stimulus exposure, the estimated number of elements processed was approximately the same as the full report span. This strongly suggests that the limiting factor in this task and in whole report tasks is either the processing capacity available for processing identity and location or the storage capacity for maintaining identity and location information of the elements processed. Graves (1976) considers both possibilities and favours the first explanation: a system with a fixed and a limited processing capacity devotes all capacity to the processing of elements in the original detection paradigm, and has to divide the capacity over processing the elements and the locations in this modified detection paradigm and in whole report tasks. However, after what has previously been said about LC and UC processing, this explanation seems unlikely. Furthermore, there is abundant evidence that the simultaneous processing of different dimensions of one input is of UC, that is, occurs in parallel without interference (see, for example, Treisman, 1969; Allport, 1971). The second possibility suggested by Graves (1976) is that visual STM can only encompass or maintain a limited number of positions of the elements and positions processed. This could occur if positional information disappears sooner from visual STM than identity information (for evidence on this point, see Townsend, 1973; Dick, 1974). It is also possible that it is not visual STM that is the limiting factor, but that the results of processing item and position have to be connected into 'identity-position units' and stored in a non-visual STM, limited in capacity or duration. This point of view can be related to Sperling's (1967) model for visual information processing tasks. In that model a 'recognition buffer-memory' converts the visual inputs into 'programs of motor-instructions', and stores these instructions. Execution of the programs constitutes rehearsal, resulting in storage of the information in AIS (auditory information storage, verbal STM) (see also Wolford et al., 1968, p. 444; Sperling, 1970). The 'recognition buffer memory' can be conceived of as an intermediate memory from which the names of the items, connected with positional information, are loaded in verbal STM.

After an impressive series of experiments, also Schneider and Shiffrin (1977) and Shiffrin and Schneider (1977) conclude that in search and detection tasks the elements are completely identified. The next quotation from their 'framework for processing in detection, search and attention tasks' summarizes their point of view.

When a set of inputs is presented (let us suppose for convenience that the inputs are visual) then each begins to undergo automatic processing. The system automatically encodes each stimulus input in a series of stages and activates a series of features in the process. For example, the letter 'M' may first be encoded in features indicating contrast, color, and position; then curvature, convexity, and angles; then a visual letter code and a verbal, acoustic-articulatory code, then the codes 'letter', 'consonant', 'capital'; and finally, perhaps, semantic and conceptual codes like 'followed by "N" ', 'middle of the alphabet', and the like. (We do not necessarily imply that these features are correct or exhaustive; if, say, amplitude components of the spatial-frequency analysis of the inputs prove to be relevant features encoded by the system, the theory we describe would be unchanged in all important respects). What features will become activated depends on the physical nature of the nervous system that was predetermined genetically, the degree and type of prior learning, the physical characteristics of the display (like duration and contrast), and the general context, both that in the environment and that generated in STS by the subject. To the extent that the subject directs the sensory receptor orientation and to the extent that internally generated information can alter the context in STS, the subject will have at least some indirect control over automatic sensory coding.

The automatic processing as described above takes place in parallel for each of the input stimuli. The processing of each stimulus is often independent, except for lateral and temporal interactions at early stages, called masking, and except for learned relationships between items that may affect processing at later stages (if adjacent letters form a word, for example). The various features that are activated are all placed thereby in STS where they reside for a short period before being lost (i.e., before returning to an inactive state in LTS). (Shiffrin and Schneider, 1977, pp. 162-3)

Recently, after a series of ingenious experiments, Logan (1978) arrived at roughly the same conclusions.

However, neither the results reported by Graves (1976) nor the framework provided by Shiffrin and Schneider (1977) answer our question as to whether the processing of an element in order to classify it as 'signal' or 'noise' studied in a detection paradigm, is equivalent to the processing of an element in a whole report task. What their studies seem to suggest is that all elements are processed in parallel, and that, given adequate exposure conditions, complete identification cannot be prevented. On what internal representation the decision 'target present' vs 'target absent' is based remains unclear. In principle, this decision can be based on the representation at any level of processing described in Shiffrin and Schneider's framework. It seems, however, that they imply that in most search and detection tasks 'completely processed letters', elements 'processed to the letter level', or 'complete character encodings' are used for this decision (see Schneider and Shiffrin, 1977, pp. 15-16).

A second issue that remains open is how the decision 'target present' vs 'target absent' is made. Schneider and Shiffrin (1977) and Shiffrin and Schneider (1977) are especially concerned with this problem. They conclude that there are two different ways: automatic detection and controlled search.

Automatic detection operates in parallel and reflects the immediate occurrence of an attention directing response that results from the presentation of a target. It proceeds without stressing the capacity limitations of the system and without subject control. With automatic detection the RTs reflect the time needed for processing the elements up to the level required for triggering the attention directing response.

Our analysis of search and detection tasks presented in this chapter presupposed a mechanism similar to this automatic detection response. Throughout the chapter it was implied that the RTs reflected the processing times. According to Schneider and Shiffrin (1977) such an assumption is, however, only justified, or automatic detection responses occur only if targets are consistently mapped (that is, the targets must be drawn from one set and the noise elements from another set of elements during the whole experiment). Furthermore, automatic detection responses require a fair amount of practice.

The experiment reported in this chapter seems to fulfil the requirements for such an automatic detection response to develop in a short time. Therefore, our conclusion that the results indicated UC parallel processing is in accord with Schneider and Shiffrin's (1977) and Shiffrin and Schneider's (1977) analysis of search and detection tasks.

In a number of experiments discussed in the present chapter, the mapping of targets was inconsistent, and in other experiments discussed a consistent mapping was used, but the amount of training given was too small. Then, according to Schneider and Shiffrin, a controlled search has to be performed. Controlled search usually operates in series. It can be set up quickly and easily, but requires attention. It is controlled by the subjects. In tasks as discussed in the present chapter it consists of a serial comparison process of the representation in memory of the predefined target against the representations in memory of the items in the display. Controlled search terminates if and when a match is found or when all comparisons are made and no match is found.

It must be clear that the notion of controlled search leads to a completely different interpretation of the RTs obtained in experiments in which inconsistent target mappings are used, or, when only low amounts of practice are given. RTs then do not reflect the processing of the information, but the controlled search of information already processed, that is, a further operation performed upon processed information stored in memory. Such an interpretation is more in line with Deutsch and Deutsch's (1963) position, and at least cannot be ruled out. (See also chapter 1, Appendix C.)

The main purpose of the discussion presented in this chapter was to get some ideas about a hypothetical processing mechanism that identifies the elements in multi-element visual displays. It will be clear that no firm conclusions can be reached. Two tentative conclusions seem justified, however.

First, there is a real possibility that in experiments intended to show the characteristics of the processing mechanism, subsequent operations performed upon already identified information are mistakenly taken as time-consuming operations of the processor. Schneider and Shiffrin (1977) and Shiffrin and Schneider (1977) make out a strong case for this point of view.

Second, there is growing and converging evidence that the processing mechanism operates in parallel over all elements presented, and that it has unlimited processing capacity. In a number of experiments designed to investigate the properties of the processing mechanism, the processor shows up as a parallel processor with limited capacity or even as a serial processor as a result of inadequately controlled experimental factors and artefacts (inadequately controlled visual acuity, lateral masking, response competition). Eriksen and Schulz (1979) especially offer strong evidence for response competition in visual search tasks. (See also Estes, 1978, p. 184.)

It will be clear that, given this state of affairs, only conditional statements can be made about parameter b in

$$\frac{\Delta X}{\Delta T} = -aX + b.$$

If the interpretation of this equation we suggested in chapter 1 is correct, then it is likely that parameter b reflects the UC parallel processing of the elements, but gives the impression of LC processing only as a result of artefacts. Parameter b can then be conceived of as a composite of processing rates for individual elements if the exposure duration is limited to one fixation. (Cf. chapter 1, Appendix B.) With extended exposures allowing fixation shifts, parameter b can be conceived of as representing the sequence of activities within fixations, as described under 'LC Mixed Processing Model'.

More in line with Schneider and Shiffrin's (1977) and Shiffrin and Schneider's (1977) analysis and with Deutsch and Deutsch's (1963) position, parameter b can also be interpreted as reflecting the serial selection of already identified information for further operations, for instance, for storage in a more enduring memory (cf. chapter 1, Appendix C). In fact, none of the alternative interpretations discussed in that appendix can be ruled out given the evidence discussed up to now.

One conclusion can be reached, however. Because it is likely that there are no capacity limitations as far as the identification of visual information is concerned, there is no need for early selection or pre-categorical selection within one fixation. Chapter 3 is devoted to a critical discussion of some evidence put forward in favour of early selection or precategorical selection.

3 The selection of information within a fixation

Summary

The topic of this chapter is the central selection of visual information (that is, selection unaided by peripheral adjustments) which results in responses depending upon a small number of elements singled out from among a large number of equally potent stimulus elements or upon one attribute from among a number of equally potent attributes. The problem considered is whether unidentified information is selected for identification (precategorical selection; Broadbent's position), or whether identified information is selected for further activities such as storage in memory or overt responding (postcategorical selection; Deutsch and Deutsch's position).

Two lines of evidence generally put forward in favour of precategorical selection are considered: (a) the evidence from the 'instructional set experiments' (an attribute selection task), (b) the evidence from the 'partial report experiments' (an element selection task). The basic evidence for precategorical selection consists of the finding that the number of correct responses increases if a properly timed selective instruction is given.

In 'modifications' of these two tasks – the 'Stroop test' (a version of the instructional set experiment) and the 'modified visual probe experiments' (a version of the partial report experiment) – strong identity-specific effects of unwanted information are found. In these two tasks Ss have to respond as fast as possible, that is, latency is the main dependent variable. It is generally assumed that in these tasks a postcategorical selection mechanism operates.

We will argue that there are no essential differences between the 'original' tasks and their 'modifications' as far as the processes going on between stimulation and response are concerned. That different selection mechanisms have been postulated for the 'original' tasks and their 'modifications' probably results from the different dependent variables used. The effects of identified unwanted information remain unobserved if the number of correct responses is used but show up as a delay in responding if latencies are used. Postcategorical selection therefore seems to offer the most parsimonious explanation.

The two-process model described in chapter 1 is used to demonstrate that the data found with the partial report experiments can be accounted for in terms of precategorical selection (selective processing) and in terms of postcategorical selection (selective remembering). So, even if a model close to Broadbent's position is taken as a starting point, post-categorical selection cannot be ruled out. It is not concluded that the postcategorical selection mechanism derived from the two-process model offers the most adequate account of the data. Given the evidence presented, none of the alternative postcategorical selection models discussed in Appendix C of chapter 1 can be excluded. The demonstration, however, shows, that 'improved performance with a properly timed selective instruction' is irrelevant for the pre- vs postcategorical selection issue.

From the discussion presented in this chapter three tentative conclusions follow.

(a) Postcategorical selection offers the most parsimonious explanation for the results obtained in the tasks discussed. (Whether the same or different postcategorical selection mechanisms operate in attribute selection tasks and in element selection tasks will be further discussed in chapter 4.)

(b) This postcategorical selection mechanism uses representations of elementary stimulus attributes such as colour or spatial position for distinguishing relevant from irrelevant information.

(c) The question whether performance is improved under selective instructions is irrelevant for the pre- vs postcategorical selection issue. Selection of information is better investigated by assessing the effects of irrelevant or unwanted information. (Chapters 4, 5, and 6 will be devoted to such an investigation.)

Introduction

When someone names the identity of a visually presented element, for instance, the name of a letter, or if someone names an attribute of a visual stimulus, for instance, the colour of a disk, he has processed the visual information, or the visual information is categorized. This translation or recoding of visual material into a form that makes verbal report possible, requires that the information derived from visual stimulation contacts information previously stored in memory.

If a subject is asked to report only a part of a multi-element stimulus array, for instance, the upper row of a matrix of letters, or if he is asked to report only one of the several attributes of a visually presented stimulus, for instance, the colour of a number of shapes, then he is able to perform according to the instruction. This even holds if the exposure duration is short enough to avoid refixation that might bring the relevant part in focus (Sperling, 1960; Haber, 1966). This central selective process, unaided by peripheral adjustments, which results in responses depending upon a small number of elements singled out from among a large number of equally potent stimulus elements (or one attribute from among a number of equally potent attributes) is the topic of this chapter. The problem we will be concerned with is whether the selective instruction has its effect prior to or after the categorization of the visual information.

From auditory information processing, two models, each taking one of these points of view, are well known.

Broadbent (1958) suggested a precategorical selection model consisting of three elements: the S system, a short-term store of high capacity in which stimuli are analysed for physical features such as location and pitch; the P system, a limited capacity processing channel, and a selective filter that allows stimuli having certain physical characteristics to go from the S system into the P system. The setting of the filter determines which stimuli enter the P system, and so the filter functions as a precategorical selection device.

Deutsch and Deutsch (1963) proposed a postcategorical selection model in which all concurrent stimuli are simultaneously processed and recognized without interference, or, simultaneously contact their location in memory. These locations have a preset weighting of importance. From the processed stimuli the one with the highest weighting of importance is allowed to transmit to further processing stages (Norman, 1968, and Morton, 1969a, present extended versions of this model).

For visual information processing tasks, proponents of precategorical selection also assume that Ss can choose which elements or attributes to encode or process, the rest of the information remaining in a relatively unprocessed state (see, for example, Sperling, 1960, 1963, 1967; Haber, 1966; Neisser, 1967; Rumelhart, 1970; Coltheart, 1972, 1975a). Proponents of postcategorical selection assume that there is no selection before categorizing or processing the information. Selection is selection of identified or categorized information (see, for example, Morton,

1969b; Keele, 1973; Gardner, 1973).

For visual information processing, two lines of evidence are generally presented in favour of central precategorical selection: (a) the results of the 'instructional set experiments' for demonstrating precategorical selection of attributes, and (b) the results of the 'partial report experiments' for demonstrating precategorical selection of elements. Two other lines of evidence, obtained with (a) the 'Stroop test', and (b) with a version of the 'visual probe experiments', however, strongly suggest postcategorical selection of respectively attributes and elements. Because the 'instructional set experiments' and the 'Stroop test' have many features in common, it seems worthwhile to consider the evidence, in order to investigate whether one selection mechanism can explain the diversity of the results obtained. Also the 'partial report experiments' and the 'visual probe experiments' have many features in common, and therefore it also seems worthwhile to investigate whether one selection mechanism is capable of handling the results obtained in these two paradigms.

(A) The 'instructional set experiments' and the 'Stroop test'

In the instructional set experiments, Ss are instructed to attend to one of several attributes of a stimulus, and to report the values of the attributes after exposure. Because of the confounding of the instructional set and the order of report of dimensions, most of the experiments in this tradition are inconclusive with respect to the pre- vs postcategorical selection issue (for reviews of the early research, see Haber, 1966; Egeth, 1967). Harris and Haber (1963) and Haber (1964a and b) tried to disentangle these two variables by separately specifying (1) the order of report, and (2) the importance of the dimensions. In their experiments, two cards of the Wisconsin Card Sorting test were simultaneously exposed during 100 msec. Each card contained a set of identical geometrical forms. The cards were different in three dimensions: number, shape and colour. One group of Ss, the object coders, was trained to remember the stimuli as objects, e.g. 'one green triangle, three red circles'. A second group of Ss, the dimension coders, was trained to remember the stimuli dimension by dimension, e.g. 'green, red; one, three; triangle, circle'. Subjects had to describe the cards completely in their reports. Before a trial the subject was either told that all dimensions were equally important (equal instructions), or, which one of the three dimensions was most important for the reports (emphasis instruction). On half of the trials the order of report was prescribed after presentation of the cards, on the other half, order of report was free.

The basic evidence for precategorical selection consists in the finding that the dimension coders, under emphasis instructions, were more accurate on the emphasized dimension than on the other two dimensions, even if the emphasized dimension was reported second or last. The object coders showed no effect of instructional set.

These findings were explained by stating that instructional set influenced the order of encoding, where encoding means 'the translation of the visual image, as it is generated on the retina by the stimulus, into some kind of memorial trace or persistence after the stimulus terminates' (Haber, 1966, p. 345). Dimension coders could vary their order of encoding as a function of set instructions, while the object coders could not because of the constraints of the English syntax. Dimension coders were therefore able to encode the emphasized dimension before the visual information had disappeared from the sensory store.

This interpretation of the data was subsequently supported by Neisser, 1967; Broadbent, 1971; Kahneman, 1973.

Harris and Haber's (1963) and Haber's (1964a and b) instructional set experiments, however, have much in common with the well-known test devised by Stroop (1935) (for an extensive review of research with this task see Dyer, 1973a). In this test, the Ss have to name as fast as possible, a set of colours (the relevant attribute) that are shaped to spell incongruent colour words (the irrelevant attribute), that is, the word 'red' written in blue, the word 'green' written in red, etc. According to Harris and Haber's terminology, all Ss have to behave as 'dimension coders' under 'emphasis instruction'. In both tasks there is an integral combination of emphasized (relevant) and unemphasized (irrelevant) attributes. In both tasks, the names for the values on the emphasized (relevant) and on the unemphasized (irrelevant) dimensions are members of the set of responses in use during the task. Both tasks are performed under time pressure; in the instructional set experiments because of the short exposure duration and the rapid fading of the icon, in the Stroop test because Ss are asked to name the colours as fast as possible.

Subjects face great difficulties in performing the Stroop test. Stroop (1935) found that colour-naming was slowed up about 75 per cent in comparison with naming the colours of a card containing rectangular colour patches. It is generally assumed, that this delayed colour-naming results from response competition or response interference. It is thought that the colour and the word are simultaneously processed (Treisman, 1969; Allport, 1971) and that the emitting of the colour-name is delayed by the simultaneous availability of the word name (see, for example, Morton, 1969b; Dyer, 1973a). The interference on the Stroop test is asymmetric, that is, the reading of the words is not delayed by the incongruent colours (Stroop, 1935). Klein (1964) furthermore showed that reading the word prior to colour-naming required only a little more time than naming the colours only. So it seems that with this task, there is a preferred order of emitting responses. If this order has to be violated, interference and delayed responding result.

Now, the basic evidence for precategorical selection in the instructional set experiments consists of the finding that dimension coders under emphasis instructions were more accurate on the emphasized dimension than on the other two dimensions, even if the emphasized dimension was reported second or last. This effect of emphasis instructions, however, was entirely due to a loss of accuracy for the unemphasized dimension under emphasis instructions. The emphasized dimension under emphasis instructions was not reported better than the comparable dimension under equal instructions. Allport (1971) states: 'Selectivity, insofar as it was acting in Harris and Haber's experiment, was acting merely to reduce the accuracy of information on certain dimensions which would otherwise have been available' (p. 104). This absence of any positive advantage on the emphasized dimension and the reduction of accuracy on unemphasized dimensions is at least as easily explained by postcategorical selection and loss of categorized information (Treisman, 1969; Allport, 1971), as by precategorical selection (Haber and Hershenson, 1974).

Haber (1964b) asked his Ss to rehearse aloud in the interval between stimulus exposure and overt recall, and found that the dimension coders started overt rehearsal considerably later than the object coders. An explanation for the reduced accuracy and the delay in overt rehearsal for the dimension coders in terms of postcategorical selection is now readily available. As in the Stroop test, the dimension coders, and especially dimension coders under emphasis instructions, have to violate a preferred order of emitting responses. This preferred order is probably the order used by the object coders: number, colour, shape, per object.

This explanation is based on the assumption that not only irrelevant words that can be read (Stroop test), but also irrelevant dimensions that have to be named such as number, shape and colour (Harris and Haber's task) might cause interference. Some positive evidence in favour of this assumption will be presented in chapters 4 and 5.

However, the task for the dimension coders under emphasis instructions is more complicated than the task for the Ss on the Stroop test. In the Stroop test Ss can fixate on each colour-word combination in turn, and the response interference mainly results from the irrelevant word fixated upon. In the instructional set experiments, two multi-attribute stimuli are simultaneously presented and refixation to bring one of the two in focus is impossible. Therefore, it is possible that the interference is not restricted to the responses to the emphasized and unemphasized dimensions within one stimulus and that also responses to the emphasized and/or unemphasized dimensions of the other stimulus can contribute to the delay in responding and the decrease in accuracy.

This would imply that an integral combination of relevant and irrelevant information as in the Stroop test is not necessary for interference to occur. Some positive evidence for this point will be presented in the next section of this chapter and in chapters 4 and 5.

In conclusion, it seems that Harris and Haber's (1963) and Haber's (1964a and b) evidence in favour of precategorical selection of attributes is more adequately handled in terms of the postcategorical selection models developed in order to explain the phenomena found with the Stroop test. That interference is readily apparent in the Stroop test, but remains hidden in the instructional set experiments, probably results from the dependent variable used. Interference primarily shows up as a delay in responding, and not necessarily in a low level of accuracy on the relevant or emphasized attribute.

(B) The 'partial report experiments' and the 'visual probe experiments'

The partial report technique was introduced by Sperling (1960). He first investigated Ss' performance in whole report tasks, that is, tasks in which Ss try to recall what they can from a display containing a number of rows with letters or digits. In the partial report task Ss were instructed to report only one of the rows of the display. The instruction was coded as a tone, the pitch indicating which row had to be reported. The tone, or cue, was presented just before or at various intervals after presentation of the visual display. The exposure duration of the matrix was 50 msec, so no useful eye movements could be made.

The basic evidence for precategorical selection, or selective processing, consists of the partial report superiority: if the cue was presented just before the stimulus, and also with cue delays up to about 200 msec, the performance on the cued row appreciably exceeded the average performance on a row under whole report instructions. The difference between the two measures declines with increasing cue delays and disappears with delays of about 400 msec.

Averbach and Sperling (1961) showed, furthermore, that the range of stimulus-cue intervals over which a partial report superiority is obtained, strongly depends on the exposure conditions used. If the post-exposure field is dark, the decline in performance under partial report is much more gradual than with a black post-exposure field.

Further investigations showed, that a partial report superiority was found if the cue specified a value on an elementary physical dimension such as location, colour, brightness, size or shape (Sperling, 1960; Von Wright, 1968, 1970; Clark, 1969; Turvey and Kravetz, 1970; Coltheart et al., 1974). If the cue, however, specified a derived property such as letters vs digits (Sperling, 1960; Von Wright, 1970, 1972), vowel vs consonant (Von Wright, 1970), or letters ending with the vowel /ɛ/ vs letters ending with the vowel /i/ (Coltheart et al., 1974) no partial report superiority is found.

From the Ss' phenomenological reports, the effects of different post-exposure fields and from the known facts of persistence of vision, Sperling (1960) concludes: 'that information is initially stored as a visual image and that Ss can effectively utilize this information in their partial reports' (p. 21). A dark post-exposure field results in a longer lasting visual image, and therefore the information needed for partial report is also available with larger cue delays. Sperling states that in response to the cue, the Ss direct their attention to the appropriate row and then read the letters necessary for the partial report (p. 24). Derived properties cannot be used for precategorical selection because the items have to be identified before these properties are known. Investigators supporting the precategorical selection view assume that elementary physical characteristics can be processed or discriminated before and independent of identification of the elements, and therefore can be used in guiding attention or processing capacity (Broadbent, 1971; Coltheart, 1972; Turvey, 1973). This interpretation seems very generally accepted and can be called, after Coltheart (1975a) 'the conventional view of iconic memory'.

However, just as there is a kind of instructional set experiment, the Stroop test, in which Ss were asked to respond as fast as possible, and in which response competition was clearly present, there is a comparable modification of the partial report experiment. It is derived from

Averbach's and Coriell's (1961) 'visual probe procedure'. In their experiments, two rows, each containing eight letters, were presented during 50 msec, simultaneously with, or followed at various intervals by, a barmarker, pointing to one of the positions in the display. Ss were instructed to name the element indicated by the barmarker (the target). Despite the differences between the two procedures (auditory vs visual cues; 3 vs 16 cues; report of a row vs report of an element), highly similar results are obtained (see Averbach and Sperling, 1961). With the visual probe procedure too, an increase in the interval between display and cue results in a decrease in proportion correct reported. At about 200 msec cue delay an asymptotic level of performance is reached, comparable to the performance in whole report experiments.

Eriksen and his associates (Eriksen and Hoffman, 1972a and b, 1973; Colegate et al., 1973; Eriksen and Eriksen, 1974; Hoffman, 1975) have used a version of this probe procedure in order to investigate the temporal course of selective attention. In most of these experiments, the letters were placed in a circular array around a fixation point in order to ensure places of equal visual acuity for all elements (Eriksen and Eriksen, 1974, used linear arrays). A line indicator was presented simultaneously with or at various intervals before the exposure of the array. (In the experiment by Eriksen and Eriksen, 1974, the target always appeared in the same position and therefore no line indicator was used.) The most important modification, however, was that Ss were instructed to respond as fast as possible to the letter indicated by the line, either by naming the letter (Eriksen and Hoffman, 1972a and b; Colegate et al., 1973) or by moving a switch left or right according to the category the letter belonged to (Eriksen and Hoffman, 1973; Eriksen and Eriksen, 1974; Hoffman, 1975).

The experiments of Eriksen and Hoffman (1973) and Eriksen and Eriksen (1974) were especially concerned with the effect of the nature of non-target letters (noise). (Keren (1976) used the same paradigm as Eriksen and Eriksen (1974) and obtained similar results.) The Ss had to move a lever in one direction if the indicated letter was a member of a set of two letters (for instance a H or an M) and in the other direction if it was a member of another set of two letters (for instance A or U). In Eriksen and Hoffman's experiment either a single target letter was presented, or a target combined with (1) letters from the same set, (2) letters from the other set, (3) a mixture of letters from both sets. In Eriksen and Eriksen's experiment either a single target was presented, or a target in combination with (1) the same letter, (2) the other letter from the same set, (3) one of the letters from the other set, (4) other letters. (Hoffman, 1975, in a similar experiment used only 3 or 5 as targets; as a result response relationship of target and noise and physical similarity between target and noise are confounded.)

The most important findings were

1 Even with the largest intervals between cue and display (350 msec; Eriksen and Hoffman, 1973) and also if the target is always in the same position (Eriksen and Eriksen, 1974) not all effects of the noise letters are completely eliminated.

2 The effect of a noise letter strongly depends on its response relationship with the target letter. Noise letters from the same set, whether physically different or not, cause little delay in responding. Noise letters from the other set give a large delay in reaction time (Eriksen and Eriksen, 1974). Noise letters belonging to neither set give intermediate delays (Eriksen and Eriksen, 1974; Hoffman, 1975).

3 The size of the effect of the noise letters depends on the distance between target and noise; the greater this distance the smaller the effect (Eriksen and Eriksen, 1974).

Eriksen and Eriksen (1974) conclude:

Since the effect of noise is strongly determined by its response compatibility with the target letter, support is given not only to the conclusion that the effects of noise are the result of response competition or interference, but further that this results from at least some of the noise stimuli being processed along with the target to the point where they are identified enough to tend to elicit appropriate responses. (p. 147)

and:

Our interpretation of the obtained spacing effect is that it represents the ease with which a S can make a spatial or location discrimination. If the S is processing essentially simultaneously, the target letter and one or more noise letters, some form of an inhibitory process has to be activated in order to prevent responses to the noise letters and to permit selection of the response appropriate to the target location . . . the more discriminable the differences in location in the display, the faster will be the selection process. (p. 148; see also p. 144)

From these quotations it is clear that the authors explain their results by postcategorical selection and response interference, and, given the data, this conclusion seems inevitable. Eriksen and Hoffman (1973) (cf. also Eriksen and Hoffman, 1972b; Colegate et al., 1973; Eriksen and Eriksen, 1974; Hoffman, 1975), in addition, propose a mechanism for precategorical selection: an attentional field with a centre of high level information extraction (radius about $1°$), surrounded by an area where only gross information is extracted. It is thought that the centre of this field does not necessarily coincide with the fovea of the eye. However, in all the experiments supporting the existence of this field, the exposure conditions were such that useful refixations could be made. Colegate et al. (1973) showed that, though two of the authors could, some of the naive Ss could not even prevent eye movements in the direction of the line indicator under these conditions. So the evidence for the existence of this precategorical selection mechanism is rather dubious, and it remains for further investigations to determine whether such an attentional field really exists. (Gatti and Egeth, 1978, demonstrated interference over distances up to $5°$! See also Merikle and Gorewich, 1979, for related results.)

Now, a perfect precategorical selection mechanism can, in response to the cue, restrict processing to the element or elements wanted for response, and thereby prevent response competition or identity-specific interference. The order of processing the elements can be made to match the desired order of report. The visual probe experiments in which Ss were instructed to report as fast as possible, however, clearly showed that Ss cannot prevent the processing of noise letters within about $1°$ of the target. Precategorical selection without additional assumptions cannot cope with this result. It has at least to be assumed that precategorical selection is imperfect (Eriksen and associates), and additional postcategorical selection mechanisms have to be introduced to solve the response conflict (Eriksen and Eriksen, 1974).

With postcategorical selection, however, the order in which the responses become available, does not necessarily coincide with the order in which the responses have to be given. A delay in responding will be readily apparent if Ss are instructed to respond as fast as possible (Eriksen's visual probe experiments), but will remain unobserved if Ss are merely instructed to name a subset of the elements presented (the partial report experiments). (What factors determine the order in which the responses become available, and whether the Ss have to use some type of inhibitory process in order to prevent incorrect responses (Eriksen and Eriksen, 1974) are problems for further investigation.)

In conclusion, because of the close resemblance between the visual probe procedure and the partial report experiments, and because the instruction allows postcategorical selection to show up in the modified visual probe experiments, but not in the partial report experiments, one selection mechanism for both tasks, postcategorical selection, seems the most parsimonious explanation. However, this explanation is tenable only if it can be shown that also the positive evidence presented in favour of precategorical selection (that is, the data on which the 'conventional view of iconic memory' is based) can be explained if a postcategorical selection mechanism is assumed.

This evidence for precategorical selection or selective processing in partial report tasks consists of (1) the partial report superiority, (2) the decline of partial report superiority with increasing cue delays, (3) the dependence of partial report superiority on the type of the postexposure fields (see Coltheart, 1975a, pp. 45-6). (The fact that a partial report superiority is obtained with various elementary physical selection criteria but not with derived properties can be interpreted in more ways, and will be discussed later on.)

The principal evidence for precategorical selection is the partial report superiority, an effect that is reliably reproducible (see Coltheart, 1975b). If the idea of selective processing is rejected, one has to propose other factors which might result in a partial report superiority.

Dick (1971) compared partial report data and whole report data and found that for comparable response positions whole report accuracy was higher than partial report accuracy. Dick's (1974) conclusion based on this analysis is 'the data do not provide any evidence for any sort of mechanism in which the S can select some parts of the contents of iconic memory to analyze in preference to other parts' (p. 585). Dick doesn't answer the question how selection operates and produces a partial report superiority.

Holding (1975), however, mentions two factors that could result in superior partial report. The first, cue anticipation, is some kind of disguised precategorical selection system. It has been adequately dealt with by Coltheart (1975a). In most partial report experiments cue randomization has been sufficient to prevent Ss from guessing at an above chance level what cue would be present next, so this factor cannot account for the superior partial report. The second factor proposed by Holding (1975) is output interference: the forgetting of already categorized information during report. Holding assumes that the execution of a response interferes with the recall of the remaining items (p. 33). In whole report tasks far more responses have to be given than in partial report tasks, and therefore categorized items in memory will undergo more output interferences in whole report tasks than in partial report tasks. This results in a spurious advantage for partial report. Output interference acts by depressing the amount apparently available in whole report tasks. So according to this view, the partial report superiority is in fact a whole report inferiority.

In this way, however, variations in size of the partial report superiority under conditions showing constant whole report performance remain unexplained. Two factors that have no or only a small effect on whole report performance but strongly influence partial report superiority are (1) the interval between stimulus and cue, and (2) the different kinds of post-exposure fields. In order to explain the cue delay effect, Holding (1975) introduces the 'rehearsal uncertainty hypothesis'.

> One possible hypothesis to account for the forgetting loss is that uncertainty about what is to be reported disrupts efficient rehearsal. A S who is attempting to hold an overload, while uncertain about what he will have to report, may lose items progressively as a result of inefficient or variable rehearsal strategies. (p. 34)

Coltheart (1975a) replies:

> It is difficult to see what kind of rehearsal could be going on in the 300-msec period over which the cue delay effect works. Moreover, the loss with increasing cue delay is much more gradual if the postexposure field is dark than if it is light (Averbach and Sperling, 1961). The rehearsal uncertainty effect cannot cope with this; it could not be argued that rehearsal strategies are less efficient, so more is lost with a white postexposure field than with a black one. (p. 46)

In conclusion, up to now the attempts to reinterpret the findings from the partial report experiments have been rather unsuccessful. The cue delay effect and the dependence of the partial report superiority on the kind of post-exposure field strongly suggest that the selection of items for report is made during the time the visual information is available (that is, during stimulus exposure and during the time the icon exists), and that the required selection is the more successful, the longer the visual information is available after appearance of the cue.

This, however, does not necessarily imply selective processing of the icon or precategorical selection as Coltheart (1975a) suggests. It is possible to explain (1) the partial report superiority, (2) the cue delay effect and (3) the dependence of the partial report superiority on post-exposure fields, as well with parallel processing during the time the visual information is available and postcategorical selection. The next part of this chapter is devoted to such an explanation.

As a starting point we take the two-process model for performance in whole report tasks as described in chapter 1. As stated in that chapter, this model necessitates only a minor change in the usual interpretations of the results of whole report experiments. (Other postcategorical selection models are presented in Appendix C of chapter 1.)

In whole report tasks, the increase in number of elements reported (ΔX) per unit time (ΔT) can be described with

$$\frac{\Delta X}{\Delta T} = -aX + b \tag{1a}$$

This equation can be considered to be a model for visual information processing in these types of tasks. The parameter 'b' can be interpreted as a 'processing parameter', reflecting the number of elements processed during ΔT, or, as the processing capacity of the system per unit time. (Because, as was shown in chapter 2, parameter 'b' can represent parallel as well as serial processing, the problem of serial vs parallel processing need not be considered here.) The parameter 'a' can be interpreted as a 'forgetting parameter', reflecting the loss of processed information during ΔT. From the equation it is readily apparent that no further increase in elements reported takes place if $aX = b$, and therefore the maximum number of elements that can be reported, X, equals b/a. This can be interpreted as a limit on the capacity of the memory that has to hold the processed elements.

This model leaves open whether selection of information occurs by precategorical selection or selective processing (connected with parameter 'b') or by differential forgetting or selective remembering (connected with parameter 'a'). It is possible to show that both ways of selecting for report (1) result in a partial report superiority, (2) result in a comparable decline of partial report superiority with increasing cue delays, and (3) show a comparable dependence of partial report superiority on post-exposure fields.

Suppose we present the Ss a 2 x 10 matrix with letters and/or digits. (We use this size of matrix in order to avoid ceiling effects in our calculations.) By varying exposure time t', we vary the total processing time $t = t' + c$, where c is the duration of the icon after exposure. We assume that c is independent of t', and that the rate of processing is constant during t.

In a whole report task, if Ss are asked to report as many elements as possible the total number of elements reported, X, as a function of processing time, is given by

$$X_w(t) = \frac{b}{a}(1 - e^{-at}) \tag{1b}$$

given X = 0 at t = 0, and given 'a' sufficiently small (see chapter 1, Appendix A).

Suppose that after report by the Ss, one of the rows is selected at random, and the number of correct responses for that row is counted. The expected mean number of correct responses, X_r, as a function of processing time is then given by

$$X_r(t) = \frac{1}{2}\frac{b}{a}(1 - e^{-at}) \tag{2b}$$

and the ultimate level of performance equals $\frac{b}{2a}$. X_r is the whole report performance per row, with which partial report performance has to be compared. X_r, therefore, represents the number of elements an S can name from one of the two rows if no selective instruction has been given. So it also represents the number of elements that can be reported from one of the two rows before the selective instruction is given.

Now suppose we present a selective cue just before or simultaneously with the stimulus. Proponents of precategorical selection assume that Ss can, in response to the cue, direct their total processing capacity, b, to the row indicated by the cue, and so restrict processing to the elements of that row. The increase in number of elements that can be reported from that row (ΔX_i), per unit time (ΔT) then equals

$$\frac{\Delta X_i}{\Delta T} = -aX_i + b \tag{3a}$$

and the number of elements reported from that row (X_i) as a function of processing time t is given by

$$X_i(t) = \frac{b}{a}(1 - e^{-at}) \tag{3b}$$

given that $X_i = 0$ at t = 0.

If, however, selective processing is impossible, the total processing capacity, b, remains divided over the two rows, and in each row $b/2$ elements are processed per unit time. If selective remembering is the mechanism by which selection takes place, then this is reflected in a smaller value of a. If it is assumed that this selection mechanism does not alter the ultimate level of performance, b/a, the minimum value for the forgetting parameter has to be set at $a/2$. So the increase in the number of elements reported, ΔX_0, per unit time equals

$$\frac{\Delta X_0}{\Delta T} = -\frac{a}{2}X_0 + \frac{b}{2} \tag{4a}$$

and the number of elements reported as a function of processing time t is given by

$$X_0(t) = \frac{b}{a}(1 - e^{-\frac{1}{2}at}) \tag{4b}$$

given $X_0 = 0$ at $t = 0$.

Figure 3.1 shows X_r (= $\frac{1}{2}X_w$), X_i (= X_w) and X_0 as a function of b, the number of elements processed per unit of time. The ultimate limit b/a was set at 6, and t was fixed at 40 (t in units of 10 msec). The values chosen for b range from .1 per unit time (Neisser, 1967, p. 103) to 1 per unit time (Sperling, 1963, p. 25; 1970, p. 200).

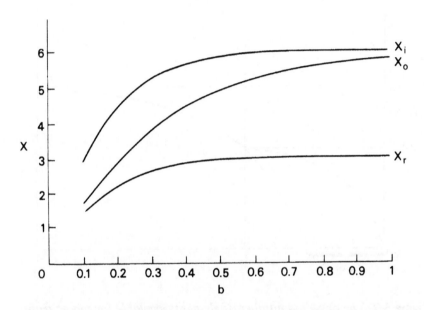

Figure 3.1 *The expected number of elements correctly reported with precategorical selection (X_i), postcategorical selection (X_o) and without selection (X_r) as a function of rate of processing (b). Exposure time, t = 40 (400 msec); ultimate limit $b/a = 6$; display consists of two rows of ten elements*

From this figure it is clear that both selection mechanisms result in a partial report superiority. The expected partial report superiority is greater for precategorical selection (X_i connected with parameter b) than for postcategorical selection (X_0, connected with parameter a). This difference, however, decreases if the rate of processing (b) increases.

71

We now show that both selection mechanisms also result in a comparable decline in partial report superiority with increasing cue delays and that with both mechanisms this decrease in partial report superiority is more gradual the longer the visual information is available for processing (that is, it depends on the kind of post-exposure field used). It is assumed that at the moment of presentation of the cue, t_c, Ss can change their processing strategy in order to obey the selective instruction. (This assumption is not essential; if it is assumed that it takes c units of time to process and respond to the cue, the change in strategy takes place at time $t_c + c = t'_c$, and the same general results follow.)

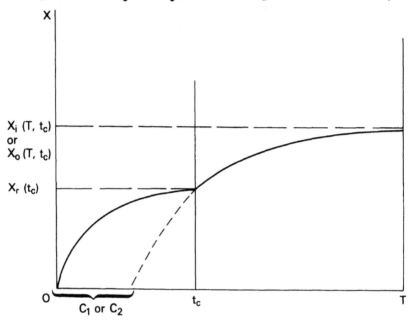

Figure 3.2 *The expected number of elements available for report from the correct row (X) during the interval O-T (solid line). Cue at time t_c. Up to time t_c this number is given by $X_r(t)$ (equation 2b); after time t_c by $X_i(t, t_c)$ (equation 3d), or $X_o(t, t_c)$ (equation 4d) (see text for further explanation)*

In Figure 3.2, the expected number of elements available for report from the cued row during the interval of time $O - T$ is shown (solid line). Up to time t_c the number of elements from the correct row available for report is given by equation (2b). At time t_c this number of elements equals

$$X_r(t_c) = \frac{1}{2}\frac{b}{a}(1 - e^{-at_c}).$$

From time t_c on, the further increase in the number of elements available for report per unit time, is given by equation (3a) for precategorical selection, and (4a) for postcategorical selection. The general solutions for these two equations are

$$X_i(t) = \frac{b}{a}(1 - e^{-a(t - C_1)})$$ (3c)

and

$$X_o(t) = \frac{b}{a}(1 - e^{-\frac{1}{2}a(t - C_2)}).$$ (4c)

As is shown in figure 2, at time t_c, $X_r(t_c) = X_i(t_c)$ and $X_r(t_c) = X_o(t_c)$. From

$$\frac{1}{2}\frac{b}{a}(1 - e^{-at_c}) = \frac{b}{a}(1 - e^{-a(t_c - C_1)})$$

it follows that

$$C_1 = \frac{1}{a}\ln(\tfrac{1}{2}(1 + e^{at_c})).$$

From

$$\frac{1}{2}\frac{b}{a}(1 - e^{-at_c}) = \frac{b}{a}(1 - e^{-\frac{1}{2}a(t_c - C_2)})$$ it follows that

$$C_2 = \frac{2}{a}\ln(\tfrac{1}{2}(e^{\frac{1}{2}at_c} + e^{-\frac{1}{2}at_c})).$$

By substituting these values of C_1 and C_2 in formulas (3c) and (4c) respectively, the expressions for the expected number of elements reported are obtained.

With precategorical selection, the expected number reported from the cued row for a cue at time t_c and a total processing time t $(t \geqslant t_c)$ is given by

$$X_i(t, t_c) = \frac{b}{a}(1 - e^{C_i})$$ (3d)

where

$$C_i = -at + \ln \tfrac{1}{2}(1 + e^{at_c}).$$

With postcategorical selection, the number of elements reported from the cued row for a cue at time t_c and a total processing time t, $(t \geqslant t_c)$ is given by

$$X_o(t, t_c) = \frac{b}{a}(1 - e^{C_o})$$ (4d)

where

$$C_o = -\tfrac{1}{2}at + \ln \tfrac{1}{2}(e^{\frac{1}{2}at_c} + e^{-\frac{1}{2}at_c}).$$

In Figure 3.3, two cue delay curves for precategorical selection (upper panel), and two cue delay curves for postcategorical selection (lower panel) are shown. The value of b was fixed at .4 (a processing rate of 4 elements per 100 msec). In order to simulate the effect of post-exposure fields, leaving icons of different durations, t values of 40 (400 msec; lower curves in both panels) and 100 (1000 msec; upper curves in both panels) were chosen. A comparison of the two panels shows that both selection mechanisms give approximately the same results. With both mechanisms (1) a partial report superiority is obtained, (2) this partial report superiority decreases with increasing cue delays, (3) this decrease is more gradual if the visual information is longer available, (4) ultimately the same level of performance as in whole report tasks is reached.

A comparison of this Figure 3.3 with fig. 7 presented by Averbach and Sperling (1961) (or Sperling, 1963, fig. 1; Coltheart, 1972, fig. 2), shows, beside a general correspondence, a difference in the shape of the cue delay curves: the curves presented here are convex, the curves found in partial report experiments appear concave. An explanation for this difference is not readily available. In the literature it is generally assumed, that during c, because of the fading of the icon, the processing rate decreases and that this causes the concave shape of the cue delay function. This interpretation, however, is incompatible with our interpretation of equation (1a). An explanation in line with our interpretation can possibly be based on the assumption that the later the selective instruction is given, the more difficult it becomes to locate or to find the relevant information.

Figures 3.1 and 3.3 show that precategorical selection (Sperling, 1960, 1963; Rumelhart, 1970; Coltheart, 1972, 1975a), in the model presented here operating by way of the processing parameter 'b', as well as postcategorical selection, in the present model connected with parameter 'a', results in a partial report superiority, a decrease in partial report superiority with increasing cue delays, and a dependence of partial report superiority on post-exposure fields. So, these three features of the data obtained in partial report experiments cannot be used to decide between the two selection mechanisms. However, the fact that in Eriksen's modification of the visual probe experiments clear evidence for response competition or postcategorical interference is found, makes postcategorical selection the most parsimonious explanation.

It cannot be concluded from the demonstration given in the previous paragraphs what postcategorical selection mechanism operates in these types of tasks. What this demonstration shows is that improved performance with a properly timed instruction as well as a dependence of performance on exposure conditions is irrelevant for the pre- vs post-categorical selection issue. Given the evidence discussed up to now, neither the postcategorical selection mechanism derived from the two-process model nor the postcategorical selection models presented in Appendix C of chapter 1 can be ruled out. (In chapter 4 we will briefly discuss (and reject) a proposal (Allport, 1977) that can be made to correspond with the postcategorical selection model described in the previous paragraphs.)

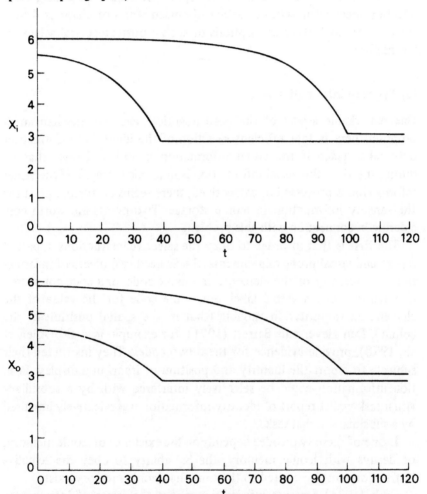

Figure 3.3 *Cue delay curves for precategorical selection (upper panel) and postcategorical selection (lower panel). Upper and lower curves represent respectively processing times t = 100 (1000 msec) and t = 40 (400 msec). Processing rate b = .4 (4 elements per 100 msec). Selective cue at times t = 0 to 120; ultimate limit* $b/a = 6$

One feature of such a postcategorical selection mechanism is apparent, however. It differs in an important way from that suggested by Deutsch and Deutsch (1963). In the partial report experiments the relevant elements cannot have a 'preset weighting of importance'. Therefore, elementary stimulus attributes such as colour or spatial position have to be used, in one way or another, by this selection mechanism, for distinguishing relevant from irrelevant elements.

In the next three sections some aspects of such a postcategorical selection mechanism will be further discussed. Parts of chapters 4 to 7 are devoted to further descriptions of such a postcategorical selection mechanism.

(a) Types of information lost

One remarkable aspect of the postcategorical selection mechanism as proposed here is that efficient selection of the identified information only takes place if the visual information is still available (that is, during the time the visual information is in iconic storage). If the visual information is processed or categorized, there seems no further need for the sensory information in iconic storage. Two points are worth considering in connection with this problem.

The first is that in order to obey the selective instructions in partial report and visual probe experiments, the Ss need two pieces of information: the identity of the element, or a name code, or a code connected in memory with a verbal label, and some code for the value of the element on the criterion variable (that is, the spatial position or the colour). Den Heyer and Barrett (1971), for example (see also Allen et al., 1978), provide evidence for these two codes. They instructed their subjects to report the identity and position of items in a display. Position information could be selectively interfered with by a subsidiary visual task whilst report of identity information was selectively impaired by a subsidiary verbal task.

If one of these two codes depends on the existence of iconic memory, or decays with iconic memory, the Ss' ability to obey the selective instruction must be limited to the time that iconic memory exists.

Dick (1974) presents information about the types of information that are lost from iconic memory (pp. 581-3) and concludes: 'The data on types of information lost suggest that physical aspects such as space or colour are lost, whereas learned aspects are not' (p. 583), and 'Thus, for visual probes, the data can hardly be interpreted in any way other than to say that S has lost exact spatial position but not other aspects of the representation ...' (p. 583). These conclusions are based on the finding by Eriksen and Rohrbaugh (1970) that with increasing cue delays the number of items erroneously reported from immediately adjacent positions increased. It is, therefore, conceivable that iconic memory limits the interval of time that selection can take place, in that the information necessary for the selection of the processed elements, that is, the spatial position, the colour, or other elementary attributes is coded in iconic memory and decays rapidly, while the information on the identity of the elements is still available.

At this point it is interesting to refer again to the experiments by Graves (1976) discussed in chapter 2. In summary, his experimental results showed that processing for identity only was far more efficient than processing for identity and position. One possible explanation suggested by Graves was based on the assumption that positional information disappears sooner than identity information.

So, while at first sight the dependence of postcategorical selection on the duration of iconic memory seems somewhat peculiar, it fits well in with the existing evidence on the kinds of information lost and the different rates at which different types of information are lost.

The second point concerns the problem of how iconic memory has to be conceptualized, that is, whether it has to be conceived as a separate store holding relatively uncoded sensory data, or as a distinguishable, but not separate, substage in an automatic stream of information processing. Of course, these two conceptualizations are connected with the points of view taken with regard to the selection of information.

Proponents of precategorical selection assume that the icon is a separate store. 'Brief displays are held in a form of storage which is of high capacity, is subject to rapid decay, and is visual in nature; this is iconic memory. Because of the rapid decay of iconic memory, items which are to be retained long enough to be reported must be transferred to PS' (Coltheart, 1975a, p. 43).

Proponents of postcategorical selection do not stress the existence of the icon as a separate store. Iconic memory can be equated with a substage in the chain of processing activities resulting from the presentation of the stimulus. Shiffrin and Schneider's (1977) analysis, for instance, is not in terms of separate stores, but in terms of levels of processing.

By *levels* we refer to a temporal directionality of processing such that certain nodes activate other nodes but not vice versa. In sensory processing, there is a tendency for increasing information reduction as successive levels are activated. Thus, a visually presented word could first be processed as a pattern of contrast regions, color, regular variations, and so forth; then lines, angles, and other similar features could be activated; then letters and letter names and verbal or articulatory codes; then the word's verbal code; and finally, the meaning and semantic correlates of the word. This sequence is meant as an example, and we do not wish to imply that these are the relevant features, that this is the only possible ordering, or that this listing is exhaustive. Such a sequence of feature encoding should occur automatically to a normally skilled reader. (Shiffrin and Schneider, 1977, p. 155; see also Shiffrin and Schneider, 1977, pp. 162-3 or chapter 2, pp. 51-2)

It will be clear that a postcategorical selection model as proposed in the present chapter has to be connected with the latter conceptualization of iconic memory: iconic memory is not a box holding relatively uncoded sensory data, but is a distinguishable level in an automatic stream of information processing (cf. Craik and Lockhart, 1972, and Posner and Warren, 1972, for similar points of view). 'It is perfectly possible to draw a box around early analyses and call it sensory memory and a box around intermediate analyses called short-term memory, but that procedure both oversimplifies matters and evades the more significant issues' (Craik and Lockhart, 1972, p. 675).

(b) The selection of attributes or dimensions

An experimental finding, generally taken as supporting the precategorical selection view, is that only cues which specify elementary physical dimensions such as colour or location result in partial report superiority, while with cues specifying a derived value such as letter vs digit no partial report superiority is found. Coltheart (1972) explains this by stating: 'simple physical characteristics such as spatial position, size, shape or colour of an item can be discriminated without the item having been identified, and so, whether an item will be identified can be controlled by the physical characteristics it possesses' (p. 65), and 'knowledge of higher order features of items . . . can only be attained after the items are transferred to a different form of memory' (p. 66), that is, after the items are identified. It is only the first part of the argument that is really relevant for the issue of precategorical vs post-categorical selection since the proponents of precategorical selection accept postcategorical selection with derived properties.

Broadbent expresses the same point of view with regard to precategorical selection: 'in selecting red from black digits each black item can be ignored after one binary choice indicating that it is irrelevant' (Broadbent, 1970, p. 55), and, 'Stimulus selection requires that every item be examined on arrival in order that the presence or absence of the desired common feature can be detected. If that feature be absent, no other feature need be examined' (Broadbent, 1971, p. 178).

However, the statement that simple physical characteristics can be discriminated without the item having been identified is not readily substantiated. Treisman (1969), Allport (1971) and Saraga and Shallice (1973) present evidence that different elementary physical dimensions are processed in parallel. After reviewing the evidence, Treisman (1969) states: 'These findings suggest that focussing on particular perceptual analyzers while excluding others may be difficult or impossible. It certainly appears to be less efficient than focussing on a selected input' (p. 265). More recently, Shiffrin and Schneider (1977) and Schneider and Shiffrin (1977) made a strong case for a similar point of view. In chapter 2 of this study we summarized their position in a lengthy quotation. (Chapter 2, pp. 51-2.)

So, it seems that Coltheart (1972) only gives an explanation of the results of partial report experiments in terms of a precategorical selection model instead of presenting evidence in favour of precategorical selection. From the results of partial report experiments it does not follow that unidentified items are selected for identification. It is just as conceivable that the physical characteristics that result in a partial report superiority are exactly the characteristics that allow easy selection of identified elements.

With postcategorical selection as conceived here, it is assumed that the element as well as the attribute necessary for selection are processed before selection takes place; and this is consistent with the evidence on the processing of attributes. Then, however, the parameter 'b' in the two-process model worked out in this chapter represents speed of processing of elements only if the selection criterion is processed faster than the element. It may be thought that this situation is represented in the right part of Figure 3.1, where the higher values of 'b' give a substantial partial report superiority. If the elements are processed faster than the selection criterion, which is probably the case with selection by derived properties such as letter vs digit or vowel vs consonant, but probably also for elementary physical dimensions if the discrimination that must be made is very difficult, then parameter 'b' reflects the time necessary for the processing of the criterion attribute. It may be thought that this is represented in the left part of Figure 3.1, where the smaller values of b give only a small partial report superiority.

In conclusion, a postcategorical selection model fits in better with the existing evidence on parallel processing of different attributes.

(c) The capacity of the processor

In the recent literature, the problem of pre- vs postcategorical selection is connected with assumptions about the capacity of the processor, that is, the limited (LC) vs unlimited capacity (UC) issue.

LC processing, especially serial processing, has been strongly connected with precategorical selection.

The prime reason for this connection between LC and precategorical selection, is that precategorical selection, or restriction of processing to stimulus elements that appear relevant as revealed by some kind of preliminary analysis, is the most efficient selection strategy for a system with LC. Broadbent (1970) states:

> capacity limitations in the system would make it helpful to be able to reject irrelevant stimuli at the time of arrival after analyzing as little information from them as possible. With stimulus set this is possible, since in selecting red from black digits each black item can be ignored after one binary choice indicating it is irrelevant. (p. 54)

Figure 3.1 also shows this greater effectiveness of precategorical selection as compared with postcategorical selection. This difference in effectiveness between the two selection mechanisms, however, does not result from the selection mechanism as such, but from the additional assumption of a capacity limitation in the processor and the assumption that the processor can direct the limited processing capacity to the relevant subset of elements. In the example previously used, the total processing capacity, b, is allocated to the relevant subset. The elements of this subset are then processed at a higher rate and a partial report superiority as shown in Figure 3.1 results. With postcategorical selection the processing rate for the subset equals $b/2$, and it is this difference in processing rates that gives the difference in partial report superiority. In a system with UC, however, precategorical selection, or restricting processing to a subset of the elements does not change the rate of processing of the elements. In the example previously used, the expected increase in the number of elements processed from the cued subset per unit time remains $b/2$, and this is the same expected increase as with postcategorical selection. So, if the processor has sufficient independent processing channels, precategorical and postcategorical selection give the same partial report superiority, or a UC processor can afford, without a loss of efficiency, to process irrelevant elements too, and select information for further activities after complete processing (Gardner, 1973, for example, proposes such a model).

In chapter 2 we already presented some evidence that UC processing sometimes appears as LC processing as a result of artefacts. In relation to the experiment reported in chapter 2, it was suggested that one feature of the results – an increase in latencies if the signal was accompanied by noise elements – could result from interference at the stage of response selection or response programming. A number of experiments discussed in this chapter, and especially the results obtained by Eriksen and Eriksen (1974) clearly support this point of view and thereby strengthen the conclusion that processing is UC. If processing is UC, the prime reason for favouring precategorical selection over postcategorical selection, the difference in effectiveness between the two selection mechanisms, disappears. Then it seems equally parsimonious to suppose that processed elements are selected for remembering or response, or that unprocessed elements are selected for identification.

Conclusion

Two lines of evidence generally put forward in favour of precategorical selection were considered: (a) the evidence from the 'instructional set experiments', and (b) the evidence from the 'partial report experiments'. In both types of experiments some measure of improved performance when a properly timed selective instruction was given was used as the basic evidence for precategorical selection. Proponents of precategorical selection assume (1) that, during, and for a short time after stimulus exposure, the input information is held in a relatively large capacity, precategorical short-term sensory store (the icon, Neisser, 1967); (2) that, in response to the emphasis instructions or a properly timed cue, the perceiver can adjust the order of identifying the elements or the attributes; (3) that this opportunity for selective processing results in superior report for cued rows over uncued rows and for emphasized dimensions over unemphasized dimensions (see, for example, Sperling, 1960, 1963; Neisser, 1967; Broadbent, 1970, 1971; Coltheart, 1972, 1975a; Haber and Hershenson, 1974).

Because in both tasks (1) identification, (2) storage of identified information, and (3) overt report are involved, improved performance does not necessarily indicate selective processing or precategorical selection, but can also reflect mechanisms at a postcategorical level. Therefore, the question of whether performance is improved under selective instructions seems inadequate for resolving the problem of precategorical vs postcategorical selection. The answers obtained indicate only that selection is possible, the conditions under which selection is possible and how effective the selection mechanism is; however, the actual mechanism by which selection takes place remains obscure.

The question whether Ss can restrict identification to a part of a stimulus, or, can focus attention at the precategorical level, is better answered by looking for effects of irrelevant or unwanted information. That is, if identity-specific effects of unwanted information are found then the irrelevant information must have been processed, and the assumption of precategorical selection has to be rejected. Two lines of evidence considered showed strong identity specific effects of unwanted information: the Stroop test (a version of the instructional set experiment) and Eriksen's modification of the visual probe experiments (a version of the partial report experiment). With both tasks, large delays in responding were observed if the irrelevant information could give rise to conflicting responses.

Of course, the instructional set experiment and partial report experiment are not really the same as the Stroop test and visual probe experiment. The essential difference between the 'original' tasks and their 'modifications' concerns the instruction given to the Ss with respect to speed of responding.

In the instructional set experiment and in the partial report tasks, Ss can respond when they want to (accuracy is the main dependent variable), while in the Stroop test and in Eriksen's version of the visual probe experiment Ss are instructed to respond as fast as possible (latency is the main dependent variable). It is conceivable that time pressure causes a change in selection strategy or alters adequacy of selection (see Kahneman, 1973, ch. 3, on the effects of arousal on selection). However, the proponents of precategorical selection agree that in the instructional set experiments and in the partial report experiments, Ss also have to perform under time pressure, because of the short exposure durations and the rapid fading of the icon.

Because of the rapid decay of iconic memory, items which are to be retained long enough to be reported must be transferred to PS (permanent storage). The capacity of PS is much less than the capacity of iconic memory, but the S can at least choose which of the items in iconic memory will be transferred to PS (the untransferred residue being rapidly lost through decay of iconic memory). (Coltheart, 1975a, p. 43; see also Haber, 1964b, p. 362)

So it seems unlikely that the selection strategies in the two types of tasks differ as a result of time pressure. The instruction to respond as fast as possible merely provides a better look at the processes going on immediately after exposure of the stimulus.

In conclusion, research on selective processing in visual information processing must be concerned with the question 'what is the effect of irrelevant information' instead of asking 'how effective is the processing of relevant information?' The Stroop test and Eriksen's modification of the visual probe experiment are two powerful experimental paradigms for providing information on the characteristics of the mechanism of central information selection.

4 The 'Stroop test' and the 'modified visual probe experiments'

Summary

In chapter 3 it was concluded that postcategorical selection offered the most parsimonious explanation for the tasks discussed in that chapter. The question of whether the same or different postcategorical selection mechanisms operate in attribute selection tasks (the Stroop test, for instance) and in element selection tasks (the modified visual probe experiment, for instance) remained open, however. This issue is discussed and investigated in this chapter.

In the experiments reported, the Stroop test (an attribute selection task) is embedded in a modified visual probe paradigm (an element selection task). If with this paradigm the same results are obtained as in the original Stroop test, then the point of view that both tasks are similar as far as the processing and selecting of information is concerned is strongly supported.

The two experiments reported in this chapter show that the phenomena found with the Stroop test can reliably be reproduced with a modified visual probe experiment. Therefore, there is no reason to maintain that this is brought about by one type of postcategorical selection mechanism in the modified visual probe experiment and by a different type in the Stroop test. In particular, the results of the second experiment show the operation of a postcategorical selection mechanism.

A discussion is devoted to the problem what common postcategorical selection mechanism can account for the results found in the original Stroop test and for the results found in the Stroop test embedded in the modified visual probe paradigm. The issue concentrated upon is the basic observation that Ss are able to find or locate the correct response. (The problem of the origin of interference is discussed in chapter 5.) First, we discuss how this locating of the correct response in the original Stroop test can be accounted for in Broadbent's (1970, 1971) conceptualization of selective attention tasks. Then we discuss how this locating of the relevant response in the modified visual probe task can be accounted for within Shiffrin's and Schneider's (1977) framework for visual information processing (this is a more recent version of Deutsch and Deutsch's theory). Both discussions lead to the same postcategorical selection mechanism: some kind of 'postcategorical filtering'.

Two stages can be distinguished in postcategorical filtering.

(a) Features having no connection with the class of allowable responses lead to, or point at the relevant features that gave rise to the correct response, or, irrelevant features serve to locate the relevant sensory information.

(b) The relevant features are used for distinguishing the correct response from the responses triggered by irrelevant information, or response selection is controlled by the relevant sensory features. The relevant features can be regarded as a tag distinguishing the correct response from the responses triggered by irrelevant information.

This conceptualization of the postcategorical selection mechanism implies that 'Both physical codes and recategorizations are available within a second or so after input' (Posner and Warren, 1972, p. 28).

The relation between 'postcategorical filtering' and the problem of 'perceptual integration' (Allport, 1977) is briefly discussed.

Two alternative ways for distinguishing the correct response from the responses triggered by irrelevant information are briefly discussed. The first is based on the notion of 'response strength', the second on the notion of 'higher level tags'. Both alternatives are rejected because it is difficult to explain how these strategies can be used in the modified visual probe paradigm.

In the last section of this chapter a number of models compatible with the results obtained in this chapter and in previous chapters are briefly discussed.

General introduction

In chapter 3 the instructional set experiments and the Stroop test, as one group of tasks, were discussed separately from the partial report experiments and the modified visual probe experiments as a second group. This strict division was maintained, because in the recent literature it is often assumed that there are essential differences between these two groups of selective attention tasks, and because it is thought that the results obtained with tasks of the two groups have to be explained by different selection mechanisms (see Treisman, 1969; Kahneman, 1973). In the present chapter we will discuss and investigate whether it is really necessary to assume that these groups of tasks are governed by different rules.

In Treisman's (1969) classification of selective attention tasks (this 'taxonomy' was subsequently adopted and elaborated by Kahneman, 1973) the instructional set experiments and the Stroop test are examples of analyser selection tasks; the partial report experiments and the modified visual probe experiments are examples of input selection tasks. Both types of tasks are defined and evaluated as perceptual attention tasks, that is, as precategorical selection tasks. With selection of analysers 'we select one or more dimensions or properties of stimuli to analyze and ignore other dimensions or properties' (Treisman, 1969, p. 285). Or, this type of attention restricts the number of dimensions analysed. With selection of inputs or sets of sensory data 'attention restricts perception by selecting which set of sensory data to analyze' (Treisman, 1969, p. 284). That is, this type of attention restricts the number of inputs analysed. In the main part of her paper, Treisman (1969) discusses the relative importance and efficiency of these two types of selective attention and of a third type, target selection.

After reviewing some evidence on the problem whether attention can be focused on one analyser, Treisman (1969) concludes: 'These findings suggest that focussing on particular perceptual analyzers while excluding others may be difficult or impossible' (Treisman, 1969, p. 295). In his chapter Attention to Attributes, Kahneman (1973) concludes: 'There is little evidence that an intention to attend to a particular dimension of experience can prevent the perceptual interpretation of other dimensions' (Kahneman, 1973, pp. 110-11).

Completely different conclusions are reached for input selection tasks. After discussing some evidence on the problem whether attention can be divided over more inputs, Treisman concludes: 'there is quite strong evidence that true division of attention is difficult or impossible and serial processing necessary both with two or more inputs and with tests for two or more targets (unless these are highly familiar and practiced)' (Treisman, 1969, p. 293). (One possible exception suggested by Treisman leads to a contradiction in her theoretical analyses and is not, therefore, further discussed here.) In his chapter on focussed attention to inputs, Kahneman (1973) states: 'The focussing of attention is very effective in preventing irrelevant stimuli from interfering with the primary task, but there is evidence that irrelevant stimuli are sometimes processed' (Kahneman, 1973, p. 135).

So, from the evidence they reviewed it appeared that Ss can easily focus attention on one input, but not on one attribute of a particular input.

The evidence reviewed also led Treisman (1969) and Kahneman (1973) to postulate two different selection mechanisms for the two types of tasks: inputs are selected by a precategorical selection mechanism ('Selective attention to inputs is the allocation of capacity to the processing of certain perceptual units in preference to others' (Kahneman, 1973, p. 135)), and attributes or dimensions of one input are selected by a postcategorical selection mechanism ('Attention to attributes affects the post-perceptual stage of response selection' (Kahneman, 1973, p. 111)).

If this point of view is accepted, then for the tasks discussed in chapter 3 we must conclude, that (a) the partial report experiments show a successful operation of a precategorical selection mechanism while in the modified visual probe experiments this mechanism faces serious difficulties, (b) the instructional set experiments show a rather efficient operation of a postcategorical selection mechanism, while in the Stroop test this postcategorical selection mechanism seems to break down.

It will be clear that this interpretation is completely at variance with the tentative interpretation we suggested in chapter 3. In section A of that chapter it was proposed that the instructional set experiments and the Stroop test are similar tasks as far as the selection of information is concerned and that a postcategorical selection mechanism sufficed for explaining the results obtained with these two tasks. This conclusion agrees with Treisman's and Kahneman's point of view. In section B of chapter 3, however, it was concluded that the partial report experiments and the visual probe experiments are identical tasks as far as the selection of information is concerned, and that also with these two tasks a postcategorical selection mechanism suffices for explaining the results obtained. The question of whether the same or different postcategorical selection mechanisms operate in both groups of tasks was left open for further investigation.

So, from Treisman's and Kahneman's analyses of selective attention tasks it follows that the issue of precategorical vs postcategorical selection is a fruitful starting point for investigating the selection mechanism in input selection tasks and in attribute selection tasks. From our analysis of selective attention tasks it follows that it is better to investigate whether the same or whether different postcategorical selection mechanisms operate in these two types of tasks. In order to decide between these two starting points it is worthwhile to have a closer look at the evidence that led Treisman and Kahneman to postulate a pre-categorical selection mechanism. This evaluation of the evidence has to be guided by one of the conclusions we reached in chapter 3. There we distinguished two types of central visual information selection tasks.

The first type investigates how effectively the selection mechanism works. With regard to this type of task we stated that answers to the question of whether or not performance is improved under selective instructions are inadequate for shedding light on the problem of pre- vs postcategorical selection. This point is illustrated in chapter 3 by the demonstration that the results obtained with partial report experiments – improved performance with a properly timed instruction – can be accounted for by a model assuming precategorical selection as well as by a model postulating postcategorical selection. In the recent past, effective selection or improved performance under selective instructions (especially the results found with the partial report experiments) was generally taken as sufficient evidence for precategorical selection. In chapter 3 we concluded that answers to the question of whether performance is improved under selective instructions only indicate that selection is possible, under which conditions selection is possible and how effectively the selection mechanism works. The actual selection mechanism remains obscure, however.

The second type of task investigates how effectively irrelevant or unwanted information is rejected. In chapter 3 it was argued that the question of whether Ss can restrict processing to a part of a stimulus or can focus attention at the precategorical level is better answered with this type of task. If identity-specific effects of unwanted information are found – that is, effects that can only result if the irrelevant information is identified – the assumption of precategorical selection has to be rejected.

If we now look at the evidence that Treisman (1969) presents in favour of precategorical selection with input selection tasks, then it appears that all this evidence is obtained with tasks of the first type. Treisman (1969) even states that it is not necessary to use tasks of the second type for investigating input selection (Treisman, 1969, p. 293). She is led to this conclusion by her analysis of the results of divided attention tasks from which, according to her opinion, it appeared that two or more inputs have to be processed in series. Our analysis of divided attention tasks in chapter 2 and the results obtained with the modified visual probe experiments strongly indicate that this interpretation must be doubted. Kahneman (1973) discusses tasks of both types.

It seems that for visual information processing, only tasks of the first type warrant his conclusion that: 'The focussing of attention is very effective in preventing irrelevant stimuli from interfering with the primary task' (Kahneman, 1973, p. 135), while mainly tasks of the second type force him to the conclusion: 'but there is evidence that irrelevant stimuli are sometimes processed at least up to the level of recognition units' (Kahneman, 1973, p. 135).

So if it is accepted that only tasks of the second type – the Stroop test and the modified visual probe experiments, for instance – can provide information on central visual information selection, then the evidence in favour of precategorical selection in input selection tasks is rather sparse.

If it is, furthermore, accepted that the processing system has unlimited capacity, then a precategorical selection mechanism for input selection tasks is not necessary (cf. chapter 2 and chapter 3).

Taken all together, it seems that it is not necessary to further investigate the pre- vs postcategorical selection issue. The question of whether the same or different postcategorical selection mechanisms operate in attribute selection tasks and in input selection tasks is a better starting point for further research. As already stated, only tasks of the second type provide information on the mechanism of central information selection. Therefore, in the experiments reported in this chapter, we investigate whether the same or different postcategorical selection mechanisms operate in the Stroop test (an attribute selection task) and in the modified visual probe experiments (an element selection task).

Of course, it is impossible to prove that in both tasks the same or different selection mechanisms operate. What we can do, however, is try to find out whether the same phenomena as found with the Stroop test can also be obtained with Eriksen's modified visual probe paradigm. If with both tasks the same phenomena are found, then there is no reason to maintain that this is brought about by one type of post-categorical selection mechanism in the modified visual probe experiments, and by a different type of postcategorical selection mechanism in the Stroop test.

In this connection, a group of modifications of the Stroop test is particularly interesting, because they show a gradual transition from the Stroop test to Eriksen's modified visual probe experiments.

The Stroop test was already described in the previous chapter. The usual procedure is to present Ss cards with (a) a series of colour patches, (b) a series of colour words, (c) a series of colour names written in non-corresponding colours. The first card is used for colour-naming, the second card for word-reading and the third card can be used for colour-naming and for word-reading. If the colours on the third card have to be named, performance is far inferior to performance on the first card; a great delay in colour-naming is found and a large number of errors is observed (the Stroop phenomenon). If the words on the last card have to be read, no appreciable differences with word-reading on the second card are found (Stroop, 1935; see also Dyer, 1973a).

The first modification was apparently introduced by Dalrymple-Alford and Budayr (1966). Instead of using lists, they measured single response latencies for tachistoscopically presented single Stroop stimuli and single colour patches. The same effects as with cards one and three of the original Stroop test were found. It seems, therefore, that the Stroop effect has nothing to do with the serial nature of the orthodox Stroop test. Sichel and Chandler (1969) and Hintzman et al. (1972) used a similar procedure. Besides the incongruent colour-word combinations (the word naming a different colour) and the neutral stimuli, also congruent colour-word combinations (word and colour name the same) were used. Hintzman et al. (1972) found that the mean response time for congruent combinations was smaller than the mean response time for the neutral stimuli.

Subsequently, Dyer (1973b) used the individual stimulus presentation procedure, but instead of integral combinations of words and colours (a coloured word), black colour names and rectangular colour patches were presented simultaneously, one to the right of the fixation cross and one to the left. Exposure durations were short enough to prevent useful eye movements. Incongruent, congruent and neutral combinations (a colour patch and a series of black Xs) were presented in a mixed sequence. Dyer concludes 'The results clearly indicate that this bilateral presentation of the colour and the word produces a large portion of the colournaming interference that occurs with individual presentation of conventional Stroop stimuli where the word and the colour are integrally combined' (Dyer, 1973b, p. 316).

Dyer's (1973b) procedure can be modified and extended in various ways. Of course, instead of asking Ss to name the colours, it is also possible to ask them in advance to read the words. It is also possible to mix word-reading trials and colour-naming trials. Then, however, an indicator or cue, for instance a barmarker, indicating the word or the colour, has to be used. The most important difference between this 'mixed' stimulus presentation technique and Dyer's (1973b) 'blocked' presentation technique seems to be in the moment that the S is told what is wanted for response. With the 'blocked' procedure, Ss know what is wanted in advance, with the 'mixed' procedure this is told during the presentation of the stimulus. The work of Sperling (1960) and Averbach and Coriell (1961) (see chapter 3), however, has shown that the difference is not between advance and simultaneous or delayed instructions, but between advance or simultaneous and delayed instructions.

With this barmarker technique it is also possible to present simultaneously two words or two colours, instead of a word and a colour. It seems that such modifications especially result in experiments identical to Eriksen's modified visual probe experiments.

In the two experiments reported in this chapter (Experiments I and II) and in the three experiments reported in the next chapter (Experiments III, IV and V), modifications of the Stroop test, or versions of the modified visual probe experiments as described in the previous paragraphs, are used. The main purpose of the two experiments reported in this chapter was to investigate whether the phenomena found with the Stroop test (an attribute-selection task) can also be obtained with the modified visual probe experiments (an input-selection task).

Experiments I and II

General method

Apparatus

A Scientific-Prototype three-channel tachistoscope, model 320 GB, was used to present the stimuli. Ss initiated stimulus exposure by means of a remote control switch. The tachistoscope was connected to an electronic timer that started counting when a stimulus card appeared, and stopped when the S spoke his response in a voice key. Latencies (RT) were recorded accurate to 1 msec. The pre- and post-exposure field consisted of a blank card with a fixation cross in the centre. The stimulus cards and the blank card appeared at a luminance of about 50 cd/m².

Stimuli

The stimulus cards contained coloured disks, half-disks or words. The words were made from Letraset 1568 capital letters. The height of a word was approximately .5° in visual angle. Geostick 9k m/m coloured disks were used as colourpatches. Their diameter was .6° in visual angle.

Procedure

Ss were run individually in a moderately illuminated room. They were instructed to initiate stimulus exposure when they clearly saw the fixation cross. They were asked to respond verbally as quick as possible while maintaining accuracy. No information was given to them about RTs or correctness of response. For each S and each condition the number of errors was counted. Only the RTs on the correct trials were included in the analysis.

Experiment I

Introduction

Dyer (1973b) introduced a new procedure for generating interference from colour words with colour-naming. Separate black colour words and non-word colour patches were simultaneously presented in a tachistoscope. One element appeared at the right, the other at the left of the fixation point. An exposure duration of 100 msec was used, so Ss could not relocate the stimulus on the retina. With this procedure the same interference with colour-naming was found as with tachisto-scopically presented integral combinations of words and colours (Dalrymple-Alford and Budayr, 1966; Hintzman et al., 1972). Dyer (1973b), however, investigated only the analogue of the colour-naming task on the conflict card (the card containing colours shaped to spell incongruent colour words). Stroop (1935), however, also used this card for word-reading. He found negligible interference from the colours on word-reading.

Experiment I was performed in order to investigate whether this result, obtained with the Stroop card, can also be reliably replicated with Dyer's (1973b) procedure of separate bilateral presentations of the word and colour aspects. If the same result is found, the evidence in favour of the point of view that the Stroop test and Dyer's task are similar types of tasks will be strongly increased.

Method

Subjects

Six Ss (four male and two female) were selected from the population of staff members of the Psychological Institute of the University of Leiden. They all had normal or corrected to normal vision and none of them was deficient in colour vision. They all had served as Ss in similar experiments before.

Stimuli

Two sets of twelve stimulus cards were prepared. The words used were 'rood' (red) and 'blauw' (blue). Each word appeared at the left and at the right of the fixation cross an equal number of times. Either only the word was presented (neutral stimuli, N), or the word combined with a colour patch having the same name (congruent combinations, C), or the word combined with a colour patch with the other name (incongruent combinations, I). Per set, this resulted in 2 (words) x 2 (places) x 3 (C, I, N) = twelve different stimuli. The cards of the two sets were mixed together and formed one series of twenty-four stimulus cards.

The distance from the fixation cross to the centre of the word or the colour patch was $1.25°$ in visual angle.

Procedure

Ss were instructed to read as fast as possible the word, while maintaining accuracy.

The stimulus duration was 150 msec.

Before the main experiment, per S, a series of twenty-four trials was run for practice. Each S saw the series of twenty-four stimulus cards four times, each time in a different random order.

Results

An analysis of variance over the mean RTs per S (a Randomized Block Factorial Design; cf. Kirk, 1968, p. 237) with (a) word to be read ('rood', 'blauw'), (b) kind of combination of stimulus elements (C, I, N), and (c) place of the element to be named (left, right) as within S factors, only revealed a significant effect for the first factor (rood, blauw), $(F (1,5) = 9.10; p < .05)$. The mean RT for the word 'rood' was 373 msec (3.5 per cent errors), the mean RT for 'blauw' was 360 msec (5.9 per cent errors).

The effect of kind of combination of stimulus elements (C, I, N) was far from significant $(F (2,10) = 0.74)$. The mean RTs for conditions C, I and N were, respectively, 367, 369 and 364 msec. The percentages of errors for these conditions were, respectively, 4.7, 6.3 and 3.1.

The linear correlation, R_1, between the overall mean RT per S and the number of errors (E) per S equalled $-.88$ ($RT = -6.6E + 396$). The linear correlation, R_2, between the differences in mean RT for the

93

incongruent and neutral stimulus combinations, (I–N), per S, and the number of errors, E, per S, equalled –.25 (I–N = –0.7E + 7.9).

Discussion

R_1 and the linear relation between RT and E indicate a strong general speed-accuracy trade-off. Each error reduces the overall mean RT by about 7 msec. R_2, however, indicates that there is only a weak linear relation between I–N and E. Therefore, the differences between conditions I and N seem not to be artificially reduced by an increase in number of errors.

The difference between condition I (a word and a competing colour) and N (only a word) can be interpreted as the amount of interference. The mean RTs for these two conditions, the linear function and the percentages of errors then show that the interference is very small, but not completely absent. This is the same result as found by Stroop (1935). He found that word-reading on the conflict card was delayed by about 6 per cent relative to words on the word card. (Colour-naming was delayed by about 75 per cent.)

The results of this experiment, together with the results obtained by Dyer (1973b), who found a highly significant amount of interference with colour-naming, lend strong support to the point of view that in the Stroop test (integral combinations of words and colours) and in Dyer's task (separate bilateral presentations of words and colours) the same processes are involved.

Experiment II

Introduction

Dyer (1973b) showed that with separate bilateral presentation of words and colours, the same interference with colour-naming is found as with colour-naming on Stroop's (1935) conflict card. In Experiment I, with the same presentation technique, virtually no effect of incongruent colours on the reading of words was found. This result parallels the word-reading performance on the conflict card (Stroop, 1935). So the basic results found with the Stroop test can be reproduced with this presentation technique.

With the experiment here reported it is investigated whether the Stroop test and Eriksen's modified visual probe experiments are similar information selection tasks. If the basic results of the Stroop test and of

Dyer's (1973b) procedure, (a) interference if colours have to be named and incongruent colour words are simultaneously presented, and (b) absence of interference if the words have to be read, also show up if the task of the Stroop test is embedded in Eriksen's visual probe paradigm, then it is parsimonious to assume that in both tasks the same selection mechanism is involved.

In the experiment here reported the method of separate bilateral presentation of elements was used. Word-reading trials and colour-naming trials were randomly mixed. A barmarker at the left or at the right indicated which element had to be named. Also combinations of two colours and combinations of two words were used. These combinations, having elements with the same relevant attribute (colour-colour or form-form), replicate the essential aspects of the modified visual probe experiments, in which a number of letters together with a barmarker are shown. As in the modified visual probe experiments, also with these combinations, interference is to be expected.

In the original Stroop test, Ss are instructed in advance to read the words or to name the colours on the conflict card. In the experiment to be reported now, Ss have no advance information about whether a colour or a word provides the information for the correct response. The selective instruction, that is, the barmarker, is presented simultaneously with the colours and the words. So the only way of getting at the correct response is by using the barmarker. As stated, if for the word-colour combinations in the experiment to be reported the same results are found as in the Stroop test, then it is parsimonious to assume that in both tasks the same postcategorical selection mechanism is at work. It is then worthwhile to further discuss what common postcategorical selection mechanism can account for the results found with the two types of tasks.

Method

Subjects

Twelve students from the University of Leiden, six male and six female, served as paid subjects. All had normal or corrected to normal vision, and none of them was deficient in colour vision.

Stimuli

Each stimulus card contained two elements. The stimulus element (a word or a colour) that had to be named was indicated by two vertical barmarkers ($1°$ x $.1°$ in visual angle) drawn with indian ink, one above and one below the stimulus element (the distance between an element and the end of the barmarker was .5° in visual angle).

The stimulus elements to be named were either colours, Cr, (a red, blue or green coloured disk), or words, Wr: 'rood' (red), 'blauw' (blue), or 'groen' (green).

Each of these colours and each of these words appeared twelve times at the left (L) and twelve times at the right (R) of the fixation cross.

At the opposite side of the fixation cross was either a colour, Ci (a red, blue or green disk, or a black outline circle of the same size), or a word, Wi ('rood', 'blauw', or 'groen', or a series of four black Xs).

The colour or the word indicated by the barmarkers was combined with (a) a colour or a colour word having the same name (congruent combinations, C); (b) a colour or a colour word having another name (incongruent combinations, I); (c) the black outline circle or the black Xs (neutral combinations, N). The frequency of the three types of combinations was equated by duplicating the stimulus cards for the congruent and neutral combinations. (For instance, there were six cards having a red disk with a barmarker at the left and a coloured disk at the right; two of these disks were red (congruent combinations), two were black outline circles (neutral combinations), one was green and one was blue (incongruent combinations).)

Altogether there were 144 stimulus cards: 2 (Wr and Cr) x 2 (Wi and Ci) x 2 (L and R) x 3 (C, I and N) x 3 (name of the elements: 'rood', 'blauw' and 'groen') x 2 (number of stimulus cards per combination).

The distance from the centre of a disk or a word to the fixation cross was 1.5° in visual angle.

Procedure

Ss were instructed to name as fast as possible the stimulus element indicated by the barmarkers. The stimulus duration was 150 msec. Before the main experiment the Ss received a random selection of 36 cards from the 144 stimulus cards for practice. Each S saw the series of 144 stimulus cards in a different random order.

Results

Table 4.1 gives the mean RTs in msec over the twelve Ss for (a) the two kinds of stimulus elements to be named, colour (Cr) and word (Wr); (b) the two kinds of irrelevant stimulus elements, colour (Ci) and word (Wi); (c) the place of the element to be named, left (L) and right (R);

and (d) the three kinds of combinations of stimulus elements, congruent (C), incongruent (I) and neutral (N) combinations.

Table 4.1   *Mean RTs (in msec) over the twelve Ss per kind of stimulus element to be named, Cr (colour) and Wr (word), type of irrelevant stimulus element, Ci (colour) and Wi (word), place of the element to be named, L (left) and R (right), and combination of stimulus elements, C (congruent), I (incongruent) and N (neutral)*

	Cr				Wr			
	Ci		Wi		Ci		Wi	
	L	R	L	R	L	R	L	R
C	571	566	591	603	613	608	570	604
I	617	631	688	670	603	621	658	627
N	583	587	590	626	595	588	579	599

An analysis of variance over the mean RTs per S with these four factors as within Ss variables (see Kirk, 1968, Randomized Block Factorial Design; p. 237) revealed:

(a) a difference between Ci and Wi (F $(1,11)$ = 11.32; p < .01). The mean RT for condition Ci was 598 msec, for Wi 617 msec. The percentage of errors in these conditions were respectively 3.2 and 3.8.

(b) An interaction between Cr/Wr and Ci/Wi (F $(1,11)$ = 14.99; p < .01) indicating a strong effect of the kind of irrelevant stimulus element when colours had to be named (mean RTs for Ci and Wi are 592 and 628 msec; the percentages errors are 2.1 and 4.9 respectively), and virtually no effect when the words had to be named (mean RTs for Ci and Wi are 605 and 606 msec; the percentages errors are 4.4 and 2.8 respectively).

(c) A difference between C, N and I (F $(2,22)$ = 22.90; p < .001). The mean RTs for these three conditions are respectively 591, 593 and 639 msec; the percentages errors 3.0, 1.2 and 6.4.

(d) An interaction between Cr/Wr and C/I/N (F $(2,22)$ = 4.00; p < .05), indicating a stronger differential effect of the kind of combination of stimulus elements when colours had to be named (mean RTs for C, N and I are, respectively, 582, 597 and 651 msec (F $(2,22)$ = 29.73; p < .001); percentages of errors 2.1, 0.5 and 8.0) than when words had to be named (mean RTs for C, N and I are, respectively, 599, 590 and 627 (F $(2,22)$ = 6.81; p < .01);* percentages of errors 3.8, 2.1 and 4.9).

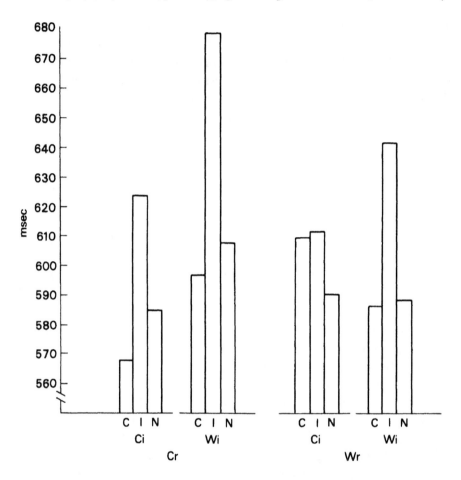

Figure 4.1 *Mean naming latencies for colours (Cr) and words (Wr) combined with irrelevant colours (Ci) or words (Wi), together forming congruent (C), incongruent (I) or neutral (N) combinations*

(e) An interaction between Ci/Wi and C/I/N (F $(2,22)$ = 3.89; p < .05) indicating a weaker differential effect of the kind of combination of stimulus elements when colours were the irrelevant elements (mean RTs for C, N and I are, respectively, 589, 588 and 618 msec (F $(2,22)$ = 6.41; p < .01);* percentages of errors 3.0, 0.7 and 5.9) than when words were the irrelevant elements (mean RTs for C, N and I were, respectively, 592, 599 and 661 msec (F $(2,22)$ = 30.46; p < .001);*

    *Tests of simple main effects.

percentages of errors 2.8, 1.7 and 6.9).

(f) A non-significant three-term interaction between Cr/Wr, Ci/Wi and C/I/N (F (2,22) = 0.97). The mean RTs for these combinations of conditions are shown in Figure 4.1. Tests of simple simple main effects showed a significant difference between conditions C, I and N for the combination Cr/Wi (F (2,22) = 20.77; p < .001), the combination Wr/Wi (F (2,22) = 10.55; p < .001) and for combination Cr/Ci (F (2,22) = 10.00; p < .001). The difference between C, I and N was not significant for the combination Wr/Ci (F (2,22) = 0.34).

(g) An interaction between Ci/Wi, C/N/I and L/R (F (2,22) = 5.36; p < .05). In Figure 4.2 this interaction is represented graphically. The figure shows that for Wi, the differential effect of the kind of combination of stimulus elements, C, N and I, is greatest, if the irrelevant word is placed at the right (R) side of the stimulus card, while for Ci the differential effect of C, N and I is greatest if the irrelevant colour is placed at the left (L) side of the stimulus card.

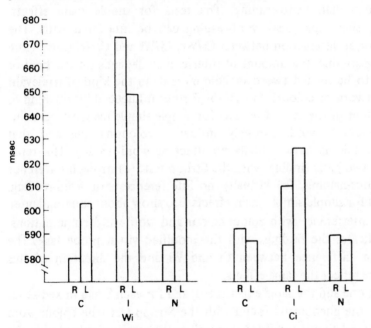

Figure 4.2 *Mean naming latencies for words and colours combined with irrelevant words (Wi) or colours (Ci) for congruent (C), incongruent (I) and neutral (N) combinations. R (right) and L (left) indicate the place of the irrelevant element on the stimulus card. The relevant element was placed at the opposite side of the stimulus card*

All further main effects and interactions were far from significant. (All remaining F-ratios < 1.)

The percentages of errors and the mean RTs generally showed the same trends, and so both reflect the relative difficulty of the different experimental conditions.

Discussion

The results of the experiment appear to support the view that the Stroop test and the modified visual probe experiments are similar tasks as far as the processing and selecting of information are concerned.

The interaction between Ci/Wi and C/I/N indicates stronger interference if words are the irrelevant elements than if colours are the irrelevant elements. The test for simple main effects, however, shows that also colours can produce interference. The interaction between Cr/Wr and C/I/N indicates that colour-naming is more susceptible for interference than word-reading. The tests for simple main effects, however, show that also word-reading can be interfered with. The absence of an interaction between Cr/Wr, Ci/Wi and C/I/N (see Figure 4.1) suggests that the amount of interference depends on the kind of element to be named (word or colour) and on the kind of irrelevant element (word or colour), but is not further influenced by the kind of combination of the two. The tests for simple simple main effects show that irrelevant words strongly influence colour-naming and that irrelevant colours have virtually no effect on word-reading. This replicates the two basic findings with the Stroop test: (a) strong interference with colour-naming, (b) virtually no interference with word-reading. The tests for simple simple main effects also show about equal and intermediate interference with colour-colour and word-word combinations. This replicates the findings with the modified visual probe task. The significant difference between Ci and Wi and the direction of this difference reflect the same effects.

So, in one and the same experiment, and for each S in a mixed series of trials, the phenomena found with the Stroop test (the colour-word and the word-colour conditions) as well as the results obtained with the modified visual probe experiments (the results of the colour-colour and the word-word conditions) are reproduced. This result lends strong support to the point of view that in the two types of tasks the same postcategorical selection mechanism operates.

The analysis of variance showed two other significant effects that require further explanation. The significant interaction between Cr/Wr and Ci/Wi indicates a difference between mean RTs for colours combined with colours (592 msec) and colours combined with words (628 msec), but no comparable difference for words combined with colours (605 msec) and words combined with words (606 msec). This seems to contradict the inference made in the last paragraph, that the amount of interference is independent of the kind of combination of the two types of elements. However, 51 per cent of this interaction is accounted for by congruent combinations (neutral combinations, 25 per cent; incongruent combinations, 24 per cent). Figure 4.1 shows that congruent colour-colour combinations (mean RT = 568 msec) and congruent relevant word-irrelevant colour combinations (mean RT = 611 msec) contribute especially to this interaction. The fast RTs with congruent colour-colour combinations suggest that a physical match can speed up colour-naming. The relatively slow RTs for congruent word-colour combinations possibly suggests that all colours, whether congruent or incongruent, have a slight delaying effect on word-reading.

The significant three-term interaction between Ci/Wi, C/N/I and L/R (Figure 4.2) was unexpected. The figure shows that the differential effect of irrelevant words is greatest if placed at the right of the fixation cross and smallest if placed at the left. The reverse effect appears for irrelevant colours. Such an interaction seems readily explainable in terms of hemispheric specialization (see, for example, Schmit and Davis, 1974; Cohen and Martin, 1975). This topic, however, is outside our line of argument and therefore will not be further discussed.

Two further implications of the results of the present experiment are worth discussing. The first concerns the processing of visual information, the second the ultimate selection of a response.

In the recent literature, the interference of colour words with colour-naming on the Stroop conflict card has been generally taken as evidence for the automatic and parallel processing of the different attributes of a stimulus (Treisman, 1969; Kahneman, 1973). Dyer (1973b) showed that this parallel processing of two different attributes also holds if the attributes are presented as separate inputs. 'Parallel processing of the separated word and color is clearly demonstrated by the facilitation and interference for color naming' (Dyer, 1973b, p. 316). By the same argument, the results of the present experiment and of the modified visual probe tasks can be seen as indicating that also two inputs with the same relevant attribute (both colours or both words) are processed in parallel. (Allport (1977) presents further evidence, obtained under conditions of severe pattern masking, for parallel processing of simultaneously presented words.) This point of view is consistent with and adds to the evidence in favour of parallel processing, presented in chapter 2.

It will be clear that the postcategorical selection mechanism investigated in our experiment differs in an important way from the postcategorical selection mechanism proposed by Deutsch and Deutsch (1963). In our experiment, word-reading trials and colour-naming trials were mixed in a random sequence, and a barmarker was used to point at the relevant element. Ss had no way of knowing in advance whether a colour or a word had to be named, and, of course, Ss had no way of knowing in advance what response had to be given. Therefore, 'central structures' with a 'preset weighting of importance' are of no use for selecting the relevant response. In one way or another, the barmarker had to be used for the ultimate selection of the response.

With the word-colour combinations in the experiment reported, the same results were found as with word-reading and colour-naming on Stroop's conflict card. So it seems parsimonious to assume that in both types of tasks the same postcategorical selection mechanism operates. We will now further discuss what common postcategorical selection mechanism can account for the results obtained with the two types of tasks. The problem we are primarily interested in is how the Ss are able to select, or to find, the correct response. (The problem of the origin of interference is further discussed and investigated in chapter 5.) First we will discuss how the finding of the correct response in the original Stroop test can be accounted for in Broadbent's (1970, 1971) conceptualization of selective attention tasks. Then we will discuss how locating the correct response in the modified visual probe task can be accounted for within Shiffrin and Schneider's (1977) framework for visual information processing tasks. This framework was already discussed in chapter 2.

Broadbent (1970, 1971) distinguishes two kinds of selective attention: stimulus set and response set (see also Kahneman's 'figural emphasis' and 'response readiness'; 1973, p. 95).

'Response set is the selection of certain classes of response (category states) as having a high priority for occurrence even if the evidence in their favour is not especially high' (Broadbent, 1971, p. 177), or 'the vocabulary of responses determines the selection, because the irrelevant stimuli are not appropriate to any one of the allowable responses' (Broadbent, 1970, p. 51). In the Stroop test, however, both the category state resulting from the word and the category state resulting from the colour are appropriate. So this kind of selection serves no function in distinguishing the response originated from the colour from the response stemming from the word in this task. Broadbent states:

> The distinctive quality of the Stroop test is however the fact that the irrelevant features are appropriate to the same set of responses as those used for reaction to the relevant features. Thus response set does not allow the shutting out of these features. . . . Intrusion errors are liable to occur, . . . and it is the guarding against these errors that takes the extra time. (Broadbent, 1971, p. 189)

So Broadbent also assumes that in the original Stroop test both responses are simultaneously available. How errors are guarded against or how it is known which response stems from the colour and which from the word, remains unclear.

The second kind of selective attention is stimulus set. 'Filtering or stimulus set is the selection of certain items for analysis and response, on the basis of some common characteristic possessed by the desired stimuli' (Broadbent, 1971, p. 177). 'The irrelevant stimuli are perfectly appropriate to the allowable responses, but are distinguished by some other feature which has in itself no connection with the class of responses allowed' (Broadbent, 1970, p. 51). In the Stroop test, the common feature that has no connection with the class of responses allowed and that distinguishes relevant from irrelevant stimuli (that is, word-colour combinations) is the location on the conflict card. But that location contains the word as well as the colour. So this kind of selection also serves no function in distinguishing the response stemming from the word and the response stemming from the colour.

Now, there are several ways in which Broadbent's model can be complemented in order to solve the problem how the response to the relevant information is distinguished from the response to the irrelevant information. The most parsimonious solution, and the solution most in line with Broadbent's analysis of selective attention tasks seems the addition of one extra step in his filter conceptualization. Filtering, or stimulus set can be conceived of as consisting of two stages:

(a) the feature that has no connection with the class of allowable responses points at the relevant features that give rise to the correct response.

(b) These relevant features are used for distinguishing the category states or the responses stemming from the word and from the colour. This additional step can be regarded as a special kind of tagging. The category state or response stemming from the relevant information is tagged with its input features, and these features are used for distinguishing this category state from the category states activated by (and tagged with) the irrelevant information.

Now we will consider how we can account for the locating of the relevant response in our modified visual probe task within Shiffrin's and Schneider's (1977) framework for visual information processing (see chapter 2). In our experiment, Ss had no advance information about what — a response stemming from a colour or a response stemming from a word — had to be given as a response. The selective instruction, that is, the barmarker, was presented simultaneously with the colours and words and pointed either at a colour or at a word. The only way for selecting the correct response was by using the barmarker. In the 'framework' it is assumed that a set of simultaneously presented inputs are automatically processed in parallel at least up to the level at which the responses, that is, verbal or acoustic articulatory codes, are available. It seems reasonable to assume that these automatic processes are very fast and that, when the selective instruction conveyed by the barmarker is understood, these responses are already available. One of the verbal codes has to be given as a response, and our problem is how the barmarker can be used for finding this verbal code.

Now it seems that this verbal code can best be regarded as a central code triggered by or aroused by specific relevant features in the stimulus (for instance, the colour of a coloured disk) and not related to or not directly connected with irrelevant stimulus features (for instance, position, size or form of the coloured disk). In this conceptualization one can only find the correct response via the relevant sensory features, that is, the colour for the colour name and the word for the word name. The barmarker cannot indicate one of the responses, because the barmarker and the response are not related in a direct way. The barmarker and the relevant sensory features are related by their spatial position. The relevant features and the correct response are related because these features gave rise to the response. Therefore, only by way of the relevant sensory features can the barmarker serve in finding the correct response. Therefore, postcategorical selection as conceived of in Shiffrin's and Schneider's (1977) framework, consists of two stages:

(a) the barmarker points at the relevant features that have triggered the correct response;

(b) these relevant features are used for distinguishing the verbal codes stemming from the word and from the colour. The relevant features can be considered as a tag distinguishing the correct response from the responses triggered by (and tagged with) irrelevant information.

We already tentatively concluded that in the Stroop test (integral combinations of words and colours; advance selective instructions) and in the modified visual probe task (separate bilateral presentations of words and/or colours; simultaneous selective instructions) the same postcategorical selection mechanism operates. We were led to this conclusion by the observation that in Experiment II, reported in this chapter, the phenomena found with the Stroop test as well as the results generally obtained with the modified visual probe task were found. The further analysis of both tasks presented in the previous paragraphs strengthens this conclusion considerably. Both the application of Broadbent's stimulus set principle to the performance in the original Stroop test and the analysis of the performance in the modified visual probe task within Shiffrin's and Schneider's framework lead to the same conclusions with regard to the separation of correct and incorrect responses:

(a) features having no connection with the class of allowable responses lead to or point at the relevant features that gave rise to the responses, or, the irrelevant features serve to locate the relevant sensory information.

(b) These relevant features are used for distinguishing the correct response from the responses triggered by irrelevant information, or, response selection is controlled by the relevant sensory features. 'Postcategorical filtering' seems an adequate name for this postcategorical selection mechanism.

This view, however, implies that the sensory features are still in the system when the responses are already available. Furthermore, the connections between the sensory features and the available responses have to be such that the selection of the response can be controlled by the sensory features from which the responses stem. So it has to be assumed that visual information at one level gives rise to, or triggers, a representation at another level, instead of being transformed from one form into another. This point of view, however, is perfectly compatible with Shiffrin's and Schneider's (1977) framework. Shiffrin and Geisler (1973), Treisman et al. (1975), and Posner and Warren (1972) also present such a point of view. 'Our studies indicate that successive codings are laid down and maintained in parallel. That is, the name code of a word is extracted from its physical code, but it does not replace the physical code. Rather both remain present and compete for the limited rehearsal capacity of the subject' (Posner and Warren, 1972, p. 25), and, 'Both physical codes and recategorizations are available within a second or so after input. Task structure determines what the subject will choose to emphasize' (Posner and Warren, 1972, p. 28). It will also be clear that this point of view is compatible with Craik's and Lockhart's (1972) levels of processing approach (see chapter 3; types of information lost).

At this point it is worthwhile to be somewhat more explicit about the assumptions underlying 'postcategorical filtering' and to relate the concept to the problem of 'perceptual integration' (Allport, 1977, 1979; see also Keele and Neill, 1978). The basic assumptions underlying postcategorical filtering are:

1 Upon presentation of a visual stimulus different 'processing domains', 'processing regions' or 'functional subsystems' are automatically activated (for instance, a 'visual domain' containing 'visual codes', a 'verbal domain' containing 'phonetic' or 'articulatory codes', a 'conceptual domain', etc.). (See, for example, Henderson, 1974; Turvey, 1975; Shiffrin and Schneider, 1977; Allport, 1977, 1979; Keele and Neill, 1978, for similar points of view.)

2 Comparisons are only possible between codes within a domain, that is, visual codes can be compared (does X look the same as Y? Is X close to Y? Is X greater than Y? Is X to the left of Y? etc.), verbal codes can be compared (see, for example, Posner et al.'s lettermatching tasks), etc. Codes from different domains, having nothing in common, are incomparable. On the level of visual codes or within the domain of visual codes the barmarker can point at the relevant element. (It seems that especially Treisman et al.'s, 1977, and Treisman's and Gelade's, 1980, research on 'stimulus integration within the visual domain' is of relevance for this and related kinds of arbitrary attribute or feature conjunctions.)

3 Codes from different domains are linked if a code from one domain has triggered or has addressed a code in a different domain or if a code in one domain has been generated from a code in another domain. These (specific) links unitize or integrate codes in different domains. (So, for people who have learned to read, neither the visual code of a word alone, nor the verbal code or the semantic code of a word alone form a perceived visual word, but the whole of unitized codes do.) In this way, the relevant features (the visual code) can be used for distinguishing the correct response (a verbal code) from responses triggered by irrelevant information, or, response selection is controlled by the relevant sensory features (that is, the visual code serves as some kind of 'tag').

So, according to this point of view, perceptual integration of visual codes and name codes occurs automatically. This is contrary to the point of view of Allport (1977, 1979) and Keele and Neill (1978). According to Allport (1977) perceptual integration has to be achieved, and there is a limited capacity for perceptual integration (Allport, 1977, p. 512). The next quotation from Allport (1977) shows how, according to his opinion, perceptual integration is achieved as far as the perception of visual words is concerned.

> Outputs of all three processing systems, visual code, phonemic code, and lexicon are generated in parallel, asynchronously, and without attentional control. . . . Lexicon outputs, ex hypothesi, take the form of abstract morphemic units, whose specification is capable of addressing, without capacity limitations, their corresponding visual or phonemic codes. That is, *with further processing*, these specifications can be translated into a description of the sound pattern or the visual appearance of the root word. Without further translation they can also be compared against the visual and/or phonemic codes generated by the immediately preceding sensory input. Conscious perception of a word (rather than a row of black squiggles) as present in a visual array is contingent on the outcome of this comparison process. (Allport, 1977, p. 528)

The essential operation required for perceptual integration is therefore the comparison process ('cross-matching' in Keele's and Neill's (1978) terminology) of lexicon outputs (lexical codes) with visual codes, (that is, 'getting this semantic information back into contact with the visual code' (Allport, 1977, p. 508)).

Two problems with this point of view will be briefly mentioned. First, a comparison operation requires, that what has to be compared is comparable, or, is in the same format. So, the lexical code has to have something in common with the visual code and what they have in common must be sufficient for an adequate and detailed comparison process (that is, must contain all information relevant for the comparison that this lexical code and this visual code belong together, and that is a lot of information). Now, Allport states that the lexical code has specifications that can be compared against the visual code generated by the immediately preceding sensory input. As stated, these specifications have to be detailed, and in the same format as the visual code. The best solution then seems to be that the lexical code has attached to it a visual code. This visual code can then be compared with the original visual code. There are two problems with this solution. First, there is an unwanted duplication of already existing and usable information (that is, two visual codes). Second, there is no reason to assume that the original visual code and the lexical code are dissociated and have to be integrated again, if, at the same time, it is assumed that a lexical code and a visual code are connected together and act as a unit (are unitized) in the comparison against the visual code. If visual codes and lexical codes can act as units, then it is parsimonious to assume that they always act as units.

Second, Allport's conceptualization of perceptual integration makes it rather difficult to explain the results obtained in a barmarker experiment like Experiment II and especially in partial report experiments (see chapter 3). The process of perceptual integration starts with lexicon outputs. Lexicon outputs have nothing in common with barmarkers, or, with high, medium or low tones. So, only a random selection of lexicon outputs can be taken for perceptual integration, and it seems that only after perceptual integration can it be checked whether the item is wanted or not. As Allport (1977) has formulated the issue now, this makes for a rather inefficient selection mechanism. He furthermore assumes that (a) whole report curves obtained under masking conditions (see chapter 1) reflect the rate of perceptual integration (that is, no differential forgetting of integrated information is assumed) and (b) that there is a limited capacity (see chapter 2) for perceptual integration (perceptual integration is 'resource limited'; Allport, 1977, p. 512). Given these assumptions, no partial report superiority is to be expected. As stated in chapter 3, however, a partial report superiority is easily demonstrated. (If, however, a number of assumptions are added about (a) the selection, and (b) the short-term forgetting of integrated information, Allport's proposal can be made to correspond with the postcategorical selection model described in chapter 3.)

Taken together, for the moment it seems preferable to take the simpler assumption that perceptual integration is an automatic consequence of stimulus presentation and does not require an active comparison process. In chapter 5 we will explain briefly why there is some reluctance to accept this point of view and why some theorists prefer to reverse the order of operations as proposed in postcategorical filtering. At the end of chapter 6, in the section The anatomy of a logogen, we will discuss one possible conceptualization of the way in which codes from the visual, conceptual and verbal domains are connected together. In chapter 7 we will briefly return to Allport's (1977) interpretation of the masking interval function.

In conclusion, we propose that in the Stroop test and in the modified visual probe task the same postcategorical selection mechanism operates. This mechanism uses the relevant features that have given rise to the correct response for distinguishing this correct response from responses stemming from (and tagged with) irrelevant information.

At this point it is worthwhile to briefly consider two alternative ways of distinguishing the correct response from the responses triggered by irrelevant information in the two types of tasks.

The first strategy is based on the notion of 'response strength'. It is possible that a word results in a stronger response tendency than a colour. For the original Stroop test, a possible strategy for emitting the correct response could then be: give the strongest response if word-reading is required, and give the weakest response if colour-naming is required. It is, however, difficult to see how such a strategy can work in the Stroop test embedded in the modified visual probe task. Ss have no advance information about whether the strongest or the weakest response has to be emitted. The assumption that the barmarker can indicate 'the strongest', 'the weakest', etc. seems too farfetched. (The same problem is encountered if the barmarker has to indicate 'the slowest' or 'the fastest'.) So, if in the original Stroop test and in the modified visual probe task the same selection mechanism operates then this strategy for distinguishing relevant from irrelevant information has to be rejected.

It can also be suggested that the responses have tags of a higher or more abstract level than the input features. The colour name can have a label 'I stem from the colour'; the word a label 'I stem from the word'. (The arguments presented below are also valid for other high-level labels such as 'I stem from the left', etc.) It is, however, as difficult to explain how the barmarker can point directly to such an abstract label as it is to explain how the barmarker can directly point at a verbal label. Again, the barmarker and such a label are not connected in a direct way (that is, the barmarker and the labels are from different domains). The barmarker points at a spatial position. That spatial position can give rise to the verbal code and to the abstract label. So, either the abstract label is an intermediate code between the sensory features and the verbal code and, as such, not needed in our conceptualization of the selection process, or the abstract label is at the same level as the verbal code, but then the detour via the abstract label is unnecessary and unwanted. So, if in the original Stroop test and in the modified visual probe task the same selection strategy is used, then this method for distinguishing relevant from irrelevant information also has to be rejected.

In the last section of this chapter, a number of models that are compatible with the results obtained in this chapter and in previous chapters are briefly discussed.

Related Models

From the evidence considered in this chapter, and in the foregoing chapters, a model for visual information processing tasks emerges consisting of two stages, parts, or sets of operations: (a) the processing, that is, the identification or categorization of visual information; and (b) the further operations performed upon the processed information, for instance, the selection of processed information for overt response, the storage of processed information in a more enduring memory or the maintaining of information in memory. It was suggested that the first set of operations is performed by a system with unlimited processing capacity, and that these processes are not under Ss' control. By way of operations of the second set, the S can cope with task demands.

Similar models were recently proposed by Keele (1973) and Shiffrin and associates.

Shiffrin and Gardner (1972), Gardner (1973), Shiffrin et al. (1973), Shiffrin and Geisler (1973) and Shiffrin (1975) propose an information processing model in which attentional effects are thought to be due to characteristics of short-term store following perceptual processing. They introduced the terms 'systemic processing' and 'cognitive processing'. 'Systemic processing is meant to refer to those stages of processing which occur automatically, with or without the subject's attempted control. . . . Usually systemic processing will correspond to the concept of perceptual contact with features in long-term store.' 'Cognitive processing refers to control processes like scanning, rehearsal, coding, and decisions carried out on the information in short-term store, before it is forgotten' (Shiffrin, 1975, pp. 170-1). Up to now, the research of the Shiffrin group has been mainly concerned with 'systemic processing', the transition from 'systemic processing' to 'cognitive processing' remaining largely a matter of speculation. Their theory assumes that the contents from short-term store are 'scanned' in order to locate important or required information (Shiffrin and Geisler, 1973, p. 57), and that a selective instruction or 'cue lets the subject rehearse and retain just those letters which must be reported' (Shiffrin and Geisler, 1973,

p. 64). Short-term store is thought to contain more levels of information, ranging from completely processed information to low-level features. It is assumed that Ss have access to all these levels, and therefore, can use this information for the location of important information (Shiffrin and Geisler, 1973, p. 79).

The latest developments in this line of theorizing were already extensively discussed in chapter 2. Schneider and Shiffrin (1977) and Shiffrin and Schneider (1977) replace the term 'systemic processing' by 'automatic processing' and the term 'cognitive processing' by 'controlled processing'.

> Automatic processing is activation of a learned sequence of elements
> in long-term memory that is initiated by appropriate inputs and then
> proceeds automatically — without subject control, without stressing
> the capacity limitations of the system, and without necessarily
> demanding attention. Controlled processing is a temporary
> activation of a sequence of elements that can be set up quickly and
> easily but requires attention, is capacity-limited (usually serial in
> nature), and is controlled by the subject. (Schneider and Shiffrin,
> 1977, p. 1)

How these two concepts are traced in the form of 'automatic detection' and 'controlled search' was discussed in chapter 2. There we also presented their framework for processing in detection, search, and attention tasks (cf. Shiffrin and Schneider, 1977, pp. 162-3).

Keele's (1973) model has its roots in the models and theories of Deutsch and Deutsch (1963), Norman (1968) and especially Morton (1969a). Deutsch and Deutsch (1963) postulated a system containing a number of 'central structures', or 'classifying mechanisms'. 'A message will reach the same perceptual and discriminating mechanisms whether attention is paid to it or not; and such information is then grouped or segregated by these mechanisms' (Deutsch and Deutsch, 1963, p. 83). Each central structure also has a preset weighting of importance. Among the structures receiving an information input, the one with the highest weighting of importance will 'switch in further processes, such as motor output, memory storage, and whatever else it may be that leads to awareness' (Deutsch and Deutsch, 1963, p. 84). Norman proposed an extended version of this model. The central structures in his model receive two inputs: a sensory input (evidence), and an importance input (pertinence). The sensory input is provided by way of an automatically performed initial analysis of the signal 'without any need for

111

sophisticated cognitive processes' (Norman, 1968, p. 523). 'Pertinence is based on the expectation of future inputs and the properties of the presently attended channel of information' (Norman, 1968, p. 527). Among the units activated, the one with the highest level of activation is selected for further processing. Morton (1969a) proposed a model for word-recognition, having much in common with Norman's model (see also Morton, 1977). In this model also the simultaneous effects of the sensory signal and contextual information, together with effects of word frequency and response bias determine which word response becomes available. The central units, counters named 'logogen', make a response available in a single channel exit from the logogen system if a threshold is reached. The sensory signal and the contextual information are thought to exert their influence by providing an information input to the logogens, thereby increasing their counts. Word frequency and response bias operate by affecting the threshold. At the moment, Morton's logogen model seems the most comprehensive model and it seems that, as a result of recent modifications, its scope will still be expanded (Morton, 1979). It can account for a variety of phenomena in word recognition tasks (Morton, 1969a) and in complex language behaviour like reading (Morton, 1964a and b). It provides a useful terminology for memory research (Morton, 1970). Auditory information processing in particular has been worked out in detail (Crowder and Morton, 1969; Morton, 1970). We shall return later to the way it accounts for the interference found in the Stroop test and related phenomena (Morton, 1969b; Morton and Chambers, 1973; Morton, 1977). However, for visual information processing the model is at least incomplete as far as the phenomena of selective attention are concerned. It is impossible to explain the selection of information for overt responding if physical features have to be used for this selection (partial report experiments, visual probe experiments). Morton (1969a) explicitly states that the logogen model is not capable of handling attention (p. 177).

Keele (1972, 1973) proposed a general model for information processing in which Morton's logogen model seems to be the central part. Two processing stages are postulated: (a) memory retrieval, and (b) subsequent operations. The model assumes that the first stage does not demand attention, that is, 'two or more sources of sensory information can activate information stored in memory simultaneously and without interference' (Keele, 1972, p. 247). The processes of the second stage, operating upon the activated memory information, selection, rehearsal, response initiation, etc., are thought to be attention-demanding and suffer from capacity limitations. As far as selective attention is concerned, the boundaries of the logogen model as formulated by Morton (1969a) lead Keele into what he calls 'an unresolved dilemma'. For competing auditory messages, he states: 'if selectivity occurs at the level of physical characteristics of the message, why does the meaning of the ignored message affect response to the selected message? If, on the other hand, selectivity occurs at the level of activated memory, why do physical characteristics of the sound, namely direction and frequency, affect selection?' (Keele, 1973, p. 151).

It will be clear that 'postcategorical filtering' at least offers a starting point for solving this dilemma.

5 The logogen model and the Stroop phenomenon

Summary

In this chapter, the origin of interference in the Stroop test and in related types of tasks is discussed and investigated. As a theoretical background we will take the logogen model, discussed in chapter 4 under related models. The core of the logogen model is the logogen system, a system of counters, one for each word in the vocabulary. Information provided by the stimulus analysers increases the counts of the logogens that correspond in whole or part with the input. Also context and frequency of occurrence of a word affect the functioning of the logogen system.

Two different explanations for interference, both in terms of the logogen model, have been proposed in the recent past.

In Morton's explanation, a response leaves the logogen system if the count in its logogen reaches its threshold. The single channel exit from the logogen system, however, accepts only one name at a time. Therefore, the first available response will occupy this channel and delay the entrance of later ones. In other words, relative naming speed is the crucial variable in determining interference. Morton's explanation is difficult to reconcile with the notion of postcategorical filtering.

In Keele's explanation, responses stay in the logogen system until a criterion, specifying what constitutes sufficient information, is reached. This criterion depends upon the relative strengths of competing logogens. This relative strength of competing logogens is, therefore, the crucial variable in determining the amount of interference. Postcategorical filtering is already part of Keele's complete explanation of performance on the Stroop test. Keele's complete explanation, however, is not consistent with the whole of its assumptions. Therefore, in this chapter a more parsimonious explanation is proposed that retains the essential characteristics of Keele's explanation: responses stay in the logogen system until actively selected and the relative strength of competing logogens is the main determinant of interference.

In summary: according to Keele's explanation responses are actively selected from the logogen system and interference takes place in the logogen system; according to Morton's explanation responses passively leave the logogen system and interference takes place in a stage after the logogen system.

The first experiment reported in this chapter showed no substantial evidence that the names of irrelevant colours become available and occupy the single channel exit of the logogen system in the passive way suggested by Morton. The results obtained in the second experiment suggest that the irrelevant colours are nevertheless processed up to a level at which their identity is known. From both experiments together it is concluded that identification is not absolute in the sense that responses passively appear in a single channel exit when the count levels in the logogens reach their threshold (Morton's point of view). It rather seems that the responses stay in the logogen system until actively selected and that interference takes place in the logogen system (Keele's point of view).

Some of the results obtained, however, suggest that the relative strength of the competing logogens is not the only factor which determines the amount of interference. It seems that postcategorical filtering is also a factor of importance. The third experiment reported is devoted to this issue. The results obtained, together with the results obtained in Experiment II (chapter 4), suggest that the amount of pure interference increases if the duration of postcategorical filtering increases.

Chapter 6 will be devoted to a further discussion of how (a) ease of discrimination of the relevant element (that is, postcategorical filtering), and (b) the relative strength of competing logogens in the logogen system, interact in determining the amount of interference.

This chapter is concerned again with the 'Stroop test' and the 'modified visual probe paradigm', or with the 'modified Stroop test', in order to investigate where the interference found in these tasks stems from. First, two explanations in terms of the logogen model for the phenomena found with the Stroop test are considered. Then the results are reported of three experiments in which the origin of interference is investigated.

General introduction

For a number of reasons it is interesting to take the logogen model as a starting point for further investigations of the Stroop test and related information selection tasks (partial report tasks, attribute selection tasks, etc.). First, and in general, it seems worthwhile to try to fit the explanations for performance in these tasks into a more comprehensive model (see chapter 4; related models). Second, our point of view that the Stroop test and Eriksen's modified visual probe experiments are similar types of tasks seems in accord with the basic assumptions of the logogen model. Third, both Morton (1969b; Morton and Chambers, 1973) and Keele (1972) investigated the Stroop phenomenon and provided explanations for it (see also Keele, 1973, and Morton, 1977). Shiffrin and Schneider (1977) devote only one paragraph to a discussion of the Stroop test (p. 152). Finally, it is interesting to see that the explanations provided by Morton and Keele are completely different.

An explanation of the Stroop phenomenon should answer two questions. First, it has to explain where the interference stems from. Second, it must explicitly state how the correct response is distinguished from the response originated from the irrelevant information. First, Morton's answers to these two questions will be evaluated. Then Keele's (1973) explanation of the Stroop phenomenon will be considered. This section will be concluded with a summary of the main differences between the two explanations.

Morton's original logogen model was already described in chapter 4. A system containing a counter or logogen for each word in the vocabulary is postulated: the logogen system. Information provided by the stimulus analysers increases the counts of the logogens that correspond in whole or part with the input. A context system is postulated that maintains the counts in logogens affected by that context at a higher level as compared with the logogens unrelated with the context. Each logogen has a threshold, determined by the frequency of occurrence of the word. If its threshold is reached, the logogen makes a verbal response available. Response bias is accounted for by the assumption that following the availability of a response the threshold of the logogen is lowered, returning to a value slightly less than the original value after a long time. A single channel exit from the logogen system is postulated.

An explanation of interference in the Stroop test (and in related types of tasks) is now readily available. Because the various stimulus analysers are supposed to operate in parallel, a number of logogens increase their counts. The finding that word-reading is faster than colour-naming (Gholson and Hohle, 1968; Fraisse, 1969), is reflected in the assumption that a logogen corresponding to a word makes its response available prior to a logogen corresponding to a colour. The word response then occupies the single channel exit from the logogen system and this will delay the colour-naming response. The absence of a reversed Stroop phenomenon with word-reading on the conflict card can be explained along the same lines: the word response is first (it is clear, that the same reasoning can be used to explain the interference effects in the modified visual probe experiments of Eriksen and Eriksen (1974), Eriksen and Hoffman (1973) and Hoffman (1975)). So, in Morton's explanation, 'the crucial variable is the relative speed of naming the various attributes of the stimuli' (Morton and Chambers, 1973, p. 389), and 'the presence of another stimulus value in a different attribute will interfere in proportion to the relative speeds of naming the attributes' (Morton and Chambers, 1973, p. 396). Morton's explanation for interference was subsequently adopted by Dyer (1973a). In his extensive review of recent research on the Stroop phenomenon, he concludes:

> Perhaps the best present explanation for response competition
> includes both Treisman's (1969) claim of an inability to focus on
> either the color or word analyzers and Morton's (1969b) assumption
> of a single response channel. The faster reading response tends to
> occupy the channel before the color-naming response can do so.
> The word response activity, however, has a very short time course
> ..., and this frees the response channel for the appropriate
> color-naming response. (cf. Dyer, 1973a, p. 118)

Morton's original explanation, however, is at least incomplete. At the output side of the logogen system, responses are available in the single channel exit or in a response buffer. The model, however, does not specify how the relevant and the irrelevant response are distinguished, and how the correct response is found from among the available ones. Allport has repeatedly pointed to this problem (Allport, 1977, 1979). (To the way in which Morton (1977) and also Allport (1977) try to solve this problem we will return further on.)

There are at least two possible ways to account for the fact that Ss can find the correct response.

(1) With the first it is assumed that the temporal order in which the responses become available is sufficient information for the Ss to distinguish between the relevant and the irrelevant response. If with the

117

Stroop test words have to be read on the conflict card, the first available response can be given. If colours have to be named, the first available response has to be suppressed and the second available response can be initiated (see Warren and Lasher, 1974). It seems that this is the only possible strategy in the logogen model as originally formulated.

While at first sight this simple strategy seems capable of accounting for the results obtained, it is not without problems. Three of these problems will be briefly mentioned.

First, for the original Stroop test this strategy can only work if the words of the word-colour combinations are always processed faster than the colours. But, while there is abundant evidence that reading a word is generally faster than naming a colour, there is also considerable evidence that, especially with small numbers of alternative stimuli and responses, the distributions of processing times for reading and naming overlap (see Morin et al., 1965; Gholson and Hohle, 1968). In general, with tasks in which the distributions of arrival times of responses for the different dimensions or elements overlap, this strategy is inadequate. For the Stroop test, Dyer concludes 'that the tagging of responses to stimuli must be different than a temporal process of suppression followed by amplification' (Dyer, 1973a, p. 119).

Second, this strategy cannot be used if the Stroop test is embedded in a modified visual probe paradigm as was done in Experiment II, reported in chapter 4. In that experiment, word-reading trials and colour-naming trials were randomly mixed, so Ss had no advance information about whether the fastest or the slowest response had to be emitted. A barmarker either pointing to a word or to a colour conveyed the selective instruction. In that experiment the same results were found as in the original Stroop test, so there is no reason to assume that different strategies are used in the two types of tasks. As stated in chapter 4, it is difficult to understand how the barmarker can directly point at 'the fastest' or 'the slowest'. So it seems reasonable to assume that in the Stroop test embedded in the modified visual probe paradigm, and therefore also in the original Stroop test, another strategy is used.

Third, this strategy cannot be used in the modified visual probe experiments. In the experiments of Eriksen and Hoffman (1973) and Hoffman (1975) the relevant element appeared in a randomly chosen position, and there is no reason to assume that that element is consistently processed fastest (the interference then remains unexplained) or slowest. The same argument holds for the colour-colour and the word-word conditions in Experiment II reported in chapter 4: there is no reason to assume that the colour or the word indicated by the barmarker is consistently processed fastest or slowest as compared to the irrelevant element. So, in the modified visual probe paradigm another strategy must be used. In chapter 4 we concluded that in this paradigm and in the original Stroop test the same postcategorical selection mechanism operates. Therefore we have to conclude that also in the original Stroop test another strategy is used.

Taken all together, it seems that order of availability cannot be used for the ultimate selection of the response. However, it seems that only this strategy can complement Morton's logogen model without adding additional explanatory components (see also Allport, 1977, 1979).

(2) With the second possible way to account for the fact that Ss can find the correct response it is assumed that the input features or relevant features are used, in one way or another, for distinguishing the correct response from the responses triggered by irrelevant information.

One such possibility was extensively discussed in chapter 4. There we searched for a postcategorical selection mechanism that could account for the results found in the original Stroop test as well as for the results found in the modified visual probe paradigm. Both the application of Broadbent's stimulus set principle to the performance in the original Stroop test as well as the analysis of the performance in the modified visual probe task within Shiffrin and Schneider's 'framework' led to the same conclusion with regard to the separation of correct and incorrect responses.

(a) Features having no connection with the class of allowable responses lead to or point to the relevant features that elicit the response, or, the irrelevant features serve to locate the relevant features.

(b) These relevant features are used for distinguishing the correct response from the responses triggered by irrelevant information, or, response selection is controlled by the relevant sensory features.

This method for finding the correct response was called postcategorical filtering.

For the Stroop test, such a method for finding the correct response was suggested by Keele (1973, p. 146). Also Eriksen and Eriksen (1974) suggest a related method for the modified visual probe tasks. 'In the case of the indicator display this selection is made in terms of determining which of the available letters matches the indicated position on the display' (Eriksen and Eriksen, 1974, p. 144). Furthermore, this two-stage method is an adequate further specification of the postcategorical selection mechanism proposed in chapter 3. There we tentatively concluded that representations of elementary stimulus attributes are used for distinguishing relevant from irrelevant information also with postcategorical selection.

As already stated in chapter 4, this method of distinguishing the correct response from responses triggered by irrelevant information implies that the sensory features are still present in the system when the responses are available. (The opposite assumption brought Holding, 1975, into great troubles in his discussion with Coltheart, 1975a.) Furthermore, the connections between the sensory features and the responses have to be such that the features can indeed be used for distinguishing the correct response from the other responses. So, it has to be assumed that visual information at one level gives rise to, or triggers, a representation at another level, instead of being transformed from one into another form.

These assumptions, however, seem contrary to Morton's original point of view. He assumed 'that little or no useful information remains in the corresponding visual store either because the course of decay is too fast or because . . . once a stimulus has been analyzed it is expunged from the system' (Morton, 1970, p. 219). Morton (1977), however, seems to have recognized the problem and presents a 'solution'. It is no longer maintained that the visual information disappears so soon. He states: 'A response is produced, from one or another source, and we then have to check the response against the stimulus to confirm that it is the one we want' (Morton, 1977, p. 126). On page 112, however, he states: 'The nature of this available response is uncertain, but since it is in some sense ready to be spoken, it is reasonable to suppose that it is in some articulatory code (as opposed to a semantic, visual or auditory code).' Here we have the problem (and the solution), already met in chapter 4 with Allport's (1977) comparison process, in a magnified form. It is extremely difficult to see how an articulatory code, as defined above, and a visual code can be checked against each other. Words like 'check', 'compare', and 'verify', used in models, have to be regarded with great suspicion, especially if (a) what is checked (see Morton, 1977, p. 112), and (b) the checking operation (see Morton, 1977, p. 126) are specified fourteen pages apart. (In his revised logogen model, Morton (1979) is not concerned with the Stroop test, so no further solutions are available.) Taken together, postcategorical filtering seems to offer a more adequate solution than Morton's (1977) proposal.

Because in Morton's (1969a) original formulation of the logogen model, in the revised logogen model (Morton, 1979) and in the application of the logogen model to the Stroop phenomenon (Morton, 1969b, Morton and Chambers, 1973, Morton, 1977), nothing is said about a connection between available responses and the physical features they stem from, postcategorical filtering implies an increase in explanatory components and a drastic change in this powerful model. That is why some theorists (see, for example, Allport, 1979) reject an order of operations as specified in postcategorical filtering and prefer the reversed order, starting with available responses or lexicon outputs.

Nevertheless, we tentatively conclude that this method for distinguishing the correct response from the other responses has to be added to Morton's explanation of the Stroop phenomenon. The two most important arguments for this conclusion are: (a) the evidence in favour of this method presented in chapter 4 and briefly discussed in the previous paragraphs; (b) the fact that most alternative methods can be ruled out. (Broadbent's response set principle, the method based on the notion of 'response strength' and the method based on the notion of 'higher-level tags' were ruled out in chapter 4. The method based on relative speed of naming the attributes was ruled out in this chapter.)

Keele (1973) presents a completely different explanation of the Stroop phenomenon in terms of Morton's logogen model. It is derived from a mathematical formulation (Morton, 1969d) that differs from the verbal statement of the model. Furthermore, Keele (1973) seems not to have been aware of Morton's (1969b) orthodox explanation of the Stroop phenomenon.

The three most important deviations from Morton's original formulation are listed below.

(a) The broadening of the concept 'logogen'. According to Keele, a logogen is 'any unit of information activated in memory, including the name of the stimulus, the meaning of the stimulus, or an appropriate response to the stimulus' (Keele, 1973, p. 88).

(b) The replacement of the 'fixed' thresholds by a variable criterion.

> Moreover, retrieval is never completed in an absolute sense. Instead there must be a criterion specifying what constitutes sufficient information to initiate a movement or perform a mental operation. If the criterion is lax, many errors are made; if it is stringent, fewer errors are made but RT is lengthened. (Keele, 1973, p. 89)

Morton's (1969a) verbal formulation excludes the possibility of such a criterion adjustment. If the threshold is reached, the response becomes available and enters the single channel exit.

(c) The dependence of the criterion on the relative strengths of competing logogens. Morton states that the logogen system is passive. 'As the system operates, no comparisons are made by any mechanism external to the Logogen System of the levels of activation in different logogens. Decisions are only made within each logogen' (Morton, 1969a, p. 167). In Keele's formulation, however, 'there is no fixed retrieval time. The time required to accumulate sufficient information to allow a decision having a certain degree of reliability depends on the relative strengths of the competing logogens' (Keele, 1973, p. 89).

The explanation of interference in the Stroop test and in related types of tasks (Keele, 1973, p. 106) is as follows:

> When one source of information is irrelevant, it typically has no effect, because the logogens activated by it are not included in the set leading to the relevant responses. But when the irrelevant information activates a conflicting logogen in the response set under consideration (the Stroop effect), the criterion of activation must be adjusted resulting in longer RTs. (Keele, 1973, p. 107)

According to Keele (1973), physical features are used for distinguishing the correct response from the response originated from the irrelevant information:

> In the case of the Stroop effect, for example, a color of ink as a stimulus activates a color name at the level of memory; a color word does the same. In order to decide which of two competing color names one should respond to, one must determine from sensory information which is the color stimulus and which is the color word. (Keele, 1973, p. 146)

So, Keele's (1973) explanation is at least complete. It accounts for interference as well as for the fact that Ss are capable of distinguishing the correct response from the response originated from the irrelevant information. Furthermore, the method he proposes is what we called postcategorical filtering. Nevertheless, there are a number of serious problems with Keele's complete explanation of the Stroop phenomenon.

First, it is not clear why a criterion adjustment has to be made only if the colours have to be named on the conflict card, and not if the words have to be read. In other words, the asymmetry in interference (Stroop, 1935; Dyer, 1973a, p. 108) remains unexplained.

Second, it is not clear how a criterion adjustment, as described by Keele (1973), can be of any use for adequate performance on the Stroop test. Of course, it is reasonable to assume that 'The longer the cumulation process takes, the more likely it is that background variability will average out, and the more likely it is that the correct logogen will have the greatest accumulation of information' (Keele, 1973, p. 89). With the Stroop test, however, there are two 'correct' logogens, one corresponding to the word and one corresponding to the colour, and not one 'correct' logogen and a number of 'incorrect' logogens with background variability that will average out. A higher criterion results in a longer cumulation process for both 'correct' logogens. Therefore, whatever the level of the criterion, the same conflict between the two activated logogens remains.

Third, if sensory information is used for determining which logogen contains the correct response, then the response can be initiated at the moment that this sensory information is found and the logogen is sufficiently activated. In other words, there is no need for a criterion that takes into account the level of activation of the logogen stimulated by the irrelevant attribute. If a criterion is postulated, then a criterion that specifies what constitutes sufficient information suffices, or, the decision can be made within each logogen.

These three arguments show that Keele's (1973) explanation of interference is no explanation at all. The problems with Keele's explanation primarily arise, because this author regards (a) interference, and (b) the strategy used for distinguishing the correct response from the other responses as two separate and independent issues that can be discussed forty pages apart (pp. 107 and 146) without reference to each other.

So the problem remains of how to account for interference in Keele's version of the logogen model. Keele's fundamental assumptions are (a) the amount of interference depends on the relative strengths of competing logogens, and (b) for the selection of the relevant response, the sensory features of the stimulus are used. As stated already, if sensory information is used for determining which logogen contains the correct response, then it is reasonable to assume that the response can be initiated at the moment that the sensory information is available and the logogen is sufficiently activated. A further accumulation of *information* in that logogen is then not necessary. It is possible, however, that it is difficult to initiate the response when also competing logogens are strongly activated. The asymmetry in interference found in the Stroop test can be explained by assuming that a word activates its logogen more strongly than a colour. It is then difficult to initiate the colour name and it is easy to initiate the word. A similar explanation can be given for the interference found in the modified visual probe experiments. Why a word would result in a stronger activation of a logogen than a colour is a matter for further investigation.

Taken all together, this leaves us with two different explanations, both in terms of the logogen model, of the origin of interference in the Stroop test and in related types of tasks. In Morton's explanation, relative naming speed is the crucial variable; in Keele's explanation, relative strength of competing logogens is the crucial variable.

These two possible explanations have not always been clearly distinguished. In his extensive review of research on the Stroop pheno- menon, Dyer (1973a), for instance, states:

> Most of these explanations have considered the phenomenon in terms of response competition with a stronger reading response to the irrelevant word aspect of the stimulus dominating and delaying the colour-naming response (Dyer, 1973a, p. 114),

as well as:

> Almost every investigator of the color-word phenomenon since Stroop (1935) has viewed the further increase in color-naming time when the patches are words as a direct result of this faster assignment of spoken words to written word stimuli than to colors and the resulting conflict between this faster response to the irrelevant word aspect of the stimulus and the response to the relevant color aspect of it. (Dyer, 1973a, p. 116)

While at first sight the difference between the two explanations seems trivial — relative naming speed and relative strength of competing logogens seem to be two different ways to characterize the same underlying factors — this difference is not trivial at all as far as the logogen model is concerned. There is an essential difference between Morton's explanation, on the one hand, and the explanation we for- warded in relation with Keele's model, on the other hand. According to Morton, responses leave the logogen system in a passive way and enter a single response channel, and interference takes place in a stage after the logogen system. According to Keele, responses stay in the logogen system until they are selected in an active way and interference takes place in the logogen system. Morton's 'passive' threshold model is changed into an 'active' selection model. (By introducing concepts like 'check' and 'compare', Morton (1977) and Allport (1977) however, again introduce an 'active' component.)

Keele's point of view is easily reconciled with the notion of post- categorical filtering: the relevant logogen contains the correct response and can be located by means of its input features. It is, however, difficult to understand how in Morton's model a free-floating response that has left the logogen system can be found by means of the sensory features from which it stems, that is, it is difficult to reconcile Morton's model with the notion of postcategorical filtering. Therefore, the problem of whether the responses leave the logogen system in a passive way (Morton's position) or stay in the logogen system until selected (Keele's position) or 'disambiguated' (Seymour, 1977) seems an adequate starting point for further investigation. In the first two experiments reported in this chapter we investigate whether Morton's explanation of interference is tenable. The third experiment reported is concerned with the relation between postcategorical filtering and interference.

For the general method for experiments III, IV and V, see chapter 4, p. 91.

Experiment III

Introduction

Dyer (1973b) showed that with separate bilateral presentations of words and colours the same interference is found as with colour-naming on Stroop's (1935) conflict card. Our experiment I showed virtually no effect of irrelevant colours on the reading of colour words. Also, with word-reading on the conflict card, virtually no effect of irrelevant colours is found. In Experiment II both effects were simultaneously obtained in a modified visual probe task. In this experiment also, intermediate interference was found with colour-colour and word-word combinations. All these findings are easily explained in terms of Morton's logogen model (Morton, 1969a and b; Morton and Chambers, 1973; see also Warren and Lasher, 1974). Morton's model specifies as the crucial variable the relative speed of naming the various attributes (Morton and Chambers, 1973, p. 388). The explanation is based on the following assumptions:

(a) The logogen system receives information from the various stimulus analysers in parallel, and all appropriate logogens increase their counts.

(b) The logogen system has a single channel exit, accepting only one response at a time.

(c) Under normal conditions, word-reading is faster than colour-naming (Morin et al., 1965; Gholson and Hohle, 1968; Fraisse, 1969) or the logogen receiving information from the word generally reaches its threshold before the logogen receiving its information from the colour.

So, with combinations of words and colours, the single channel exit is first occupied by the word name. If the word has to be read no delay in responding is to be expected (Experiments I and II). If the colour has to be named, the channel has first to be freed from the irrelevant word response before the colour-name response can be made (Experiment II; Dyer, 1973b). If, as in Experiment II, two words or two colours are simultaneously presented, the response stemming from the irrelevant element will occupy the response channel before the response to the relevant element on about 50 per cent of the trials. So with these combinations intermediate interference is to be expected.

One strong prediction following from Morton's logogen model is that under appropriate conditions the Stroop effect can be reversed (Morton and Chambers, 1973, p. 388). If an experimental situation is created in which colour-naming is faster than word-reading, the colour names should interfere with the reading of the words, and the interference from the words on the naming of the colours should disappear. Gumenik and Glass (1970) and Dyer and Severance (1972) reduced word-reading speed by placing a mask over the conflict card. The mask consisted of opaque white lines, ¼ in. wide, and separated by ¼ in. Through the mask, three fragments of the word were visible. This procedure produced interference with word-reading (Gumenik and Glass, 1970; Dyer and Severance, 1972) and decreased the effect of the colour words on colour-naming (Gumenik and Glass, 1970).

It will be clear, however, that these findings do not exclusively support Morton's explanation of interference. These results can also be taken as supporting the explanation that we forwarded in relation to Keele's model.

Gumenik and Glass (1970), for instance, explained their results in terms of response strength. 'Introduction of the mask, in the present experiment, weakened the reading response while leaving the color naming response unaffected' (Gumenik and Glass, 1970, p. 248). This formulation is in accord with Keele's model, in which it is assumed that responses stay in the logogen system until selected, and a further specification of this explanation in terms of 'relative strength of competing logogens' is easily made.

It is also possible that performance in Gumenik and Glass's (1970) and Dyer and Severance's (1972) tasks is seriously hampered in another way, as a result of the special method for weaking the reading response. In chapter 4 and in the general introduction to this chapter we argued that in the Stroop test and in related types of tasks the sensory features of the stimulus are used for distinguishing the correct response from the responses originated from irrelevant information. This way of finding the correct response was called postcategorical filtering. The masking procedure, however, destroys the sensory features of the word stimulus, while the colour features remain intact. Therefore, also, the ease of locating the correct logogen can account for the interference found by Gumenik and Glass (1970) and Dyer and Severance (1972).

The main purpose of the experiment to be reported now was to investigate whether a reversed Stroop effect could be obtained with intact words. First, by manipulating exposure times, we attempted to create a condition in which colour-naming was faster than word-reading. A preliminary experiment showed that an exposure duration of 150 msec resulted in about equal word-reading and colour-naming times. An exposure duration of 50 msec resulted in a mean RT of 522 msec for a word-reading group and of 488 msec for a colour-naming group (t = 1.35; df = 5; NS). Because further reductions in exposure durations resulted in a strong increase of errors for the word-reading group, this exposure duration was used in the main experiment.

In order to further investigate the effect of extent of overlap of distributions of processing times for words and colours, three exposure conditions were used:
(a) a 50 msec pre-exposure of the colour patch;
(b) simultaneous exposure of word and colour patch;
(c) a 50 msec post-exposure of the colour patch.
Especially under conditions (a) and (b) colours will be generally processed earlier than words, and, according to Morton's model, a reversed Stroop effect is to be expected. Furthermore, according to Morton and Chambers (1973), the reversed interference will decrease from conditions (a) to (c): 'our position is that, in a task which involves the naming of one value of a stimulus, the presence of another stimulus value in a different attribute will interfere in proportion to the relative speeds of naming the attributes' (Morton and Chambers, 1973, p. 396).

Two groups of Ss were used; the first had instructions to read the word as fast as possible, the second should name the colours.

Because Morton and Chambers (1973) consider relative speed of naming the various attributes as the crucial variable, it follows from their model that the decrease in interference over conditions a, b and c for word-readers is paralleled by an increase in interference over the same conditions for colour-namers.

However, because a 50 msec exposure duration results in faster colour-naming in comparison with word-reading, the average interference from words on colour-naming should be smaller than the interference from colours on word-reading.

Dyer's (1973b) method of separate bilateral presentations of words and colours was used. The combinations of words and colours were either congruent, incongruent or neutral.

Method

Subjects

Twelve students from the University of Leiden, six male and six female, served as paid subjects. All had normal or corrected to normal vision and none of them was deficient in colour vision.

Stimuli

Six sets of twenty-four stimulus cards were prepared. The colours used for the colour patches were red, blue and yellow; a black outline circle of the same size was used as a neutral colour. The words used were 'rood' (red), 'blauw' (blue), and 'geel' (yellow); a series of four black Xs was used as a neutral 'word'.

Cards in set 1 contained one of the three colour words, combined with one of the three colours or the circle. Each word appeared an equal number of times to the left and to the right of the fixation cross. This resulted in 3 (words) x 2 (places) x 4 (colours and circle) = 24 combinations of words and colours. There were six congruent combinations (C), twelve incongruent combinations (I) and six neutral combinations (N). The cards in set 2 contained one of the twenty-four possible combinations of the three colours, two places and four words (colour words or Xs). This set also contained six congruent, twelve incongruent and six neutral combinations.

The cards in set 3 contained only colour words and the cards in set 4 only a colour or a black circle. The cards from sets 3 and 4 were combined in such a way that the same twenty-four combinations of words and colours as in set 1 resulted.

The combination of the cards from sets 5 and 6 resulted in the same twenty-four combinations of colours and words as in set 2.

The distance of the centre of a colour patch or of a word from the fixation cross was 1.25° in visual angle.

Design

One group of Ss (three male and three female) was randomly chosen and assigned to the word-reading condition. The other Ss formed the colour-naming group.

Three exposure conditions were used: (a) pre-exposure of the irrelevant element (PR) (a card with a colour from set 4 followed by a card with a word from set 3 for word-readers; a card from set 5 followed by a card from set 6 for colour-namers); (b) simultaneous exposure of relevant and irrelevant element (S) (cards from set 1 for word-readers; cards from set 2 for colour-namers); (c) post-exposure of irrelevant element (PO) (a card from set 3 followed by a card from set 4 for word-readers; a card from set 6 followed by a card from set 5 for colour-namers).

Each S served in six blocks of trials. Each block consisted of three parts: one part devoted to twenty-four consecutive trials in one of the three exposure conditions. The order of the kind of combination of stimulus elements (C, I, N) within a series of twenty-four trials was random. A latin square was used to balance the order of exposure conditions (PR, S, PO) within blocks and within Ss.

Procedure

The stimulus duration was set at 50 msec. In the simultaneous exposure condition a card from set 1 or 2 was exposed for 50 msec. In conditions with pre- and post-exposure, first a card from set 4 (5) or 3 (6) was exposed for 50 msec, immediately followed by a 50 msec exposure of its complement from set 3 (6) or set 4 (5).

In the conditions in which an irrelevant word or colour was pre-exposed, 50 msec were subtracted from the times recorded.

Word-readers were instructed to read the word as fast as possible and to neglect the colour patch. Colour-namers were instructed to neglect the word and to name the colour of the colour patch as fast as possible.

Each S served in three sessions on three separate days. At the beginning of each session, twenty-four practice trials were given.

Results

An analysis of variance was performed over the mean RTs per S, with word-readers vs colour-namers as a between block variable and exposure condition (PR, S, PO) and the kind of combination of stimulus elements (C, I, N) as within block variables (see Kirk, 1968, split plot design, ch. 8).

There was a significant difference in mean RTs for the two groups of Ss (F $(1,10)$ = 6.35; p < .05). The mean RT for word-readers was 563 msec (5.2 per cent errors), the mean RT for colour-namers was 506 msec (1.4 per cent errors). Also, a significant effect of the kind of combination of stimulus elements was found (F $(2,20)$ = 30.56; p < .01).

The mean RT for congruent (C) combinations was 526 msec (2.2 per cent errors); for incongruent (I) combinations, 544 msec (4.4 per cent errors); and for neutral (N) combinations, 534 msec (2.2 per cent errors). However, the two-term interaction between groups of Ss and the kind of combination of stimulus elements (word-readers/colour-namers x C/I/N) was also found to be significant (F (2,20) = 13.84; p < .01). For the word-reading group, the mean RTs for combination C, I and N were 560, 566 and 562 msec. For the colour-namers, these mean RTs were 491, 522 and 505 msec. Furthermore, there was a significant three-term interaction between groups of Ss, exposure conditions and the kind of combination of stimulus elements (word-readers/colour-namers x PR/S/PO x C/I/N) (F (4,40) = 2.97; p < .05). In Figure 5.1 this interaction is graphically represented.

In order to further investigate this interaction, separate analyses of variance (a randomized block factorial design; see Kirk, 1968, p. 237) were performed on the data from the group of word-readers and from the group of colour-namers.

For the word-readers, only a significant interaction between exposure conditions (PR, S and PO) and the kind of combination of stimulus elements (C, I and N) was found (F (4,20) = 2.87; p < .05). This interaction is represented in the left panel of Figure 5.1. For none of the three exposure conditions did Duncan's New Multiple Range test show a significant difference in mean RTs between the different kinds of stimulus combination (C, I, N). The percentages of errors for conditions C, I and N were, respectively, 4.3, 6.3 and 4.0; for conditions PR, S and PO, these percentages were, respectively, 6.5, 5.2 and 3.9.

For the group of colour-namers, only a highly significant effect of the kind of combination of stimulus elements was found (F (2,10) = 27.63; p < .001). The mean RTs for conditions C, I and N were, respectively, 491, 522 and 505 msec (see also Figure 5.1, panel at the right). Duncan's New Multiple Range test revealed significant differences between conditions C and I for all three exposure conditions (p < .01) and a significant difference between conditions N and I when the irrelevant word was pre-exposed (p < .05). The percentages of errors for conditions C, I and N were, respectively, 0.0, 2.6 and 1.5; for conditions PR, S and PO, these percentages were, respectively, 0.9, 1.9 and 1.5.

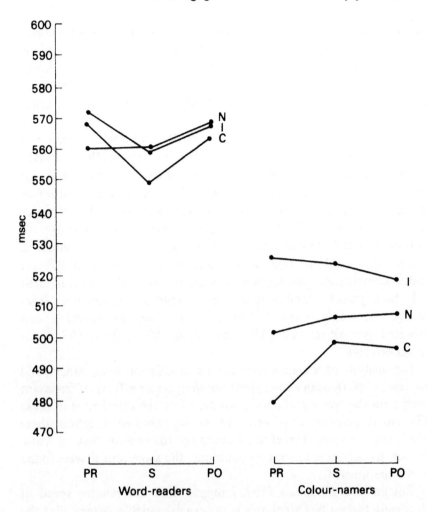

Figure 5.1 *Mean RTs for congruent (C), neutral (N) and incongruent (I) colour-word combinations for word-readers (left panel) and colour-namers (right panel) and for the three exposure conditions: pre- (PR), simultaneous (S) and post- (PO) exposure of irrelevant elements*

Discussion

From the present results, three points are of special relevance.
(a) The significant difference between the mean RTs for the word-reading group and the colour-naming group (57 msec) shows that the procedure of slowing down word-reading with respect to colour-naming was successful (see also Fig. 5.1).

(b) The significant interaction between groups of Ss (word-readers/ colour-namers) and the kind of combination of stimulus elements (C/I/N) indicates that an effect of the kind of combination is clearly present for the colour-naming group, but virtually absent for the word-reading group (mean RTs and percentages of errors show that interference is not completely absent).

The analysis of variance over the mean RTs for colour-namers and the results of Duncan's test show that for colour-namers the mean RTs for incongruent combinations are larger than the mean RTs for congruent combinations (see also Fig. 5.1). A significant amount of interference was found only with pre-exposure of the irrelevant word. So, in this condition, the same effects as in Dyer's (1973b) study with separate bilateral presentations of words and colours were obtained. Figure 5.1 also shows that for the colour-namers the mean RTs for neutral combinations are midway between the mean RTs for congruent and incongruent combinations. So, besides interference from incongruent words, some facilitation from congruent words is also indicated (see Dyer, 1971; Hintzman et al., 1972; Dyer, 1973b, for similar effects).

The analysis of variance over the mean RTs for word-readers, and the results of Duncan's test, show no comparable effects of irrelevant colours on the reading of colour words. While the differences in mean RTs and in percentages of error are in the expected direction, these differences are small. Therefore, it seems fair to conclude that for word-readers, for all three exposure conditions, the same results were found as in Experiment I.

Morton and Chambers (1973) suggest that the relative speed of processing the various attributes is the crucial variable, determining the amount of interference. In the present experiment, however, in spite of successful experimental manipulation of processing times, the same asymmetry in interference as already found by Stroop (1935) was obtained (Dyer, 1973a, mentions a number of other unsuccessful attempts to create interference by manipulating processing times). In the present experiment, virtually no effect of the kind of combination of stimulus elements was found with relative fast processing of the irrelevant attribute (see the results of the word-reading group) and a differential effect was found with relative slow processing of the irrelevant attribute (see the results of the colour-naming group). This result seems rather damaging for Morton's logogen model in its present form, if applied to this modified Stroop task. Furthermore, the results of the preliminary experiment mentioned in the introduction – about equally fast word-reading and colour-naming with an exposure duration of 150 msec — cast serious doubts on an explanation of interference in terms of relative processing times for the results of Experiments I and II. In both experiments an exposure duration of 150 msec was used and virtually no reversed Stroop effect was obtained. Therefore, as far as word-colour combinations are concerned, the results of Experiments I, II and III are not in accordance with the assumption that relative speed of processing is the crucial variable in determining interference. While an effect of irrelevant words on the naming of colours is easily demonstrated for a broad range of exposure conditions, no substantial reversed Stroop effect was obtained. So factors other than relative processing speed seem to be responsible for the asymmetry in interference obtained in experiments II and III.

(c) As the left panel of Figure 5.1 shows, the significant interaction between exposure conditions (PR, S, PO) and the kind of combination of stimulus elements (C, I, N) for word-readers is not readily interpreted as a decrease in differential effect of the kind of combination of stimulus elements over exposure conditions. For colour-namers (right panel of Figure 5.1), this interaction was not significant. Figure 5.1 and the results of Duncan's test, however, suggest a slight decrease of differential effect of the kind of combination of stimulus elements over exposure conditions. Morton's and Chambers's (1973) suggestion that the attributes will interfere in proportion to the relative speeds of naming the attributes (p. 396) possibly holds for colour-naming.

A number of other investigations, however, suggest that this interpretation has to be doubted. Dyer (1971) and Dyer and Severance (1973) also investigated the amount of interference as related to the pre-exposure time of the incongruent colour word. Dyer (1971) reports a significant decrease of colour-naming RTs and a significant interaction between the kind of combination of stimulus elements (C, I, N) and pre-exposure time. Dyer and Severance (1973), however, found no effect of the interval factor. The amount of interference was found to be constant for the different word-to-colour intervals. The results of Dyer (1971) can be taken as supporting Morton's point of view (see Dyer, 1973a, p. 118), but the results of Dyer and Severance (1973) are not in accord with this point of view. Van der Heijden and Frankhuizen (1975) also investigated the effect of pre-exposing the irrelevant colour word over a range from 0 to 125 msec. The results of this experiment are presented in Figure 5.2. No convincing effect of pre-exposure interval on mean RTs for incongruent word-colour combinations and on the amount of interference was found. So the same results were found as in Dyer and Severance's (1973) study. The reasons for this discrepancy in results are not clear, but the evidence in favour of Morton and Chambers's (1973) position seems not very convincing.

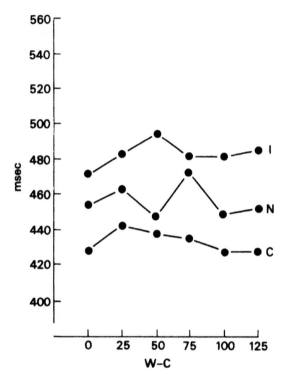

Figure 5.2 *Average colour-naming times (means of medians per S) for colour-word combinations (W–C) for congruent (C), incongruent (I) and neutral (N) combinations of stimulus elements for five pre-exposure times of the irrelevant element (from van der Heijden and Frankhuizen, 1975)*

All these results together make it rather doubtful that relative speed of processing is the crucial variable and that attributes interfere in proportion to their relative speed of processing, as suggested by Morton and Chambers (1973). In other words, it seems that processing is not absolute in the sense that responses passively appear in a single channel exit when the count level in the logogen reaches a fixed threshold. Rather, it seems that responses stay in the logogens until they are actively selected.

Experiment IV

Introduction

Gumenik and Glass (1970) and Dyer and Severance (1972) found interference from irrelevant colours on the reading of the words on Stroop's (1935) conflict card when word-reading was artificially delayed, relative to colour-naming, by fragmenting the words with a patterned mask. In Experiment III, virtually no differential effect of irrelevant colours on the reading of colourwords was found with a procedure that reduced word-reading speed relative to colour-naming by manipulating exposure duration and moment of presentation of a word relative to a colour. It seems that there are two relevant differences between their experiments and Experiment III on which an explanation for this difference in results can be based.

The first difference concerns the use of intact against the use of fragmented words. In the introduction it was suggested that fragmenting the words possibly not only results in delayed word-reading, but can also have an effect during the locating of the response because the masking method destroys the word features.

The second difference concerns the use of integral combinations of words and colours vs the use of separate bilateral presentation of words and colours. It is possible that only with integral combinations of words and colours are both attributes processed in parallel, while with separate bilateral presentations an irrelevant colour can be excluded from processing. Given this point of view, Morton's logogen model remains an adequate explanation of the original Stroop phenomenon, the absence of a reversed Stroop effect with word-reading on the conflict card, the reversed Stroop effect found by Gumenik and Glass (1970) and Dyer and Severance (1972), the Stroop effect found with separate bilateral presentations of words and colours (Dyer, 1973b; Experiments II and III) and the absence of a reversed Stroop effect with separate bilateral presentations of words and colours (Experiments I, II and III). The effects found with colour-colour combinations (Experiment II) would then be beyond the range of Morton's logogen model.

The assumption that irrelevant colours can be gated if presented as separate inputs, however, is contrary to our basic assumption: the automatic parallel processing of different inputs (cf. chapter 4, related models). Furthermore, in Experiment II a clear differential effect of irrelevant colours was found with colour-colour combinations, and this was taken as evidence for parallel processing of the two colours. An

135

alternative interpretation for this result is possible, however.

The assumption of serial processing with two colours together with the finding that a physical match (two identical colours) is detected early in the processing sequence (see, for example, Posner, 1969) easily leads to a completely different explanation for the effects found with these combinations. If a physical match is detected (congruent combinations) no search for the relevant element is needed. One of the two identical elements can be taken, and after processing this element, the correct response can be given. If only one colour patch is detected (neutral stimuli) also no search is needed. After processing that element, the correct response can be given. If, however, two different colours are detected (incongruent combinations) a search for the relevant element is necessary. It can be thought that this search, or the processing of the information conveyed by the barmarker, took the additional time with incongruent combinations.

One method for investigating whether colours produce interference at the input side of the processing system or at the output side, can be derived from Klein's (1964) well-known experiment (see also Proctor, 1978). Klein investigated the Stroop task by using conflict cards with different kinds of words. On each card the same four colours had to be named. Six different 'conflict cards' were used: (1) the original conflict card, (2) a card with colour words different from the colour names, (3) a card with colour-related words such as grass and sky, (4) a card with common words, (5) a card with rare words, and (6) a card with nonsense syllables. The interference from the words on colour-naming was found to decrease with these six types of cards; the highest amount of interference was found with card 1, the least with card 6.

This result is often taken as indicating that the amount of interference depends on the meaning relation between the irrelevant words and the colour names, and on the frequency of occurrence of the words in the language (Klein, 1964; Morton, 1969b; Morton and Chambers, 1973; Dyer, 1973a). These factors can exert their influence only after processing of the word and not prior to the naming system (Morton and Chambers, 1973) or prior to memory contact (Keele, 1972). (Klein's results fit in with Morton's (1969b) explanation of the Stroop phenomenon in terms of relative processing speeds (see Morton, 1969b, p. 340; Morton and Chambers, 1973, p. 396). There are a number of reasons to assume that the mean reading speed for the different kinds of words decreases over the six cards: words of card 1 are read fastest, words of card 6 slowest.)

Another explanation for Klein's results is possible, however. His data show an increase in RTs of 85 per cent with colour naming on the original conflict card (card 1) and an increase of 41 per cent with 'distant' colour words (card 2), both if compared with a card containing coloured asteriks. (The other cards showed increases in naming times between 35 per cent and 12 per cent; Dyer, 1973a, p. 112.) So, interference was less than half when the incongruent colour words were replaced by colour words that did not belong to the set of responses in use. However, members of both sets of 'incongruent' colour words have a strong semantic relation with the colour-name response that has to be given. It therefore seems that meaning relatedness does not primarily account for the difference in interference with these two types of cards. A close look at the words used by Klein (1964) for his cards shows that (a) respectively, 4, 2, 1, 0, 0, 0 of the four words of cards 1 to 6 had exactly the same first two letters as the words from the response set, (b) respectively, 4, 4, 3, 4, 3, 3 of the words in the response set matched in length with the words on the six cards. With appropriate weightings, for instance 4 and 1, a linear combination of these two factors is an appropriate predictor for the differences in performance with the six types of cards. (Also Morton, 1969b, reports two experiments with results comparable to those of Klein, 1964, in which physical similarity and meaning relatedness are confounded; see Experiments VII and VIII, p. 340.) Independent evidence for the interfering effects of the first letters of colour words was obtained by Dalrymple-Alford (1972), Singer et al. (1975) and Regan (1978). So, a variable of prime importance seems to be whether the irrelevant word is capable of activating a logogen that gives rise to one of the responses from the response set in use. After mentioning a number of unsuccessful attempts to show that any nameable symbol will cause interference, Kahneman (1973) also concludes: 'It seems that the interference effect occurs primarily when the printed word elicits a coding response which is relevant to the task' (p. 110). In order to explain the interference obtained with cards 2 to 5, the assumption that an input activates all logogens that correspond in whole or in part with it is essential. This assumption is generally made, however (see Morton, 1969a, pp. 165-6; Morton, 1970, p. 206; Keele, 1973, p. 88; Kahneman, 1973, p. 68).

Whether a coding response is relevant to the task is not known prior to the logogen system or the naming system, but has to be assessed by such a system. Therefore with this second explanation of Klein's (1964) results also, the interference is thought to occur after the information has contacted memory or at the output side of the processing system.

The experiment to be reported is concerned with the problem of whether two different explanations are necessary for colour-colour combinations and colour-word combinations, or, with the problem of whether colours are processed in series or in parallel. A modification of Klein's paradigm was used. Only colour-colour combinations were used. There were two types of 'incongruent' combinations: (a) relevant colours combined with an irrelevant colour that could also appear as a relevant colour (incongruent combinations, IN), (b) relevant colours combined with an irrelevant colour that never appeared as a relevant colour (irrelevant combinations, IR). If the irrelevant colour is simply gated, or if processing of colours is serial, both kinds of combinations will result in about equal mean RTs. With both kinds of combinations, no physical match is found. For both conditions, an equal amount of additional time is needed for the search of the relevant element. If, however, both colours are processed in parallel, larger RTs are to be expected with IN combinations than with IR combinations. Both explanations of Klein's (1964) results lead to this prediction. According to the first explanation, the meaning relation between the name of an irrelevant colour and the names in the response set in use is the crucial variable. With IN combinations, the name of the irrelevant colour belongs to the response set and is therefore identical in meaning with one of the members of the set of responses. With IR combinations this name is not included in the response set. The greatest amount of interference is therefore to be expected with IN combinations. According to the second explanation, the physical similarity between the irrelevant colour and the set of colours that have to be named is the crucial variable. With IN combinations, the irrelevant colour belongs to the set of relevant colours. With IR combinations, the irrelevant colour is not included in the set of relevant colours. Therefore, the greatest amount of interference is to be expected with IN combinations.

Three groups of Ss took part in the experiment. Three different colours were used. For each group of Ss one of the three colours was used as the 'irrelevant' element that had never to be named. RTs for the condition in which one of the two relevant elements was presented together with this element (IR combinations) were compared with RTs for incongruent combinations (IN), congruent combinations (CC) and single colours (SC).

Method

Subjects

Nine Ss were selected from the population of staff members of the Psychological Institute of the University of Leiden. They all had normal or corrected to normal vision and none of them was deficient in colour vision. They had all served as Ss in similar experiments before.

Stimuli

Twenty-four stimulus cards were prepared. Three colours were used: red, blue and yellow. There were two types of colour patches, half-disks and disks. Disks and half-disks were placed to the left or to the right of the centre of the stimulus card. The horizontal distance between the fixation cross and the centre of the disk or a half-disk was $1.5°$ in visual angle. Eight cards contained a red, eight a blue and eight a yellow half-disk, each colour appearing four times at the right and four times at the left. A half-disk at one side and of one colour was either presented singly, or together with a red, a blue or a yellow disk at the other side.

Design

The Ss were randomly assigned to one of three groups of three Ss, depending on which two colours they had to name. For the first group of three Ss only stimulus cards containing yellow or blue half-disks were used, for the second group red and blue half-disks, and for the third group red and yellow half-disks.

For each group of Ss the following four types of stimulus cards, corresponding with four experimental conditions can be distinguished: (a) cards containing only a half-disk (single colour condition, SC), (b) cards containing a half-disk and a disk of the same colour (congruent colour condition, CC), (c) cards containing a half-disk and a disk of the colour not used for the half-disks in that group (irrelevant colour condition, IR), (d) cards containing a half-disk and a disk of the other colour used for the half-disks in that group (incongruent colour condition, IN).

Procedure

Ss were asked to name as fast as possible the colour of the half-disk while maintaining accuracy. The stimulus duration was 150 msec. Before the main experiment each S received thirty-two practice trials (two series of sixteen stimulus cards). For each S the RTs on correct trials of eight series of sixteen stimuli were used in the analyses. The order of the stimuli within a series was randomized before the presentation of the series.

Results

Table 5.1 shows the mean naming times in msec (RT) for the three groups of Ss, for half-disks at the left (L) and at the right (R) and for the four experimental conditions (SC, CC, IR and IN). Also mean RTs per group of three Ss ($\overline{X}$) and overall mean RTs for the four experimental conditions (OM) are included. An analysis of variance over the mean RTs per S, with colours to be named as a between-block variable, and experimental conditions and left vs right as within-block variables (see Kirk, 1968, Split-plot design; ch. 8), revealed only a highly significant effect of experimental conditions (F (3,18) = 29.5; p < .001). As Table 5.1 shows, the mean RT for condition SC was 474 msec, for condition CC 474 msec, for condition IR 494 msec and for condition IN 541 msec. (The percentages of errors for these conditions were respectively 1.0, 0.7, 6.9 and 13.9). The mean RT for condition IN differed from the mean RTs in the other three experimental conditions (Duncan's New Multiple Range test, p < .01.) The mean RT for condition IR differed from the mean RTs for conditions SC and CC (Duncan's New Multiple Range test, p < .05). The percentages of errors are in accordance with this order of difficulty of the experimental conditions.

Separate analyses of variance over the data of each group of Ss, with colour to be named, experimental condition, and left vs right as factors (see Kirk, 1968, Randomized Block Factorial design; p. 237) showed, besides the significant effect of experimental conditions (group 1, F (3,6) = 5.69; p < .05; group 2, F (3,6) = 35.62; p < .001; group 3, F (3,6) = 6.31; p < .05), only two significant interactions for group 3: L/R x yellow/red (F (1,3) = 19.95; p < .05) and L/R x yellow/red x SC/CC/IR/IN, (F (3,6) = 9.91; p < .01). Table 5.2 gives the data necessary for the evaluation of these interactions.

Discussion

Duncan's test shows that the mean RTs for IN combinations and also the mean RTs for IR combinations significantly exceed the mean RTs for SC and CC combinations. The test furthermore shows that the mean RTs for IN combinations significantly exceed the mean RTs for IR combinations. The latter difference provides evidence against the serial processing hypotheses as elaborated in the introduction. If processing

140

of colours is serial, the same mean RTs for the two conditions are to be expected. With both kinds of combinations, no physical match is found and in both conditions an equal amount of additional time is needed for the search of the relevant element. As elaborated in the introduction, the difference indicates that the irrelevant colour is not gated or excluded from processing. Without processing of the irrelevant element, no differential effect of the kind of irrelevant element (IN or IR) is to be expected. Only if the irrelevant colour is processed, or, after the information has activated the logogen system can such a difference between IN and IR combinations result. Therefore, the results of the present experiment are in accordance with our general point of view with regard to the processing of visual information (chapter 4, related models). Different explanations for the results found with colour-colour combinations and relevant colour-irrelevant word combinations do not seem necessary.

Table 5.1 *Mean RTs (in msec) for the three groups of Ss for half-disks at the left (L) and at the right (R) for the single-colour condition (SC), the congruent-colour condition (CC), the irrelevant-colour condition (IR) and the incongruent-colour condition (IN)*

			Experimental Condition			
			SC	CC	IR	IN
Group 1	Blue/Yellow	L	475	474	511	541
		R	486	473	493	531
	(X̄) Mean	RT	481	474	502	536
Group 2	Red/Blue	L	444	452	478	539
		R	438	448	454	520
	(X̄) Mean	RT	441	450	466	530
Group 3	Red/Yellow	L	504	507	527	562
		R	501	450	497	555
	(X̄) Mean	RT	502	498	512	558
Overall mean RT (OM)			474	474	494	541
Errors (%)			1.0	0.7	6.9	13.9

Table 5.2 *Mean RTs (in msec) for group 3 (relevant colours red and yellow, irrelevant colour blue) for red and yellow half-disks, placed at the left (L) and at the right (R) for the single-colour condition (SC), the congruent-colour condition (CC), the irrelevant-colour condition (IR) and the incongruent-colour condition (IN), and averaged over the four kinds of stimulus combinations ($\overline{X}$)*

		Experimental Condition				
		SC	CC	IR	IN	$\overline{X}$
Red	L	491	488	523	587	522
	R	488	462	463	537	488
Yellow	L	516	525	530	537	527
	R	514	517	532	572	534

As stated, Duncan's test also showed a significant difference in mean RTs between IR combinations (494 msec) and SC combinations and CC combinations (474 msec). There are at least two different types of explanations for this 20 msec difference. First, the difference in RTs can reflect the additional search-time (that is, the time needed for post-categorical filtering) required with IN and IR combinations as compared with SC and CC combinations. Second, this difference can reflect interference from irrelevant elements on the naming of the relevant element. In the introduction, two explanations were advanced that could account for such an interfering effect. (a) According to the first one, IR elements elicit their own names as responses, and the semantic relation between this name and the responses used determines the interference. (b) According to the second explanation, the interference arises because an irrelevant colour (an IR element) elicits a coding response in the response set in use (for instance, a yellow colour patch also activates the 'red' logogen). The results of the present experiment are not sufficient to decide between these possibilities. One observation, however, is pertinent to this issue and seems to rule out the possibility mentioned under (a). While the Ss made a considerable number of errors with the IR combinations, 6.9 per cent, they never used the name of an IR element as a response. This is to be expected with the interference explanation mentioned under (b), and not with the one mentioned under (a). However, the 'additional search time explanation' is also consistent with this result. In the next experiment and in chapter 6 we will return to this issue.

The interactions found with the third group of Ss (Table 5.2) are not easily accounted for. These interactions, however, do not contradict the general conclusion from this experiment: the colours in colour-colour combinations are processed in parallel, and the interference effects found with incongruent colour-colour combinations are not different from the interference effects found with relevant colour-irrelevant word combinations. With colour-colour combinations (this experiment), the same effects are found as with colour-word combinations (Klein, 1964; Proctor, 1978).

The results of this experiment strongly suggest that in colour-colour combinations irrelevant colours are processed. What, however, about irrelevant colours in word-colour combinations? None of the first three experiments showed a convincing effect of colours on word-reading! The results of this experiment and Experiment II together, however, suggest that the irrelevant colours are indeed processed. In Experiment II word-reading trials and colour-naming trials were randomly mixed. It seems most likely that such a procedure forces Ss into the same mode of processing on each trial. Experiment II showed that with relevant-colour/irrelevant-word combinations, both elements are simultaneously processed. The results of the present experiment indicate that two colours are also simultaneously processed. It seems, therefore, most likely that also with the relevant word-irrelevant colour combinations both elements are simultaneously processed, or that also in that condition the colours are not gated.

In Experiment II an exposure duration of 150 msec was used, resulting in about equal mean naming times for words and colours ($F (1,11) = 0.14$, NS; mean RT for word-reading was 605 msec, mean RT for colour-naming 610 msec). However, virtually no differential effect of irrelevant colours on word-reading was found. In Experiments I and II no differential effect of irrelevant colours was found either. But given the results of Experiment II there is also no reason to assume that in these experiments irrelevant colours were gated or excluded from processing. This view is in accord with Treisman's (1969) point of view (see also Kahneman, 1973, p. 123) and corresponds with our general point of view with regard to the processing of visual information (chapter 2 and chapter 4, related models).

From this point of view, two further conclusions follow. First, Experiments I, II and III show that at least for relevant word-irrelevant colour combinations relative processing speeds cannot be regarded as

143

the crucial variable determining interference. From Experiment III it also follows that with the same combination of relevant and irrelevant elements the amount of interference is not in proportion to the relative speed of processing colours and words. In none of these experiments was substantial evidence found that the names of the incongruent colours delay word-reading in the same way as the incongruent colour words can delay colour-naming. In other words, no evidence was found that the colour names become available and occupy the single channel exit of the logogen system in the passive way suggested in Morton's (1969a) logogen model.

Furthermore, the fact that in Experiment II (chapter 4) approximately the same results were found with colour-colour combinations and with word-word combinations strongly suggests that there are no essential (qualitative) differences between colour-naming and word-reading in this type of task. We therefore have no reason to conclude that words that are read behave differently or become available as responses in the passive way as suggested by Morton.

As elaborated in the general introduction to this chapter, from Keele (1973) an explanation of the Stroop phenomenon can be derived in which it is assumed that responses stay in the logogen system until actively selected and in which the locus of interference is placed in the logogen system. In this explanation, the 'relative strength of competing logogens' within the logogen system determines the amount of interference. In chapter 6 we will present an explanation for the results obtained in Experiments I and II of chapter 4 and for the results obtained in the experiments reported in this chapter in which this 'relative strength of competing logogens' is the major determinant of interference.

Second, the reversed Stroop effect found by Gumenik and Glass (1970) and Dyer and Severance (1972) does not really support Morton's (1969b) and Morton's and Chamber's (1973) point of view with regard to the origin of interference in the Stroop test. In these experiments word-reading was delayed by fragmenting the words with a mask. In Experiment III word-reading was slowed down relative to colour-naming by manipulating exposure duration and moment of presentation of the word stimulus. Both procedures appeared successful in slowing down word-reading with respect to colour-naming. However, only with fragmented words was a substantial reversed Stroop effect found. This experiment suggests that integral combination vs separate bilateral presentations of word and colour is not the important variable. The only relevant difference between the two types of experiments seems to be the method used for slowing down word-reading. One possible explanation for the differences in results obtained is based on the assumption that fragmenting the word has an effect during post-categorical filtering. To this possibility we will return in chapter 6.

Experiment V

Introduction

In Keele's (1973) explanation of the Stroop phenomenon, the basic assumptions are (a) the amount of interference depends on the relative strengths of competing logogens within the logogen system, and (b) for the selection of the relevant response the sensory features of the stimulus are used. In our attempt to make Keele's explanation more parsimonious, we furthermore assumed that the selection process starts when the sensory features are available and the logogen is activated (a further accumulation of information in that logogen is then not necessary), and that the response is initiated when the selection process is finished. In other words, it was assumed that the relevant response is selected in an active way from among the activated logogens by means of sensory features.

For this modified version of Keele's explanation, the ease of selection of the relevant response (or logogen) is the crucial variable in determining the amount of interference. The results obtained up to now strongly suggest that two different aspects have to be distinguished with regard to this selection process.

The first aspect concerns postcategorical filtering, that is, the locating of the relevant information. If the sensory features of the elements are used for the selection of the correct response, then the ease and the speed with which the discrimination between the sensory features from the relevant and the irrelevant logogens can be made is an important variable. This point of view corresponds with Eriksen's and Eriksen's (1974) view with regard to the response selection process in the modified visual probe tasks: 'This response selection must be made in terms of the target letter's location in the display. As with discrimination tasks in general, the more discriminable the differences in location in the display, the faster will be the selection process' (1974, p. 148).

The second concerns the level of activation of the logogens from among which the relevant one has to be selected, or, the relative strengths of the competing logogens. This aspect of the selection process will be further discussed in chapter 6. It will be argued there that this relative strength of the competing logogens is the major determinant of pure interference or postcategorical interference.

This distinction between (a) the time needed for postcategorical filtering or the search time, (t_s); and (b) the amount of pure interference, or postcategorical interference (PI), is possibly of some value for clarifying and investigating a discrepancy in the results obtained up to now. In the foregoing experiments two types of stimuli with relevant colours were used: colour-word combinations and colour-colour combinations. In Experiment II a simultaneous barmarker was used to indicate the relevant element and all stimuli contained two elements (that is, also the neutral stimuli contained two elements, the relevant one and a 'neutral' element). Therefore, for that experiment there is no reason to believe that it was easier to make the spatial discrimination, or, to locate the relevant element with one combination than with another combination (that is, equal t_ss for all combinations). In that experiment a larger amount of interference (the difference between mean RTs for incongruent and neutral combinations) was found with colour-word combinations (71 msec) than with colour-colour combinations (39 msec). Given equal t_ss for all combinations, these figures can be regarded as estimates of pure interference or postcategorical interference, PI.

The results of Experiments III and IV, however, suggest the reversed order of difficulty. For the colour-word combinations of the colour-naming group in Experiment III, 17 msec interference was found. In Experiment IV, in which only colour-colour combinations were used, the amount of interference found was 67 msec. For Experiment IV (and for the same reason for Experiment I), however, it is rather doubtful whether the difference between I and N can be interpreted as an estimate of postcategorical interference, PI. In this experiment, the neutral stimuli contained a single colour patch (that is, no 'neutral' colour was used, and it is difficult to find an adequate 'neutral' colour patch). The incongruent combinations contained two elements. It is therefore likely that the search for the relevant element (that is, postcategorical filtering) took more time with incongruent stimuli than with neutral stimuli. Therefore, part of the difference I-N, the amount of interference, consists of this difference in search-times. So the difference I-N cannot be taken as an adequate estimate of the amount of pure interference or postcategorical interference, PI. In the colour-word condition of Experiment III, the neutral stimuli contained a 'neutral' element (that is, a series of black Xs). If it is assumed that, as far as postcategorical filtering is concerned, such a series of Xs acts in the same way as a black colour word, then for this experiment the difference I-N gives an adequate estimate of pure interference or post-categorical interference, PI. Therefore, a comparison between these two experiments is not justified because such a comparison involves different time components.

Let us state this argument in a more formal way. Latencies with incongruent (I) combinations include a general time component in common with latencies for neutral stimuli (A), a search-time, or, the time needed for postcategorical filtering $t_{s(i)}$, and the amount of pure interference or postcategorical interference, PI. Latencies for neutral stimuli include the same general time component (A), and also a search-time, $t_{s(n)}$.

In general (and especially in experiments in which no 'neutral' elements are used) in an experiment including I and N stimuli, $t_{s(i)} \neq t_{s(n)}$. For instance, it is easy to locate a colour patch if only one element is presented ($t_{s(n)}$, neutral stimuli), and it probably takes more time to locate a relevant colour patch distinguished by its form if it is presented together with another different colour patch, ($t_{s(i)}$, incongruent stimuli). Therefore, the difference in latencies between conditions I and N equals

$$(A + t_{s(i)} + PI) - (A + t_{s(n)}) = (t_{s(i)} - t_{s(n)}) + PI \qquad (1)$$

and this difference can not be used as an estimate of pure interference or postcategorical interference, PI.

Furthermore, a comparison of the differences between latencies for I and N stimuli over different experiments provides no information over the relative duration of pure interference in the experiments compared. In general, search-times differ from one experiment to another (for instance, it seems reasonable to assume that it is easy to find a relevant colour with colour-word combinations but that the search for the relevant colour takes appreciably more time with colour-colour combinations). Therefore, the differences, I-N, include different time components ($t_{s(i)} - t_{s(n)}$), that obscure the differences in PI between experiments.

It is, however, rather doubtful whether the argument presented in the previous paragraphs can completely account for the reversed order of difficulty found between Experiment II (I-N = 71 msec (C, W) and 39 msec (C̱, C)) and Experiments III and IV (I-N = 17 msec (C̄, W) and 67 msec (C̱, C)). As already stated, it seems reasonable to assume that the differences I-N from Experiments II and III provide fair estimates of pure interference or postcategorical interference, PI. In Experiment IV, however, the neutral stimuli contained only one single colour

147

patch. Therefore, the difference I-N includes the difference in search-times between I and N stimuli, and is an estimate of $(t_{s(i)} - t_{s(n)})$ + PI. Experiment IV, however, also included a condition with irrelevant colour patches (IR combinations). The difference IR-N was 20 msec. If it is assumed that no postcategorical interference is involved with this kind of combination, than the difference IR-N is an adequate estimate of $t_{s(i)} - t_{s(n)}$. (See also the discussion of Experiment IV.) (I-N) − (IR-N) gives therefore an adequate estimate of PI in Experiment IV. This estimate of PI (47 msec) still appreciably exceeds the 17 msec PI found in Experiment III, and therefore the reversed order of difficulty remains.

A possible explanation for this pattern of results is that the amount of postcategorical interference (PI) increases with increasing duration of postcategorical filtering (t_s). As stated, it seems reasonable to assume that it is easier to find a relevant colour with colour-word combinations (Experiment III) than with colour-colour combinations (Experiment IV). The task of discriminating between a coloured disk and a black colour word seems much easier than the task of discriminating between a coloured half-disk and a coloured disk. In other words, t_s in Experiment IV exceeds t_s in Experiment III. If PI increases with t_s, the amount of PI in Experiment IV (C̲, C combinations) can exceed the amount of PI in Experiment III (C̲, W combinations), while with equal t_ss (Experiment II) the amount of PI for C̲, W combinations exceeds the amount of PI for C̲, C combinations.

There are, however, several other differences between Experiment III and Experiment IV besides ease of locating the relevant element (exposure duration, number of relevant responses, etc.) and a direct comparison is impossible. The experiment reported further on, however, allows for a valid comparison.

In the experiment, we tried to get independent estimates of $(t_{s(i)} - t_{s(n)})$ and of PI for colour-colour and colour-word combinations from separate experiments. The experiment consisted of two parts, a position-naming and a colour-naming part.

In the first part of the experiment, separate series of colour-colour and of colour-word combinations were presented. The neutral (N) stimuli contained a single circular colour patch, the incongruent (I) stimuli contained a circular colour patch and an incongruent coloured half-disk (colour-colour combinations) or an incongruent black colour word (colour-word combinations). Ss had to indicate as fast as possible the position of the circular colour patch by saying 'links' (left) or 'rechts' (right). If it is assumed that in this position-naming task no response competition is involved, the difference between the mean latencies for I and N stimuli can be used as an estimate of $(t_{s(i)} - t_{s(n)})$ for colour-colour and for colour-word combinations. The latencies for incongruent combinations include a general time component in common with the latencies for neutral stimuli, (B), and the search-time needed to locate the relevant element, $(t_{s(i)})$. Latencies for neutral stimuli include the same general time component, (B), and a search-time $(t_{s(n)})$. The difference in latencies between conditions I and N is therefore an estimate of

$$(B + t_{s(i)}) - (B + t_{s(n)}) = (t_{s(i)} - t_{s(n)}). \tag{2}$$

In the second part of the experiment the same stimuli were used. Again separate series of colour-colour and of colour-word stimuli were presented. In this part, Ss had to name as fast as possible the colour of the circular colour patch by saying 'rood' (red) or 'blauw' (blue). As already stated, the difference in latencies between conditions I and N equals

$$(A + t_{s(i)} + PI) - (A + t_{s(n)}) = (t_{s(i)} - t_{s(n)}) + PI. \tag{1}$$

Subtracting (2) from (1) gives

$$(t_{s(i)} - t_{s(n)}) + PI - (t_{s(i)} - t_{s(n)}) = PI.$$

So, this subtraction procedure yields estimates of differences in search-times $(t_{s(i)} - t_{s(n)})$ and of pure PIs for colour-colour and colour-word combinations and a valid comparison over experiments can be made.

It will be clear that this procedure is a direct application of Donders's (1969) subtraction method. For a recent, verbal evaluation of this method, see Taylor (1976), pp. 178-9.

Method

Subjects

Eight students of the University of Leiden (five male and three female) participated in the experiment. They all had normal or corrected to normal vision and none of them was deficient in colour vision.

Stimuli

Two sets of twenty-four stimulus cards were prepared. The stimulus element to be named or located was a red or blue circular colour patch .9 mm in diameter. In the first set (colour-colour condition, CC), each colour patch was placed six times at the left and six times at the right of the centre of the stimulus card. At the opposite side was either a coloured half-disk in the incongruent colour (incongruent combinations, I) or the opposite side was left empty (neutral stimuli, N). In the second set (colour-word condition, CW) the neutral stimuli were identical to those in the first set, but instead of coloured incongruent half-disks, incongruent colour words were used, that is, 'blauw' (blue) and 'rood' (red).

Each possible combination of colour of colour patch, position of colour patch and kind of combination was represented three times in each set of twenty-four stimulus cards.

The distance from the centre of a disk, half-disk or word to the fixation cross was 1.25° in visual angle.

Design

The two parts of the experiment, position-naming and colour-naming, were run on two consecutive days. The first day all subjects performed in the position-naming part and the second day in the colour-naming part. In each part, 3 x 24 stimuli of one of the conditions, CC or CW, were presented, followed by 3 x 24 stimuli of the remaining condition. The order of presentation (CC-CW or CW-CC) was balanced over Ss and over the two parts of the experiment. So, in the position-naming part, half of the Ss started with the CC condition and the other half with the CW condition; in the colour-naming part, half of the Ss had the same order of conditions, the other half a reversed order of conditions.

Procedure

On the first day the Ss were instructed to name the position of the coloured disk, that is, 'links' (left) or 'rechts' (right). On the second day they were asked to name the colour of the disk, that is, 'rood' (red) or 'blauw' (blue). On both days the Ss were asked to react as fast as possible while maintaining accuracy. The S spoke his response in a voice key connected to the electronic timer. At the beginning of the first part of the experiment thirty-six practice trials were given; at the beginning of each new series of 72 stimuli with another kind of irrelevant element twenty-four practice trials were given.

The stimulus duration was 150 msec.

Results

Position-naming

Table 5.3 shows the mean position-naming times in msec (RT) for the eight Ss and for the different experimental conditions. Row $\bar{X}$ gives the mean RTs for the major experimental conditions (CC, CW x I, N). The numbers in parenthesis are the numbers of errors. An analysis of variance was performed over the mean RTs per S, with order of presentation (CC-Cw vs CW-CC) (F (1,6) = 10.0; p < .01). The mean irrelevant element (CC, CW) and kind of combination (I, N) as within block variables (see Kirk, 1968, Split-plot design, ch. 8).

A significant difference in mean RTs was found for order of presentation (CC-CW vs CW-CC) (F (1,6) = 10.07; p < .01). The mean RTs for CC-CW and CW-CC were respectively 479 and 590 msec. Also a significant difference in mean RTs was found for kind of combination (I vs N) (F (1,6) = 39.15; p < .01). The mean RTs for the incongruent and neutral combinations were 543 and 526 msec respectively. Separate t-tests revealed significant differences between I and N for CC (t = 2.742; df = 7; p < .05) and for CW combinations (t = 2.320; df = 7; p < .05). Neither the difference between conditions I for CC and CW combinations nor the difference between conditions N for CC and CW combinations appeared significant (t = .852 and t = .535 respectively; df = 7). Furthermore the three term interaction (CC-CW, CW-CC x CC, CW x 1, N) appears to be significant (F (1,6) = 6.33; p < .05). Table 5.4 gives the data necessary for evaluating this interaction.

Table 5.3 *Mean position-naming times (in msec) per S and over Ss ($\bar{X}$) for the two kinds of irrelevant elements (CC and CW), the two kinds of combinations (I and N) and the order of presentation (CC-CW and CW-CC). The numbers in parenthesis are the numbers of errors per 36 trials*

		CC		CW	
		I	N	I	N
CC-CW	S_1	529(0)	499(0)	526(1)	513(0)
	2	552(0)	510(0)	492(0)	483(0)
	5	467(1)	410(0)	380(1)	398(0)
	6	513(1)	499(0)	453(2)	438(1)
CW-CC	3	619(0)	596(0)	659(0)	628(0)
	4	633(1)	645(2)	648(3)	625(0)
	7	598(0)	592(0)	545(1)	537(0)
	8	499(0)	488(0)	571(0)	550(0)
	$\bar{X}$	551(0.4)	530(0.3)	534(1.0)	522(0.1)

Table 5.4   *Mean RTs (in msec) for the two orders of presentation (CC-CW, CW-CC), the two kinds of irrelevant elements (CC, CW) and the two kinds of combinations of elements (I, N). The numbers in parenthesis are the numbers of errors per 36 trials*

	CC		CW	
	I	N	I	N
CC-CW	515(.5)	480(0.0)	463(.75)	458(.25)
CW-CC	587(.25)	580(.5)	606(1.0)	585(0.0)

Colour-naming

Table 5.5 shows the mean colour-naming times in msec (RT) for the eight Ss and the different experimental conditions. The same analysis of variance was used as for the results of the position-naming part. Only a significant difference in mean RTs was found for kind of combination of elements (I vs N (F (1,6) = 48.34; p < .001). The mean RTs for the incongruent and neutral combinations were 534 and 493 msec respectively. Separate t-tests revealed significant differences between I and N for CC (t = 12.178; df = 7; p < .001) and for CW combinations (t = 3.594; df = 7; p < .01). Neither the difference between conditions I for CC and CW combinations, nor the difference between conditions N for CC and CW combinations appeared significant (t = .509 and t = .327 respectively; df = 7).

Discussion

From the significant effects obtained in the analyses of variance over the position-naming data, two seem to be of minor importance. (a) The significant difference between the two groups of Ss was unexpected. It is likely that this effect is only the result of the small samples of Ss used. (b) The three-term interaction CC-CW, CW-CC x CC, CW x I, N (see Table 5.4) suggests that the second of the two localization tasks is performed fastest, and that the difference between I and N is smaller for the second task than for the first. These trends appear as a significant three-term interaction because of the way the data are entered in the analysis of variance matrix. The remaining significant effect − the difference between I and N − was expected and in the expected direction.

Table 5.5 *Mean colour-naming times (in msec) per S and over Ss ($\bar{X}$) for the two kinds of irrelevant elements (CC and CW), the two kinds of combinations (I and N) and the order of presentation (CC-CW and CW-CC). The numbers in parenthesis are the numbers of errors per 36 trials*

		CC		CW	
		I	N	I	N
CC-CW	S_1	$504_{(1)}$	$471_{(0)}$	$474_{(2)}$	$464_{(0)}$
	3	$654_{(0)}$	$603_{(0)}$	$722_{(1)}$	$640_{(1)}$
	5	$494_{(4)}$	$442_{(3)}$	$497_{(1)}$	$426_{(2)}$
	7	$564_{(0)}$	$520_{(0)}$	$558_{(0)}$	$535_{(0)}$
CW-CC	2	$539_{(0)}$	$505_{(0)}$	$483_{(0)}$	$435_{(0)}$
	4	$542_{(2)}$	$501_{(0)}$	$494_{(1)}$	$487_{(0)}$
	6	$490_{(1)}$	$428_{(0)}$	$427_{(1)}$	$418_{(0)}$
	8	$524_{(1)}$	$488_{(1)}$	$581_{(4)}$	$525_{(0)}$
	$\bar{X}$	$539_{(1.1)}$	$495_{(.5)}$	$530_{(1.3)}$	$491_{(.4)}$

The analysis of variance over the data obtained in the colour-naming task showed only a significant effect of kind of combination of elements, I vs N. This difference was expected and in the expected direction.

Two of the non-significant results are worth mention. (a) The t-test revealed no significant difference between the RTs for incongruent stimuli for CC and CW conditions in the position-naming task (mean RTs were 551 and 534 msec respectively). Therefore the supposition that the search for the relevant colour takes appreciably more time with colour-colour combinations than with colour-word combinations is not substantiated by the data obtained in this experiment. The data at most suggest that the search with colour-colour combinations takes somewhat more time than the search with colour-word combinations. (b) Furthermore, the t-test showed no significant difference between the corresponding mean RTs in the colour-naming task. (The mean RTs for the incongruent combinations in the colour-colour and the colour-word condition were 539 and 530 msec respectively; in Experiment II these RTs were 624 and 679 msec respectively!

In Table 5.6 the results obtained with the double subtraction method, outlined in the introduction, are presented. In the two columns under 'Position-naming' the estimates of the differences for I and N combinations $(t_{s(i)} - t_{s(n)})$ for the 8 Ss separately and averaged over the 8 Ss ($\overline{X}$) for CC and CW combinations are given. The difference in estimated differences in search-times for CC and CW combinations is not significant (t = .762). In the two columns under 'Colour-naming' the corresponding estimates of search-time plus pure interference time $(PI + (t_{s(i)} - t_{s(n)})$ are given (t = .554; N.S.). The last two columns, under PI, contain the estimates of pure interference or postcategorical interference for incongruent colour-colour combinations (PI_{cc}) and for incongruent colour-word combinations (PI_{cw}) (t = .159, N.S.).

Table 5.6 *Amount of pure interference or postcategorical interference, PI, estimated by the method outlined in the introduction to this experiment (for further details see text)*

	Position-naming		Colour-naming		PI	
	CC	CW	CC	CW		
S	$(t_{s(i)}-t_{s(n)})$	$(t_{s(i)}-t_{s(n)})$	$(PI+(t_{s(i)}-t_{s(n)})$	$(PI+(t_{s(i)}-t_{s(n)})$	PI_{cc}	PI_{cw}
1	30 (0)	13 (1)	33 (1)	10 (2)	3 (−1)	−3 (1)
2	42 (0)	9 (0)	34 (0)	48 (0)	−8 (0)	39 (0)
3	23 (0)	31 (0)	51 (0)	82 (0)	28 (0)	51 (0)
4	−12 (−1)	23 (3)	41 (2)	7 (1)	53 (3)	−16 (−2)
5	57 (1)	−18 (1)	52 (1)	71 (−1)	−5 (0)	89 (−2)
6	14 (1)	15 (1)	62 (1)	9 (1)	48 (0)	−6 (0)
7	6 (0)	8 (1)	44 (0)	23 (0)	38 (0)	15 (−1)
8	11 (0)	21 (0)	36 (0)	56 (4)	25 (0)	35 (4)
$\overline{X}$	21 (.1)	12 (.9)	44 (.6)	38 (.9)	23 (.5)	26 (0)

If we assume that the double subtraction method gives indeed estimates of pure interference, then the table shows that about equal amounts of pure interference, PI, are found with CC combinations and with CW combinations (23 msec and 26 msec respectively). It therefore seems that the discrepancy in results mentioned in the introduction does not disappear if the time component due to postcategorical filtering is eliminated. The results of this experiment seem to suggest that (a) somewhat more time is needed to locate the relevant element with incongruent CC combinations than with incongruent CW combinations (mean RTs are 551 and 534 msec respectively), and (b) under these conditions about equal amounts of pure interference (PIs) are found for incongruent CC and incongruent CW combinations. In Experiment II (chapter 4) (a) equal amounts of time were needed for locating the relevant element with incongruent CW and incongruent CC combinations, and (b) appreciably more pure interference was found with incongruent CW combinations than with incongruent CC combinations.

As explained in the introduction, such a pattern of results suggests that PI increases with t_s. (The overall mean RTs of experiment II and of this experiment (about 600 msec and 515 msec respectively) and the estimated mean amount of pure interference in the two experiments (about 71 msec and 39 msec in experiment II and 26 and 23 msec in this experiment for CW and CC combinations respectively) substantiate this point of view.)

There is some further evidence in the literature from other types of experiments suggesting that PI increases with t_s, or, at least, that can be interpreted as suggesting this relation (see Eriksen and Hoffman, 1973, exp. I, fig. 2; Dallas and Merikle, 1976a, exp. II; cf. Humphreys (in press) experiments I and II (tables 1 and 3); note also that Stroop-type response competition is found in Humphreys (in press) experiment I, but not in experiment II; see Kahneman and Henik (1977), who observed that: 'In the terms of the group-processing model, the groups that appear late in the queue for processing resources tend to suffer most from the presence of irrelevant material in the array' (1977, p. 329); Biederman and Tsao, 1979. It is likely that their patch (control) condition involves colour-colour interference. Therefore, their interference measure underestimates pure interference).

In section 4 of chapter 6 we extensively discuss Dallas's and Merikle's (1976a) experiments. There we will argue that, because of Ss' selection strategies, it is often difficult to find convincing effects of t_s on amount of interference, PI. Also at the end of section (b) of chapter 7 this issue is briefly discussed in terms of a 'selection strategy' and an 'inhibition strategy'. In the next chapter we will further speculate on how (a) ease of discriminating the relevant element (that is, postcategorical filtering), and (b) the relative strength of competing logogens interact in determining the amount of pure interference, PI.

6 A tentative model for performance in the 'modified Stroop test'

Summary

In the first three sections of this chapter a tentative model for performance in the tasks used in the two preceding chapters is formulated. As in chapter 4, related models, two stages are distinguished in this model (a) the processing (that is, identification or categorization) of visual information, and (b) the further operations performed upon this processed information.

The first stage, the processing of the information, is accounted for by postulating a system of counters or logogens. A logogen is defined as a transducer in which 'programs of motor instructions' are activated by stimulus features. These logogens differ in (a) the sets of critical features that can increase their counts, and (b) in their output. The level of activation of a logogen is determined by 'response readiness' or 'response set' and by the momentary stimulation conditions. It is assumed that during the presentation of the stimulus the count of the logogens with input sides corresponding to stimulus features increases linearly, and that after exposure of the stimulus the count decreases according to an exponential decay function. So, unless further operations are performed, stimulation has only a transient effect in the logogen system.

Three further operations performed upon this processed information are distinguished: (a) postcategorical filtering, (b) selection, and (c) response initiation and execution.

In postcategorical filtering it is assumed that the physical features of the stimulus are used for locating the relevant response. In terms of the logogen system as here defined this means that the input side of the logogens (that is, the representation of the stimulus features) is used for locating the relevant logogen. If the 'program of motor instructions' of this logogen is executed, then the correct response is given.

It is assumed that the 'programs of motor instructions' can only be executed in the order of their level of activation or count level. 'Selection' can result in a reordering of the levels of activation. Because it is assumed that after stimulation the counts in the logogens automatically decrease, a selection mechanism capable of keeping the count level of the relevant logogen on its maximum (or on the level at the moment that the logogen was located) until the count levels of the other logogens are sufficiently decreased, can perform this job.

With some specific assumptions added about the duration of post-categorical filtering, the maximum levels of activation of logogens activated by words and by colours and about the time-course of activation of the logogens, the model gives an adequate numerical account of the data obtained in the experiments reported in chapters 4 and 5.

This model maintains the essential characteristics of Keele's (1973) explanation of interference: responses stay in the logogen system until actively selected, and the relative strength of competing logogens is the main determinant of postcategorical interference.

In the last two sections, some attempts to broaden the scope of the model are described.

In section 4 ('Some related results') first a highly interesting analysis of performance in a more orthodox version of the Stroop-task is discussed (Schulz, 1979; integral combination of words and colours). It seems that the outcome of Schulz's analysis is in line with what is expected from the tentative model. Then the model is confronted with the results obtained in a highly unorthodox version of the Stroop-task (Dallas and Merikle, 1976a and b; word-word combinations). In order to cope with these results, the logogen system has to be redefined as a lexicon (that is, a combined logogen system and semantic system) in which activation spreads.

In section 5 ('The anatomy of a logogen') the concept 'logogen' is redefined. Three interconnected (that is, unitized) types of codes are distinguished within a logogen: a visual code, a semantic code and a verbal or articulatory code. One suggestion is made about how these three codes are connected. A selection of issues that can be discussed in terms of the resulting framework is briefly mentioned.

At the end of chapter 4, in the section on 'related models', a model for visual information processing was suggested, consisting of two stages, parts, or sets of operations: (a) the processing, that is, the identification or categorization of visual information; and (b) the further operations performed upon the processed information, for instance, the selection of processed information for overt response, or, the storage of processed information in a more enduring memory. In this chapter we will discuss how this general model can be made more specific, so that it can account for the results obtained with the 'modified Stroop test', reported in chapters 4 and 5.

1 The processing of visual information

It was, furthermore, suggested that the first set of operations is performed by a system with unlimited processing capacity and that these processes are not under Ss' control. The results of the experiments reported in chapters 4 and 5 seem to confirm this assumption. As stated in the respective discussions, the results of Experiments II and IV in particular can be taken as additional supportive evidence for this point of view. It seems, therefore, that the first processing stage can be adequately represented with a model assuming a system of counters or logogens (Morton, 1969a and b; Keele, 1973). (A system of 'cognitive demons' (Selfridge, 1959), 'dictionary units' (Treisman, 1960), 'programs of motor instructions' (Sperling, 1967), classifying structures as proposed by Deutsch and Deutsch (1963) and Norman (1968), 'category states' (Broadbent, 1971), 'recognition units' (Kahneman, 1973), 'pathways' (Posner and Snyder, 1975a), or a system of 'nodes' (Schneider and Shiffrin, 1977), and also a 'lexicon' (that is, a combined logogen system and semantic system; see, for example, Allport, 1977) can serve the same function.) In principle, Morton and Keele agree on the definition of a logogen and therefore we can start with Morton's definition:

> Each logogen is defined by its output, which can be represented by the set of phonological features (P_i), and by the sets of acoustic, visual, and semantic attributes (A_i), (V_i), and (S_i), respectively. ... A logogen is basically a counting device that is incremented whenever there is an output to the logogen System of an attribute from any source, which is a member of one of its defining sets. (Morton, 1970, p. 206)

There is, however, a basic difference between Morton's and Keele's points of view with regard to the further properties of the logogen system. According to Morton's formulation, the system is passive. Each logogen has a critical threshold value. If the count in a logogen exceeds this threshold, the logogen makes an 'implicit response' available that enters an output buffer via a single channel exit. In Keele's formulation, 'A logogen may, when activated, lead to mental operations, such as rehearsal or counting, or to immediate bodily movement' (Keele, 1973, p. 88). According to this point of view, responses remain in the system until one is actively selected (see Keele, 1973, pp. 136-9; see also chapter 5, general introduction). The series of experiments reported in the previous chapters provide two pieces of information that lead to a rejection of Morton's point of view.

First, no evidence was found that responses passively leave the logogen system. Experiment III was especially concerned with the assumption that relative naming speed is the crucial variable in determining interference. No evidence, however, was found that in a situation with relatively fast colour-processing, word-reading was seriously interfered with. As described in the discussion of Experiment III, the results of Experiments I and II are also not in accordance with the prediction following from Morton's model. From the results of Experiments I to IV together it was concluded that colour names do not occupy the single channel exit of the logogen system in the passive way as suggested in Morton's (1969a) model. The results of Experiments II and IV together suggest that there is no reason to assume that colour words behave differently or that, in contrast with the responses to the colour patches, the responses to the colour words automatically occupy the single channel exit.

Second, abundant evidence was presented for the point of view that the physical features of the stimulus are needed for the ultimate selection of the correct response. In Morton's model the implicit responses leave the logogen system. The response is then, however, detached from its physical features and additional provisions are necessary to explain how a free-floating 'implicit response' can be located by use of the physical features it stems from. Allport's (1977) and Morton's (1977) proposals were discussed and criticized (see chapters 3 and 4). The assumption that the 'implicit responses' stay in the logogen system until one of the logogens is selected, offers a more adequate starting point for a solution of this selection problem.

For these two reasons (and especially for these two reasons together) it seems better to abandon Morton's threshold idea. The logogen system, then, is a system of counters. These counters differ in (a) the sets of critical features, input features or stimulus features that can increase their counts, and (b) in their output. In order to indicate that the 'implicit responses' remain in the logogen system, it seems better to use Sperling's (1967) 'program of motor instructions' instead of 'set of phonological features', to characterize the output side of a logogen. A logogen, then, is a transducer, in which 'programs of motor instructions' are activated by stimulus features. (Possibly more levels have to be distinguished within a logogen (see, for example, Stirling, 1979). For our present purposes however, a transducer as defined above is sufficient. At the end of this chapter we will return to this issue.) The level of the count of a logogen at a given moment can be regarded as the level of activation of the program of motor instructions at that moment. In the next part of this chapter it will be proposed that this level of activation is the major determinant of postcategorical interference.

Two factors are thought to determine this level of activation. The first concerns the momentary stimulation conditions. It is assumed that during and possibly for a short time after the presentation of a stimulus, the logogens having input sides corresponding with stimulus features increase their counts, while after exposure of the stimulus these counts decrease to the original level. In the sequel, furthermore, we make the simplifying assumptions that during the presentation of the stimulus the count increases linearly (this assumption is not essential and is not further used), and that after exposure of the stimulus the count decreases according to an exponential decay function. In Fig. 6.1, the hypothetical time-course of activation of two logogens is shown. The maximum level of activation and the time-course of decay are arbitrarily fixed. (Fig. 6.1 can be interpreted as a 'smoothed' version of Vanthoor's and Eijkman's (1973) fig. 3, in which the estimated time-course of the iconic memory signal is depicted; Dyer (1971), and Compton and Flowers (1977), among others, provide evidence for transitory activation that decays rapidly over time.)

The second concerns 'response readiness' or 'response set' (Broadbent, 1971, p. 177). In all the experiments reported in chapters 4 and 5 the Ss were constrained to make only responses belonging to a predefined set. In order to account for the fact that no other responses were emitted by the Ss and for the fact that irrelevant information (that is, an IR element) showed only a minor effect (see Experiment IV), additional assumptions are necessary. The assumption that logogens with programs of task-relevant responses have a higher initial count during the whole experiment as compared with the other logogens, seems capable of accounting for this effect. This assumption is readily related to Norman's (1968) pertinence concept or to the effect of the context system in Morton's (1969a) logogen model.

Following Morton (1969a, 1977), we assume, furthermore, that both kinds of activation, external activation and internal activation, simply add. For our present purposes we do not need this assumption. In chapter 7 we will briefly return to this issue.

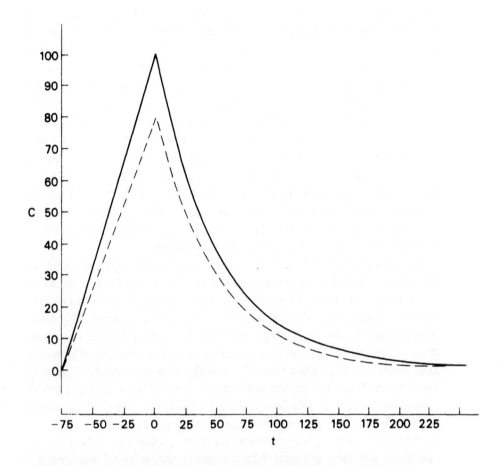

Figure 6.1 *Hypothetical time-course of activation of two logogens: one reaching a maximum count, C, of 100; the other a maximum count of 80*

2 The further operations performed upon the processed information

Keele (1973) and Shiffrin and Geisler (1973) present lists of possible further operations that can be performed upon the processed information (see Keele, 1973, pp. 136-7; Shiffrin and Geisler, 1973, pp. 57-9). For the series of experiments now under discussion two of these operations are of importance: (a) the localization of the relevant response (that is, postcategorical filtering) and (b) the selection of this response.

(a) The localization of the relevant response. In chapter 3, in relation to the partial report experiments, and especially in chapter 4, evidence was presented that the physical features of the stimuli are used for locating and selecting the relevant response. This method for locating the correct response was named postcategorical filtering. In terms of the logogen system as here defined — a logogen is a transducer linking physical features with programs of motor instructions — this means that the input side of the logogens is used for locating the relevant logogen. In this way the unnecessary connection between precategorical selection models or filter/attenuation models and selecting by way of physical features of the stimulus is disjoined. Furthermore, Keele's paradox (see chapter 4, related models; Keele, 1973, p. 151) can be partially solved. Because logogens are transducers, selectivity at the level of physical characteristics, as well as interactions at the level of identified or categorized information are possible.

The assumption that the input features of the logogens are used for locating the relevant logogens entails that all existing knowledge about the selection of visual information by way of physical features (see, for example, Coltheart, 1972; Broadbent, 1970; see also chapter 3) is easily incorporated in the postcategorical selection model as here proposed. Also, concepts like 'perceptual grouping' (see, for example, Kahneman and Henik, 1977; Humphreys, in press), 'moving attention through visual space' (van der Heijden and Eerland, 1973; Shulman et al., 1979), 'attention switching' (Keele and Neill, 1978), etc. can find a place in the postcategorical selection model as here proposed.

However, locating the relevant logogen is only one aspect of the complete selection process. While locating the relevant logogen is a necessary condition for the subsequent initiation of the correct response, the experiments reported in the previous chapters also show that it is not a sufficient condition. In other words, a number of experiments clearly show that under some conditions the response is not immediately initiated at the moment that the relevant logogen is located. For instance, in Experiment IV two types of incongruent colours were used: a colour with a name belonging to the response set in use and a colour with a name not belonging to the response set in use. The RTs for naming the relevant colour patches strongly depended upon the kind of incongruent element used. For this experiment, the task of locating the relevant element, or of choosing the relevant logogen, seems exactly the same for the two conditions. Comparable results were obtained in Experiment II. In that experiment barmarkers were used to indicate the relevant element. For this experiment, it is, therefore, difficult to support the position that locating the relevant element differs from one condition to another. Nevertheless, appreciable differences in RTs for the different experimental conditions were found. Experiment V was explicitly concerned with this issue. From the differences I-N found in that experiment, the time component due to differences in postcategorical filtering was eliminated. A time component, PI (representing pure interference or postcategorical interference), remained. This evidence indicates that besides locating the relevant logogen, in some conditions another time consuming selective operation is needed before the relevant response can be initiated. Further suggestions about this selective operation will be made under (b).

(b) The selection of responses. In Morton's (1969a and b) original formulation of the logogen model, the 'implicit responses' enter the single channel exit of the logogen system in the order in which the logogens they stem from reach their thresholds. So, the interaction of the logogen system with the various factors that can increase the counts of the logogens, results in a 'fixed', or 'preferred' order of availability of 'implicit responses'. In this way, the traffic between the logogen system and subsequent stages in the processing sequence seems adequately regulated; for most tasks, task-relevant and appropriate responses are first available.

In part 1 of this section, however, a number of reasons were given for rejecting the passive thresholds. Therefore, some other principle, governing the transition between the logogen system and subsequent parts in the processing sequence, has to be postulated. More specifically, for the experiments now under discussion, a rule specifying in what order the 'programs of motor instructions' are executed, or, the responses are initiated, has to be worked out. Evidence for a preferred order of emitting responses was already discussed in chapter 3. There it was mentioned, that Klein (1964) showed that reading the word prior to colour-naming on the Stroop conflict card required only a little more time than naming only the colours. This result, and also the results found by Haber (1964a and b) and Harris and Haber (1963) with the instructional set experiments, was taken as indicating that there is a preferred order of emitting responses, and that interference and delayed responding result if this order has to be violated (see chapter 3). This suggestion can now be worked out in more detail, in terms of the logogen system as described in part 1. The assumption that 'programs of motor instructions' can only be initiated and executed in order of their count level, or in order of their level of activation, seems to serve the same function as the thresholds in Morton's logogen model, as far as the transition of the logogen system to overt responses is concerned. (All further properties of Morton's model can be taken over without changes.) With certain further assumptions, this assumption leads to the rule, that a located response can only be initiated if (a) its count or its level of activation is highest, and (b) exceeds the count of the next highest logogen by a certain amount, δ. A system capable of performing this task was already proposed by Deutsch and Deutsch (1963). In their model the system is used, however, for locating the relevant information. In the present formulation, the system is concerned with the order in which the responses are given. (At the end of part 3 of this chapter, the parameter δ will be further commented upon.)

In order to account for the results of the experiments reported in the previous chapters two further assumptions have to be made.

The first concerns the way in which the effect of a word stimulus and of a colour stimulus differ in their effects on the logogen system. From (a) the asymmetry in interference found with the Stroop test (a strong interfering effect of irrelevant words on colour-naming and virtually no effect of irrelevant colours on word-reading (Stroop, 1935; Experiments I and II)) and (b) the remarks just made about the order of overt responses it can be concluded that a word results in a higher ultimate count of its corresponding logogen than a colour. (This parallels directly Morton's assumption that words generally give a faster increase in count level than colours.) This assumption can readily be related to explanations of the Stroop phenomenon in terms of response strength; the higher the level of activation of a logogen, the greater its response strength.

The second assumption concerns the selection operation that makes it possible to respond with the colour name, while also the logogen corresponding with a conflicting colour word is activated. Figure 6.1 can be interpreted as showing the time-course of two hypothetical logogens, one activated by a colour word (solid line) and one activated by a colour (dashed line). During the whole interval of time that the logogens are activated, the count in the 'word logogen' exceeds the count in the 'colour logogen'. If 'programs of motor instructions' are executed in the order of their counts, the colour-name response can be made only after the word response. Colour-name responses, however, can be given without first producing the word response. Therefore, a further selection operation has to be assumed, as a result of which the count of the 'colour logogen' ultimately exceeds the count of the 'word logogen'. This operation will be called 'selection'. In the recent literature a number of mechanisms has been proposed that can accomplish this task. For instance, the count of the relevant logogen can be increased by adding a 'pertinence input' (Norman, 1968, pp. 526-7), by adding 'an additional input of attention or effort' (Kahneman, 1973, p. 9), by 'additional stimulation from the region of relevant perceptual information' (Klein, 1964, p. 585), or by actively inhibiting logogens activated by the irrelevant information (Neill, 1977, 1978; see also section (b) of chapter 7). For the series of experiments reported in the previous chapters, a comparable but somewhat simpler mechanism will suffice. Two considerations are at the basis of this mechanism.

The first concerns the amount of time necessary to locate the relevant logogen, or, for postcategorical filtering. Averbach and Coriell (1961) and Eriksen and Collins (1969) present estimates in the order of 100-200 msec (see also Kahneman, 1973, pp. 83-4). Also, Hoffman (1975) presents evidence that locating the relevant element takes an appreciable amount of time, in the order of 150 msec. These estimates are obtained in experiments in which cues are used that are easily discriminated. The duration of locating the relevant information will be appreciably greater if more inconspicuous cues or features have to be used (see, for example, Broadbent, 1970, p. 58). (From the position-naming part of Experiment V, chapter 4, only estimates of the differences in duration of postcategorical filtering can be obtained. So this experiment provides no information about the absolute duration of postcategorical filtering.) It will be clear that the selection mechanism can start only after the relevant information is found, or after the relevant logogen is located.

The second consideration concerns the hypothetical time-course of activation of the logogens, as described under 1 (see figure 6.1). For the experiments under consideration (a) the relatively long time needed for locating the relevant logogen as compared with the exposure times used, and (b) the hypothetical time-course of activation of the logogens have as a consequence, that the selection mechanism can start only when the count of the logogen is near its maximum, or when the count is already decaying. A mechanism capable of keeping the level of the count of the relevant logogen on its maximum (or on the level at the moment that the logogen was located) will then suffice. The level of the count in the relevant logogen then remains constant, while the count levels of the other logogens involved decrease. Ultimately, the count level of the relevant logogen will be highest and will exceed the count level of the next highest logogen by the amount δ. It is at this selection stage that 'effort' is required (Kahneman, 1973), that the system is 'resource limited' (Norman and Bobrow, 1975) or has a limited capacity (see chapter 2).

Therefore, in the present model, there are three further operations performed upon the processed information:

(a) the relevant logogen is located by using the physical features (postcategorical filtering);

(b) its count, or level of activation is maintained (selection);

(c) its response is executed at the moment its count is highest and exceeds the count of the next highest logogen by an amount δ.

It will be clear that in this model the essential characteristics of Keele's (1973) explanation of interference are maintained: responses stay in the logogen system until located (postcategorical filtering) and actively selected. The relative strength of competing logogens determines the selection time and is therefore the main determinant of pure interference, or postcategorical interference, PI.

(It is important to note that the arguments presented in the previous paragraphs do not imply that postcategorical filtering is the only possible control operation for finding the correct logogen. Postcategorical filtering is better conceived of as one of the possible strategies of a 'selector mechanism' (Keele and Neill, 1978). This strategy, however, seems to be essential for tasks like the Stroop test, partial report tasks, etc. Other tasks, however, can require different strategies. For some tasks (for instance, tasks in which only one single item is presented), simply emitting a response after a certain interval of time, will, according to the model here described, lead to adequate behaviour; see also section 5 of this chapter: 'The anatomy of a logogen'.)

3 A numerical example

In Table 6.1, the results of the experiments reported in chapters 4 and 5 are summarized. From Experiment III, only the results found in the simultaneous exposure conditions are included. As already described in the discussion of Experiment III, the results of experiments in which the irrelevant material is pre- or post-exposed are rather ambiguous (see also Dyer, 1973a, pp. 110-11; Dyer and Severance, 1973, p. 439); attempts to interpret the diverse results of these experiments in terms of the model will not be described. From Experiment V only the results of the colour-naming part and the results obtained with the double subtraction method are included.

In this part a numerical example will be given in order to show how the model described can account for the main features and general trends of the data presented in Table 6.1. Because the absolute time-course of activation of the logogens is unknown (in fact, the t values on the time axes in Figure 6.1 have to be replaced by t + c values), only relative search-times, t_ss, and estimated amounts of pure interference, PIs, can be related. Furthermore, because these estimates of post-categorical interference, PI, are strongly influenced by speed-accuracy trade-offs and by differences in the neutral conditions (see the results of Experiment II, for example), no attempts will be made to fit the data obtained.

As Table 6.1 shows, the mean RTs for congruent combinations are about the same as the mean RTs for neutral combinations. The assumption that with congruent combinations both inputs activate the same logogen and that the response is initiated at the moment that the correct logogen is located (as with neutral combinations), is sufficient to account for this result.

Table 6.1 *Summary of results of Experiments I to V (chapters 4 and 5). Column S gives the kind of combination of the stimulus elements (relevant word (W) or colour (C) and irrelevant word (W) or colour(C)). Column T gives the exposure time in msec. In columns C, I(N) and N the mean RTs and the percentage of errors (in brackets) for congruent, incongruent and neutral stimuli are given. Column I-N shows the amount of interference (that is, the difference between columns I(N) and N) in msec and in percentage of errors. Column PI gives the estimated amounts of pure interference or postcategorical interference for those experiments for which this estimate is available (see the introduction to Experiment V, chapter 5)*

Exp.	S	T	C	I(N)	N	I-N	PI
I	W, C	150	367 (4.7)	369 (6.3)	364 (3.1)	5 (3.2)	
II	C, C	150	568 (1.4)	624 (4.9)	585 (0.0)	39 (4.9)	39 (4.9)
	C, W	150	597 (2.8)	679 (11.1)	608 (0.7)	71 (10.4)	71 (10.4)
	W, C	150	610 (4.9)	612 (6.9)	591 (1.4)	21 (5.5)	21 (5.5)
	W, W	150	587 (2.8)	642 (2.8)	589 (2.8)	53 (0.0)	53 (0.0)
III	W, C	50	549 (4.0)	559 (6.0)	560 (5.0)	−1 (1.0)	−1 (1.0)
	C, W	50	498 (0.0)	523 (3.7)	506 (0.0)	17 (3.7)	17 (3.7)
IV	C, C	150	474 (0.7)	541 (13.9)	474 (1.0)	67 (12.9)	
V	C, C	150		539 (3.0)	495 (1.4)	44 (1.7)	23 (1.4)
	C, W	150		530 (3.6)	491 (1.1)	39 (2.5)	26 (0.0)

As stated, the further operations performed upon the processed information are thought to consist of (a) the search of the relevant logogen, and (b) the selection of the relevant response. If the relevant information is found at time t_s, the response can be initiated at time t_i, if at that moment the count level of the relevant logogen, $C_r(t_s)$ exceeds the count level of the logogen next highest in count, $C_i(t_i)$, by an amount δ. Therefore, from

$$C_r(t_s) - C_i(t_i) = \delta, \tag{1}$$

the value t_i has to be obtained. The amount of postcategorical interference, PI, is then given by $t_i - t_s$.

By using the assumptions that (a) the selection mechanism starts if the counts are already decreasing, and (b) that the counts decrease according to an exponential decay function, (1) can be rewritten as

$$Re^{-\alpha t_s} - Ie^{-\alpha t_i} = \delta. \tag{2}$$

Here R and I are the count levels for the relevant and the irrelevant logogen respectively, at the time $t = 0$ (see the time axes in Figure 6.1), and α is the rate parameter of the decay function. The t_i values can be calculated with

$$t_i = \frac{1}{-\alpha} \, Ln \, (\frac{Re^{-\alpha t_s} - \delta}{I}). \tag{3}$$

For the example, the parameters of the decay functions from Figure 6.1, and a δ value of 20 were used. The word-count decay function and the colour count decay function in Figure 6.1 are, respectively, $C_w = 100e^{-.02t}$ and $C_c = 80e^{-0.2t}$; t in units of 1 msec. (For fitting the model to the data, values for $\alpha(c)$, $\alpha(w)$, $C(c)$, $C(w)$ and δ have to be estimated.) In Table 6.2 values for t_i and for $t_i - t_s$ (the amount of pure interference or postcategorical interference, PI) are given for the four kinds of combinations of relevant and irrelevant words and colours, (C, C; C, W; W, W) and for three values of t_s (0, 25 and 50 msec). Three features are readily apparent from this table.

(a) A comparison of rows C, W and W, C of Table 6.2 shows that the model accounts for the asymmetry in interference, as found by Stroop (1935) among others. The table also shows that at $t_s = 0$, that is, with fast locating of the relevant information, no interference from colours on words is to be expected. In Experiment I, the Ss knew in advance that the words had to be read, and this made fast location of the relevant information possible. Therefore, the model is in accordance with the outcome of Experiment I: virtually no effect of irrelevant colours on word-reading.

(b) In Experiment II a strong effect of irrelevant words on colour-naming, a weak effect of irrelevant colours on word-reading and intermediate effects of words on word-reading and of colours on colour-naming was found. Table 6.2 shows that the model is capable of accounting for this order of amount of postcategorical interference for all values of t_s. In Experiment II barmarkers were used to indicate the position of the relevant element. It is therefore likely that more time was needed for locating the relevant element than in Experiment I. In the model this is represented by a value of $t_s > 0$. A comparison of the PI values for Experiment II in Table 6.1 and the $t_i - t_s$ values in Table 6.2 shows that with $t_s = 50$ msec, a reasonable correspondence between observed and predicted values is obtained.

Table 6.2 *Expected moment of initiation of response (t_i) and expected amount of postcategorical interference ($t_i - t_s = PI$) for four kinds of incongruent combinations of stimulus elements (relevant word ($\underline{W}$) or colour ($\underline{C}$) and irrelevant word (W) or colour (C)) and for three starting times of the selection mechanism ($t_s = 0$, 25 and 50 msec) (values in msec after beginning of decay of counts)*

S	$t_s = 0$		$t_s = 25$		$t_s = 50$	
	t_i	$t_i - t_s$	t_i	$t_i - t_s$	t_i	$t_i - t_s$
$\underline{C}$, C	14	14	52	27	107	57
$\underline{C}$, W	26	26	63	38	118	68
$\underline{W}$, C	0	0	34	9	78	28
$\underline{W}$, W	11	11	45	20	89	39

(c) Experiment V was concerned with the relation between amount of pure interference or postcategorical interference, PI, (($t_i - t_s$) in the model here described) and the time needed for postcategorical filtering, or the search-time (t_s in this model). The results of the experiment suggested that (a) somewhat more time is needed to locate the relevant element with incongruent $\underline{C}$C combinations than with incongruent $\underline{C}$W combinations, and (b) under these conditions about equal amounts of postcategorical interference, PI, for incongruent $\underline{C}$C and incongruent $\underline{C}$W combinations are found. As can be seen in Table 6.2, the model exactly predicts this result. The estimated amounts of pure interference, PI, in the easy discriminating task ($\underline{C}$W combinations, 26 msec) and in the more difficult discriminating task ($\underline{C}$C combinations, 23 msec) correspond fairly well with the predicted values for $t_i - t_s$ in Table 6.2 for $\underline{C}$W combinations at $t_s = 0$ (26 msec) and for $\underline{C}$C combinations at

$t_s = 25$ (27 msec).

It is, furthermore, worthwhile to note that the positioning of Experiment II at $t_s = 50$ msec and of Experiment V at $t_s = 0$ msec (C̲W combinations) and at $t_s = 25$ msec (C̲C combinations) not only accounts for the amounts of postcategorical interference, PI, found, but also for a large part of the difference in overall mean RTs between the two experiments (Experiment II about 600 msec, Experiment V about 515 msec). Furthermore, the positioning of Experiment I (W̲C combinations) at $t_s = 0$ and of the C̲W condition of Experiment V at $t_s = 0$ is consistent. Both experiments involve comparably easy search tasks.

It seems that there are two relevant differences between Experiment IV and the C̲C condition of Experiment V. The first consists of the inclusion of a second type of incongruent combinations, IR combinations, (combinations with an irrelevant element that never appeared as a relevant element) in Experiment IV. The experiment showed that for this type of combination about 20 msec (5.9 per cent errors) more time was needed than for the neutral stimuli. Of course, in the model this difference is completely accounted for by the additional time needed for postcategorical filtering with incongruent combinations in comparison with neutral combinations (that is, by t_s). Therefore, the assumption that also an IR element can elicit a coding response in the response set in use (see the discussion of Experiment IV in chapter 5) is not needed for accounting for this result. The second difference concerns the change of roles of disks and half-disks. In Experiment IV the half-disk was the relevant element and the disk was the irrelevant element. In Experiment V these roles were reversed. This difference might have caused a somewhat smaller value for I-N for Experiment V.

As stated, the assumption that also an IR element can elicit a coding response in the response set in use is not needed for accounting for the additional amount of time needed with this kind of combination. The model, however, does not rule out such a possibility. In Experiment IV, the relevant element was located relatively fast. Table 6.2, however, shows that a weakly activated logogen can interfere with the selection of a strongly activated logogen only if the latter is located relatively late. This effect is apparent in row W̲, C (relevant word, irrelevant colour). The model predicts no postcategorical interference, PI = $t_i - t_s$, with this combination of stimulus elements (that is, no reversed Stroop effect) if the relevant logogen is located fast ($t_s = 0$) and a considerable amount of postcategorical interference if located late ($t_s \geqslant 50$). Preliminary (unpublished) experiments confirmed this prediction. The 'postcategorical filtering explanation' forwarded to account for the reversed Stroop effect found by Gumenik and Glass (1970) and Dyer and Severance (1972) can now be made more explicit in terms of the model. Fragmenting the word by means of a patterned mask destroys the word as a unit. Under such conditions, the connection between visual code and verbal code has possibly been weakened. Phrased in terms of the model: locating the relevant logogen takes an appreciable amount of time. In the model this is represented by a higher value for t_s, and with a higher value of t_s, postcategorical interference from weakly activated logogens on strongly activated logogens is also predicted. Gumenik and Glass (1970), however, also found decreased postcategorical interference from the masked words on the naming of the colours. Because there is no reason to expect that fragmenting the coloured words speeds up locating the relevant colour information, other factors must also be involved. One reasonable possibility is that fragmenting the inputs also has its effects on the maximum count levels ultimately reached. The procedure can result in a smaller maximum count level for the logogen corresponding to the word, while the maximum count level of the logogen corresponding to the colour remains unchanged (the colour is not destroyed by the mask). Of course, all effects found by Gumenik and Glass (1970) can be accounted for solely in terms of the effect of the mask on the maximum level of the counts. Such an explanation then comes down to Gumenik's and Glass's response strength explanation.

In Experiment III, postcategorical interference was found with $\underline{C}$, W combinations and no interference with $\underline{W}$, C combinations, while a pilot experiment had shown — and this was confirmed by the results of Experiment III — that colours were processed faster than words. At first sight, this result seems paradoxical; some kind of retroactive action is exerted by a signal that is processed later on a signal that is processed earlier. This effect, however, is readily explicable in terms of the model here presented if one assumption about the effect of reducing exposure duration — the procedure used in Experiment III to lengthen word processing time — on the time-course of activation of the logogens is added. According to the model, postcategorical interference is to be expected if on time t_s, the difference in counts between the logogen activated by the relevant input and the logogen activated by the irrelevant input is smaller than some value δ. Up to now, only situations were considered in which it was assumed that the logogens involved reached their maximum level of activation at the same moment (at $t = 0$; see Figure 6.1). However, it seems possible that under certain exposure conditions, logogens corresponding to different kinds of inputs (words and colours for instance) reach their maximum level of activation at different moments of time, and therefore also start decaying at different moments of time. In Figure 6.2 the hypothetical time-course of activation of two logogens, a (solid line) and b (dashed line), activated by different kinds of inputs under such exposure conditions is shown. Both logogens ultimately reach the same maximum level of activation (50), but at different moments of time: a at t = 0, b at t = 50. The decay functions for a and b are, respectively,

$$Ca = 50e^{-.01t}, \text{ and } Cb = 50e^{-.01(t-50)}.$$

The fact that both logogens reach ultimately the same maximum level of activation is not essential for the further arguments. In the example given in Figure 6.2, the values of the decay function of logogen b will exceed the values of the decay function for logogen a for all maximum count levels of logogen b larger than 31.

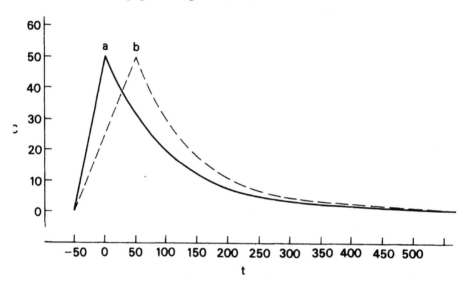

Figure 6.2 *Hypothetical time-course of activation of two logogens, a (solid line) and b (broken line). A reaches its maximum level of activation (C = 50) at t = 0; b reaches its maximum level (C = 50) at t = 50. Decay functions for a and b are, respectively, Ca = 50e$^{-.01t}$ and Cb = 50e$^{-.01(t-50)}$*

Now it seems reasonable to assume that if stimulus elements are presented in isolation, a stimulus, giving rise to a time-course of activation as represented with a in Figure 6.2, will lead to faster responding than a stimulus resulting in a time-course of activation as represented

172

with b. If, however, an incongruent combination of the two elements is simultaneously presented, and if the relevant element is located when also the count of logogen b is already decaying (that is, $t_s > 50$), the selection of logogen a will be interfered with, and virtually no post-categorical interference with the selection of logogen b will be found. In Experiment III a stimulus exposure duration of 50 msec was used. It is, therefore, to be expected that the process of locating the relevant logogen is finished only if all counts are already decreasing (in Figure 6.2, $t_s > 50$). Therefore, in order to account for the paradoxical effect found in the simultaneous exposure condition of Experiment III and for the result of the preliminary experiment reported in the introduction of Experiment III (faster colour-naming than word-reading), one additional assumption suffices: a reduction in exposure duration results in a delayed increase of the counts of the logogen corresponding to the word relative to the increase in count of the logogen corresponding to the colour. In Figure 6.2, a can be interpreted as the time-course of activation of the 'colour logogen', b as the time-course of activation of the 'word logogen'.

The implicit rejection of a possible 'retroactive action' as described in the previous paragraphs easily leads to unfounded conclusions. An example can be found in Shallice and Warrington (1977). They investigated selective attention in acquired dyslexia. An explanation in terms of 'implicit response interference' for their patients' difficulties with reading letters within words was rejected with the following argument:

> If competition between responses was the operative factor in
> producing the patients' difficulties, target dots should be at least
> as affected as the target numbers, as verbalisation of the number
> of dots would occur more slowly than verbalisation of the number.
> The clear superiority of performance with dots therefore strongly
> suggests that the difficulty is not produced at an implicit response
> level. (Shallice and Warrington, 1977, p. 36)

The argument presented in relation to Fig. 6.2 makes it clear that their conclusion is in no way warranted. In chapter 7, at the end of section (b), we will briefly return to the role of selective attention in acquired dyslexia.

Figure 6.2 also gives some cues for an explanation of the effects found with pre- and post-exposure of the relevant material in Experiment III. With an appropriate choice of parameters (t_s, δ, and separation of moment of reaching the maximum count level) the interference effects found in these conditions can be accounted for. Because of the ambiguous results found in experiments concerned with pre- and post-exposure of the relevant information (see the discussion of Experiment III), this issue will not be further pursued.

At this point it is worthwhile to briefly return to the search task, reported in chapter 2. Recently, Stirling (1979) showed, that in the Stroop task, interference is also found if Ss have to respond with newly learned verbal responses (for instance, the response 'D' assigned to the colour red). In the search task, Ss had to respond 'yes' if there were Es and they had to respond 'no' if there were only Fs. So, the element E was connected with the verbal response 'yes', and the element F in some way with the verbal response 'no'. Combinations like EF, EFF and EEF can be regarded, therefore, as 'incongruent combinations' and greater mean RTs are to be expected with these combinations than with one E (a 'neutral combination') or with EE and EEE ('congruent combinations'). That was found in the experiment. Whether there are still other factors of importance in this type of search task (for instance, postcategorical filtering) is a matter for further investigation.

Two further remarks about the tentative model seem in order.

The first concerns the assumption of constant differences, δ, between the count level of the relevant logogen, C_r (the 'signal') and the count level of the irrelevant logogen, C_i (the 'noise'). Instead of a fixed difference between signal level and noise level, in the literature more often a fixed ratio between the two levels is proposed. (Keele's 'relative strength' hints at this position.) For those who prefer an analysis in terms of a fixed ratio, a simple reformulation of the model suffices. Assume that the time-course of activation of the logogens as a function of time, C_t, is not given by

$$C_t = Ce^{-at},$$

as we proposed, but by

$$C_t = {}_eCe^{-at}.$$

(With this assumption, Figures 6.1 and 6.2 depict the logarithm of the count level of the logogens as a function of time t, that is, C in the figures equals logarithm C_t.) If the relevant information is found at time t_s, the response can be initiated at time t_i if at that moment the ratio of the two count levels equals some constant, e^δ. Therefore, from

$$\frac{e^{Re^{-\alpha t_s}}}{{}_eIe^{-\alpha t_i}} = e^\delta \qquad (4)$$

the value t_i has to be obtained.

This can be done by first taking logarithms at both sides. Equation (4) then reduces to equation (2) and the same predictions as from the original model result. (In the next parts we will continue our analysis in terms of fixed differences, δ. A similar reformulation in terms of fixed ratios, e^{δ}, as presented above, is rather easy, however.)

The second remark concerns the value of parameter δ. It was assumed that a response can only be initiated if (a) its count is highest, and (b) exceeds the count of the next highest logogen by a certain amount δ. This assumption was needed for explaining the interference effects in conditions in which the two logogens had equal counts (colour-colour and word-word condition). For the other conditions, the simpler assumption that the count of the relevant logogen, $c(a)$, must not be smaller than the count of the irrelevant logogen, $c(b)$, suffices. However, the latter assumption also easily leads to the inclusion of a parameter δ in the model for colour-colour and word-word conditions. Assume that the counts for logogen a and logogen b are normally distributed with mean $\overline{c(a)}$ and $\overline{c(b)}$. For word-word and colour-colour combinations, $\overline{c(a)} = \overline{c(b)}$, as represented in the model. On 50 per cent of the trials, $c(a) \geqslant c(b)$, and the response can be initiated after locating the correct logogen. On 50 per cent of the trials, $c(a) < c(b)$ and the selective operation is necessary before response initiation. If the mean difference between $c(a)$ and $c(b)$ for these trials equals $2\delta'$ (that is, $c(a) + 2\delta' = c(b)$ for all $t \geqslant 0$), then δ' is the mean of the positive differences between $c(a)$ and $c(b)$ over all trials. Parameter δ in the model reflects the effects of these positive differences. Therefore, the rule that a response can be initiated if there is no stronger alternative response, suffices.

4 Some related issues

The model presented in this chapter was designed to account for the results obtained in what we called, the 'modified Stroop task' (that is, separate bilateral presentations of words and colours, colours, words, etc.). Recently, Schulz (1979) has presented a highly interesting analysis of performance in a more orthodox version of the Stroop task. In two experiments, integral combinations of words and colours were used in the single-trial reaction time version. Both experiments had one block of colour-naming trials and one block of word-reading trials. In both blocks, congruent, incongruent and neutral combinations were presented in a random order. So, RTs for six different conditions were obtained: C, I and N colour-naming RTs and C, I and N word-reading RTs. The

RTs were decomposed into potentially meaningful components by fitting two different linear models to the data. (That is, for each model, six equations for six unknown parameters were solved.) With the best-fitting model, only two consistent and reliable significant components were found in the two experiments (neglecting the time component common to all conditions). These components were also connected with the largest processing-time parameters. The first component was connected with all colour-naming conditions and indicates that colour-naming takes more time than word-reading. The second component is unique for incongruent combinations under colour-naming and indicates that these combinations require an additional amount of time.

It will be clear that the outcome of this decomposition is completely in line with what is expected from the model presented in this chapter. For Schulz's task, there is reason to expect neither differences in the duration of postcategorical filtering between the six conditions nor that postcategorical filtering takes an appreciable amount of time (word-reading trials and colour-naming trials were blocked and there was no uncertainty about position). The overall difference between colour-naming and word-reading is one of the assumptions of the present model (see Fig. 6.1). A difference between these two tasks will show up especially if the tasks are blocked. Furthermore, with fast locating of the relevant information only one further RT component is to be expected according to our model. This component was termed pure or postcategorical interference, and, given Schulz's six conditions, this component will only show up with incongruent combinations under colour-naming (see Table 6.2). So the results of Schulz's analysis of performance in the Stroop-task with integral combinations of colours and words correspond with our analysis of performance in the Stroop-task with separate bilateral presentations of words and colours.

Schulz's interpretation of the results is completely at variance with the interpretation presented in this chapter. He interprets the unique time component for incongruent combinations under colour-naming as the time for a 'different' match and the subsequent search for a colour name.

Now, the detection of incongruence seems to require a match. How can a match be performed, if no colour-name, i.e. a verbal colour-code, is already present? We think that it is a performance by hypothesis-testing: The verbal word-code suggests a verbal colour-code which makes further search unnecessary in the case of congruence, whereas disproof of the hypothesis is an incongruent result by default in the sense that incompatibility of codes is taken for a mismatch. (Schulz, 1979, p. 392)

As elaborated in chapters 4 and 5, words like 'compare', 'check' and 'verify' used in models have to be regarded with great suspicion. It seems that the list has to be extended with 'match' and 'test'. It is extremely difficult to see how it is known that the suggested verbal colour-code (that is, a duplicate of the verbal word-code) corresponds with a verbal colour-code, if no colour name, that is, a verbal colour-code is already present. In other words, even the words 'hypothesis-testing' fail if comparisons between incomparable codes are involved in one way or another! (In his experiments Schulz used an exposure duration of 500 msec. To the issue of short exposure durations vs extended exposure durations we return in the next chapter.)

In four experiments, Dallas and Merikle (1976a and b) investigated performance in a highly unorthodox version of the Stroop-test. Their investigations were primarily concerned with word-word combinations. According to our definition, word-word conditions also belong to the 'modified Stroop task' (see Experiment II, chapter 4), and it is therefore interesting to see whether our tentative model is capable of explaining the results that they obtained. All their experiments involved conditions in which two words were simultaneously presented, one above and one below a fixation point. Barmarkers were used to point at one of the two words. Ss were instructed to name that word as fast as possible. The non-reported word was either semantically related to the reported word or was a non-associated word. In all experiments it was found that RTs were faster when the non-reported word was semantically related than when it was a non-associated word. (See Allport, 1977, exp. II, for related results.)

It will be clear that, without further assumptions, there is nothing in our model that can explain this result. One further assumption, however, seems to suffice in order to account for this result. Assume that logogens corresponding with semantically related words are connected in such a way, that an increase in level of activation in one of these logogens is also reflected as an increase in activation in the connected logogens. (The logogen system is redefined as a lexicon or as a lexical memory, in which, during the time the logogens increase in counts, activation spreads; see, for example, Collins and Loftus, 1975, for a related point of view.)

As a first approximation, we can work out this assumption in the following way. Suppose there are two logogens, corresponding to words

A and B respectively. Presented in isolation, word A results in a maximum count level C_A, word B in a maximum count level C_B. If these two words are non-associated (that is, the corresponding logogens are not connected), simultaneous presentation of words A and B will also result in maximum count levels C_A and C_B respectively. If the two words are matched in frequency, length, etc., we can assume that $C_A = C_B = C$.

If the two words are semantically related (that is, their logogens are connected), simultaneous presentation of the two words results in some kind of reciprocal recurrent activation (see Cornsweet, 1970, pp. 295-300 for an inhibition analogy). If we assume that only two logogens are involved, the maximum level of activation of the logogens corresponding to words A and B, M_A and M_B, can be found by solving

$$M_A = C_A + \alpha M_B; 0 < \alpha < 1 \tag{5}$$
$$M_B = C_B + \alpha M_A; 0 < \alpha < 1 \tag{6}$$

in which α is the proportion of activation that spreads ($\alpha < 1$) and C_A (and C_B) are the count levels that are reached if words A and B are presented in isolation. The first equation can be read as: with simultaneous presentation of words A and B, the maximum level of activation of the logogen corresponding with word A (M_A) equals the maximum count level reached by that logogen if word A is presented in isolation, (C_A), plus a fraction ($\alpha < 1$) of the maximum count level of the logogen corresponding with word B (M_B). By substituting 6 in 5 (or 5 in 6) we can solve for M_A (or M_B)

$$M_A = C_A + \alpha(C_B + \alpha M_A),$$

or,

$$M_A = \frac{C_A + \alpha C_B}{(1 - \alpha^2)}.$$

For $C_A = C_B = C$, this equation reduces to

$$M_A = M_B = \frac{C}{1 - \alpha} = C'.$$

We therefore have maximum count levels of C if the logogens are not connected, and of C' if the logogens are connected. Because $\alpha < 1$, it follows that $C < C'$. (For instance, with C = 80 and α = .20, C' = 100.)

Table 6.2 shows, that according to our tentative model, less interference is to be expected if the two logogens start with a higher value of C (see the word-word condition; C = 100), than when they start with a lower value of C (see the colour-colour condition; C = 80). So the semantic facilitation effects observed by Dallas and Merikle (1976a and b) are easily explained in terms of our tentative model if the logogen system is redefined as a lexicon in which activation spreads. (Possibly it is better to distinguish more levels in a logogen than we have done up to now; to this issue we will return at the end of this chapter. The analysis presented in the previous paragraphs, however, shows that at the present we do not need such an assumption.) It will be clear that according to our interpretation 'semantic facilitation' has to be interpreted as 'less interference'.

Three further remarks about the data reported by Dallas and Merikle (1976a and b) and about their interpretations of the data, and one general remark about the extension of our tentative model have to be made.

In the second experiment reported by Dallas and Merikle (1976a) only word-word combinations were presented. The two words were either semantically related (R) or non-associated (NR). The display duration was 125 msec. The barmarker either preceded display onset by 250 msec (the pre-cue condition or 'selective' condition), or followed display onset by 250 msec (the post-cue condition or 'non-selective' condition). In the pre-cue condition, the difference NR-R was about 15 msec, while in the post-cue condition, this difference was about 80 msec (overall mean RTs were also appreciably larger (more than 250 msec) in the post-cue condition than in the pre-cue condition). Dallas and Merikle conclude:

> These results are inconsistent with any interpretation stating that
> there is unimpaired semantic analysis of non-attended material . . . .
> For such an interpretation to be supported, equivalent effects of
> non-reported material should have been found in both the selective
> and non-selective conditions. On the other hand, since the present
> results show greater semantic interaction in the non-selective than
> in the selective conditions, they are consistent with any of the
> general class of theories specifying that selective attention produces
> an unequal degree or level of analysis for attended and non-attended
> material . . . (Dallas and Merikle, 1976a, p. 20)

This conclusion, however, is in no way justified. A basic assumption of our tentative model is: 'unimpaired semantic analysis of non-attended material', and our model exactly predicts the results obtained by Dallas and Merikle. A comparison of rows C̲, C and W̲, W in Table 6.2 shows this feature of the model. Row C̲, C gives the amount of interference obtained with two logogens reaching a maximum count-level of 80. This row can be interpreted as reflecting the effects found with two non-associated words (NR). Row W̲, W gives the amount of interference

179

obtained with two logogens reaching a maximum count-level of 100. This row reflects the effects found with two words that are semantically related (R). The table shows that the difference between the two rows increases with increasing t_s, that is, the later the starting time of the selection mechanism, the greater the difference between NR and R ($\underline{C}$, C and $\underline{W}$, W in Table 6.2). The data presented by Dallas and Merikle (1976a), therefore, offer strong support for the model presented in this chapter. Ironically, our model belongs to the class of models rejected by Dallas and Merikle (1976a) on the basis of this data! (Dallas and Merikle (1976b) offer an interpretation for related results in terms of processes related to the response-execution stage, that is much more in line with our point of view.)

In the first experiment reported by Dallas and Merikle (1976a) a completely different pattern of results was found. The only major difference with the second experiment, described in the previous paragraph, was that this experiment included a third condition in which the target word was paired with a non-word (a pseudo-random letterstring). In this experiment the difference NR-R was about the same in pre- and post-cue condition. Because the inclusion of the third condition is the only major difference between the two experiments, it seems reasonable to attribute the different patterns of results in the two experiments to the presence of the non-words in the first experiment (cf. Dallas and Merikle, 1976a, p. 20). According to Dallas and Merikle, the presence of the non-words can have induced a different strategy in the post-cue condition. 'One may speculate that the strategy ... was to analyse the display for the presence of a non-word .... On many trials this "non-word" cue would have been available prior to the visual report cue' (Dallas and Merikle, 1976a, p. 19). The remaining problem is how this strategy can have its effects on NR-R. According to Dallas and Merikle (1976a) this is because processing capacity is withdrawn from semantic analysis. 'If subjects in the postcue condition were analysing the display for the presence of a non-word, attention may not have been directed towards analysis of its semantic characteristics' (Dallas and Merikle, 1976a, p. 19). It will be clear that this point of view is opposite to our basic assumption of automatic parallel processing of visual information. An alternative explanation, in line with our point of view, starts with the assumption that the non-word condition induces a fast selection strategy for all combinations in the post-cue condition. It is in no way clear, whether the strategy of waiting for 250 msec, until the cue comes, is the most efficient strategy in this type of tasks. A different, and possibly more efficient, strategy is (a) to select the target with word/non-word pairs, and (b) select one of the two words at random (or select both words, one after another) with word-word pairs and then wait for the cue. (This is a well-known strategy in experiments involving delayed cueing; see, for example, Sperling, 1960, pp. 8-10.) It will be clear, that, given such a selection strategy, a great number of further assumptions are needed before the tentative model outlined in this chapter can be used to describe the results. In other words, the model as formulated up to now, can only be used for interpreting the results of experiments for which the moment of initiating the selective operation is approximately known or can be inferred without reasonable doubt. The first experiment reported by Dallas and Merikle (1976a) shows that this condition is not easily met. Their second experiment, however, shows that this condition can be met.

Dallas and Merikle (1976b) reported the results of two similar experiments in which only a post-cue condition was investigated. (Exposure durations were 150 msec in the first and 1000 msec in the second experiment, but roughly similar results were obtained. In the next chapter we will return to the issue of short vs extended exposure durations.) The post-cue appeared more than a second after stimulus onset. Even with this long interval between stimulus onset and moment of presentation of the cue, RTs were significantly shorter when the two words were semantic associates than when they were non-associates. It will be clear that neither Morton's logogen model nor the tentative model outlined in this chapter are capable of handling this result without adding further assumptions. It is, however, worthwhile to briefly discuss what type of model offers an adequate starting point for handling this result. It seems that Morton's model offers no starting point at all. Long before the appearance of the selective cue, the responses have left the logogen system and have entered the response buffer. Further ad hoc assumptions are needed to explain any facilitation or interference at this level. Our tentative model seems to offer a more adequate starting point. One assumption of the model is that the initial level of activation of the logogen is reflected during the whole time-course of activation of the logogen (see Fig. 6.1). Because it is assumed that the words stay in the logogens until actively selected, a differential effect of activation level is to be expected at all selection times, t_s. It therefore depends upon the further assumptions one is willing to make about the duration of activation of the logogens whether Dallas's and Merikle's results can be explained or not. Two issues are of importance in connection with this argument: (a) the time-course of activation of the logogens depicted in Figure 6.1 and used in the numerical example was arbitrarily chosen and other time parameters will suffice; (b) again, it is not known what the Ss do in the interval of time until the cue comes (see Sperling, 1960, pp. 8-10). In the next chapter, in relation to whole report experiments, another possible strategy for lengthening the duration of activation of logogens will be discussed. The essential point, however, seems to be, that Dallas and Merikle's results can better be understood in terms of a model involving activated programs of motor instructions (that is, our tentative model) than in terms of a model involving logogens with fixed thresholds in which words become available in a passive way (that is, Morton's model). In a sense, we can therefore agree with Dallas's and Merikle's interpretation:

> While the present findings do not rule out a contribution of early
> processing stages, they suggest that caution should be exercised
> when interpreting the effects of semantic context. In any case,
> semantic context appears to affect late stages in the word-
> recognition process, suggesting that any conceptualization of
> semantic context effects must consider the contribution of the
> response-execution stage. (Dallas and Merikle, 1976b, p. 444)

At this point, one further remark with regard to the extended tentative model is of importance. In section 1 of this chapter, two factors were distinguished that could determine the level of activation of the logogens: (a) the momentary stimulation conditions (external activation), and (b) 'response readiness' or 'response set' (internal activation). This distinction parallels Norman's (1976) and Lindsay's and Norman's (1977) distinction between 'data driven' (bottom-up) and 'conceptually driven' (top-down) processing. Data driven processing can be defined as operations or activations resulting from or triggered by incoming sensory data. Conceptually driven processing, at the other hand, starts with high level expectations. It will be clear that the 'spread of activation' concept, as elaborated in the previous paragraphs, belongs to the province of data driven processing. Semantic context effects as observed by Dallas and Merikle (1976a and b) are, in this conception, simply the result of stimulus presentation. No higher level expectations are involved. This must not be taken to mean that these effects are of minor importance as compared with internally generated context effects. In a number of experiments, similar or related effects have been found with sequentially presented information under various different conditions (for example, Warren, 1972, 1974; Jacobson, 1973,

1974; Jacobson and Rhinelander, 1978; Conrad, 1974; Posner and Snyder, 1975b; Taylor, 1977; Humphreys, 1978; Sperber et al., 1979). Of course, to cope with the detailed results of these experiments, further assumptions are necessary. (as far as pattern-masking is concerned, some of these will be briefly discussed in the next chapter.) It seems, however, that the 'spread of activation' concept, especially if connected with assumptions about time delays in the connections between logogens, can provide a fruitful starting point for explanations of behaviour in continuous language tasks such as reading and listening. This issue will not be further pursued, however. In the next chapter we will briefly return to one possible way in which external activation (that is, the results of data driven processing) and internal activation (that is, the results of conceptually driven processing) interact. (See Neely (1977) for a similar distinction between 'data driven' and 'conceptually driven' semantic priming effects; see also Posner and Snyder (1975d) and Taylor (1977) for a related distinction.)

5 The anatomy of a logogen

At the end of this chapter we will briefly speculate about the 'anatomy' of a logogen. These speculations serve only the function of indicating one line along which the model can be elaborated in order to broaden its scope. What follows is only a raw sketch. Nevertheless, the perspective is intriguing and that is why this section is included.

In section 1 of this chapter we defined a logogen as a transducer in which 'programs of motor instructions' (that is, a verbal code) are activated by stimulus features. (In the system these features are also represented as a visual code.) This definition was sufficient for explaining the results obtained with the modified Stroop task. In section 4 of this chapter, in relation with Dallas's and Merikle's (1976a and b) experiments, however, we had to redefine the logogen system as a lexicon (that is, a combined logogen system and semantic system) in which activation spreads between logogens corresponding with semantically related words.

In chapter 4, in relation to 'postcategorical filtering' we distinguished a number of different 'processing domains', or 'functional subsystems', for instance, a 'visual domain' containing 'visual codes', a 'verbal domain' containing 'phonetic' or 'articulatory codes', a 'conceptual domain', etc. We assumed that 'Codes from different domains are linked if a code from one domain has triggered or has addressed a code in a different domain or if a code in one domain has been generated from a code in another domain. These (specific) links unitize or integrate codes in different domains' (cf. p. 106).

Given this notion of 'processing domains', we can make the concept 'lexicon' more explicit by distinguishing three, interconnected, types of codes within a logogen: a visual code (that is, the visual representation generated by a stimulus), a semantic code and a verbal or articulatory code. The problem is how to connect these three codes in order to get a fruitful starting point for discussions about a number of experimental tasks and observed phenomena and in order to be capable of spanning a number of theoretical concepts.

Figure 6.3 depicts a set of relations that (a) seems to provide such a starting point, and (b) is consistent with the results discussed in this chapter.

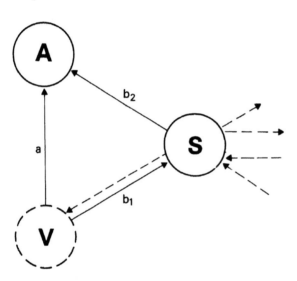

Figure 6.3 *The anatomy of a logogen. V is visual representation; S is semantic code; A is articulatory code (for further explanation see text)*

In this conceptualization, the visual code, V, (in fact, one of several possible visual representations, $V \in [V']$), can be connected with the verbal or articulatory code, or, the code of articulatory instructions, A, in three ways.

1 The visual code, or a subset of the features represented in the visual code, is capable of triggering directly the verbal or articulatory code

via connection a. Activation of A via a can be considered as resulting from an automatic application of overlearned visual-verbal coversion rules; for words and word-like letter-strings some kind of learned extra-lexical 'pronunciation' rules. (Possibly this direct route can also be temporarily established; see, for example, Keele, 1973, p. 91: 'The repetition effect: bypassing memory retrieval'.) Let us call this route 'reading' (that is, 'barking at words').

2 The visual code, or a subset of the features represented in the visual code triggers one (likely more) semantic code, S, in the conceptual domain via b_1, and this semantic code triggers the verbal or articulatory code via b_2. In this way, the input to A via b_2 depends on access to 'semantic memory'. The route via b_1 and b_2 can be called the 'naming route', because it is assumed that it is in operation with items that have to be named, like pictures, colours, forms, etc. (see also Morton, 1979).

3 The visual code, or a subset of the features represented in the visual code, directly triggers A via a (as under 1), and the visual code or a (not necessarily the same) subset of the features represented in the visual code triggers A via b_1 and b_2 (as under 2). It is assumed that if both routes are activated, activation via a and via b_2 'adds' at A. In this way, a special status is given to real words as compared with 'pseudo-words' or non-word figures or colours, etc. Words can be 'read' (route a), but, in a sense, words are also pictures or forms that can be 'named' (route b_1, b_2). Words have picture-like properties, but pictures do not have word-like properties.

An essential notion is that the whole of codes and interconnections activated by a given stimulus item forms the unitized logogen. Further assumptions that have to be added mainly concern the properties of the conceptual domain, or the properties of the semantic codes, S. Examples of properties that can be added are: the conceptual domain is diffusely activated (see Keele and Neill, 1978); activation spreads within the conceptual domain (see, for example, Neely, 1977). This is indicated by the dashed arrows to and from S; effects of 'context' operate in the conceptual domain; activation at level S can have its effects at level V (see the dashed arrow pointing back from S to V), etc.

In the next paragraph a selection of issues that can be discussed in terms of this framework is briefly mentioned. Only some hints for a more precise inclusion in the framework are given. It is to the reader and to the present author to work out these (and other) issues in more detail.

1 Learning to read. The 'whole-word' (look-and-say) method vs the 'analytical' method. The route via S vs route a.

2 The reading of non-words. Up to now Morton's logogen model does not include a 'mechanism' for the reading of non-words or pseudo-words. Route a.

3 The 'word-superiority effect' (see, for example, Reicher, 1969; Wheeler, 1970; Krueger and Shapiro, 1979). Route a for non-words, route a plus the route via S for words.

4 Acquired dyslexia (see, for example, Allport, 1979). Deep dyslexia and surface dyslexia. Selective impairment of route a and selective impairment of route via S.

5 Semantic confusions (see, for example, Allport, 1977). Route via S.

6 Reading vs naming (Fraisse, 1969; Gholson and Hohle, 1968). Route a plus route via S vs route via S.

7 The locus of interference in Stroop-like tasks (Seymour, 1977, Stirling, 1979). Interference at level A and/or at level S.

8 'Postcategorical filtering' (this study). A selective operation performed at level V.

9 Stimulus set and response set (Broadbent, 1970, 1971). Selective operations performed at level V and selective operations performed at level S.

10 Data driven vs conceptually driven processing (Lindsay and Norman, 1977). Effects of context in S.

11 Two coding systems for representing the world (see, for example, Kolers and Smythe, 1979). A pictorial system ('imaging': route from S to V) and a verbal system (route from S to A). 'Imaging, as is true too of an internal dialogue, is a way of expressing one's thoughts to oneself; the descriptions are pictorial in the one case and linguistic in the other' (Kolers and Smythe, 1979, p. 181).

12 The effects of semantic cues on the resolution of words presented dichoptically (see, for example, Rommetveit and Blakar, 1973; Lema-Stern and Gottwald, 1979). The effects of level S on level V).

13 Pre-attentive analysers (Neisser, 1967; Kahneman, 1973). The effect of level S on level V.

14 Various category effects in visual information processing (Egeth et al., 1972; Allport, 1977). The effects of S on A and V.

15 Various kinds of visual/verbal/semantic dissociations (see Morton, 1977, p. 125 and Wickelgren, 1979, p. 123, for examples). Depending on which S and which A has the highest level of activation in the set of all logogens that are activated on a certain moment.

As stated, the set of relations depicted in Fig. 6.3 is consistent with the logogen concept as used in the first two sections of this chapter. As far as our explanation of the results obtained with the modified Stroop-task is concerned, the assumption that pure interference effects for this type of task obtain only at the level of articulatory codes (that is, at level A), suffices. The 'spread of activation' concept, introduced in relation with Dallas and Merikle's (1976a and b) experiments is now formulated in a more precise way. Instead of 'relations between logogens' (that is, relations between the whole of unitized codes), we now have 'relations between semantic codes' (that is, at level S). (This entails that a higher coefficient of 'recurrent activation' has to be postulated between related codes at level S (that is, in the conceptual domain) in order to get the same results as obtained in the numerical example discussed in connection with Dallas's and Merikle's experiments.)

One further general remark has to be made. The conceptualization as represented in Figure 6.3 is rather similar to Morton's (1979) conceptualization in his revised logogen model and to Nelson's (1979) sensory-semantic model of picture and word encoding. The three conceptualizations differ, however, as far as a great number of additional assumptions are concerned. Nevertheless, their similarity can possibly offer a starting point for integrating present views in different fields of research such as visual and auditory information processing, memory, word recognition, language, etc.

This, as far as the anatomy of a logogen is concerned. In the next chapter we do not need this elaborate version. Therefore, we return to our first definition: a logogen is a transducer in which 'programs of motor instructions' are activated by stimulus features.

7 Further speculations and reinterpretations

Summary

This chapter presents a discussion about how the postcategorical selection model developed in chapter 6 can be extended so that it is capable of accounting for the results found with whole report experiments (see chapter 1) and partial report experiments (see chapter 3). Separate discussions are devoted to the three main differences between the 'modified Stroop test' (that is, the task for which the postcategorical selection model was devised) and whole report tasks: (a) short exposure duration vs extended exposure durations, (b) one response vs several responses, and (c) immediate responding vs delayed responding.

(a) The selection mechanism described in chapter 6 functions by maintaining the count level of the correct logogen until the count level of the other logogens are sufficiently decreased. Short exposure durations seem to ensure such an automatic decrease of count levels. Additional assumptions are necessary to account for this decrease under conditions with extended exposures. Fixation durations under normal viewing conditions are rather short, however, and therefore conditions with extended exposures can be regarded as conditions in which a quick succession of stationary 'tachistoscopic' stimuli is presented. With regard to the relation between fixations and iconic memory (iconic storage can be identified with the activated input sides of the logogens), two positions can be taken: (1) the icon fades within a fixation, and (2) the icon fades during the saccadic eye movement or the next fixation. Both positions are compatible with the assumption of a count decrease during stimulus exposure. The first position, together with the assumption of a fast decrease of the counts of the logogens whose response is executed, is taken as a starting point for further speculations.

(b) In this section the results of a whole report experiment from Sperling (1967) and Sperling's interpretation of these results are discussed. Sperling's precategorical selection model is rephrased as a postcategorical selection model. This reformulation leads to the hypothesis that, given optimal exposure conditions, the results of whole report experiments reflect the activities of a serial selection mechanism. A concatenation of selective operations as specified in the model presented in chapter 6 indeed predicts the mathematical relation between number of elements reported and exposure time as found by Sperling (1967) and as found in the experiment reported in chapter 1. From among the models described in Appendix C of chapter 1, the postcategorical selection model most in accordance with this analysis is briefly discussed. This model is also compatible with recent STM notions. Again, Allport's (1977) perceptual integration hypothesis is briefly discussed.

(c) The results of whole report experiments seem incompatible with the assumption of immediate, vocal or subvocal, execution of responses. A faster operation has to be postulated as a substitute for this responding, and a store is needed in which the results of this substitute operation can be kept until the responses can be executed. This issue is made more specific in terms of a single-store model and in terms of a multi-store model.

It will be clear that the discussions offered in this chapter are not intended as a summary of firm conclusions based upon the results obtained in previous chapters. They merely indicate some fruitful directions for further research within this area of investigation.

The Stroop test and Eriksen's modified visual probe experiments are powerful experimental paradigms for providing information on the characteristics of the mechanisms of central information selection, because both paradigms are concerned with the question 'what is the effect of irrelevant information?' instead of asking 'how effective is the processing of relevant information?' (cf. chapter 3). In chapters 4 and 5 the results of a number of experiments in which modifications of these paradigms were used were presented and in chapter 6 a tentative model, accounting for the characteristics of central visual information selection in these types of tasks was described. These experimental tasks have as characteristics (a) the short exposure duration, (b) only one response has to be given on a trial, and (c) this response has to be given as fast as possible. In the present chapter we will speculate further on how the model presented in chapter 6 can be extended and/or modified in order to account for the results of other visual information processing experiments, especially for the results of whole report experiments (see chapter 1). Whole report tasks have as characteristics (a) a range of exposure durations, including longer exposures; (b) more responses have to be given on a trial; (c) no explicit instructions are given about the speed of responding. Therefore, the following three issues have to be considered:

(a) short exposure durations vs extended exposure durations;

(b) one response vs several responses;

(c) immediate responding vs delayed responding.

(a) Short exposure durations vs extended exposure durations

In the experiments reported in chapters 4 and 5 the exposure durations used were so short that Ss could not make useful eye movements. This fact not only characterizes these experiments, but was also used in the model developed in chapter 6. According to this model, response initiation is possible only if the irrelevant information is sufficiently decayed; in addition, the time necessary for the selective operation was made dependent upon the decay of the irrelevant information. The short exposure durations used ensured the rapid decay of information and a selection mechanism as described in chapter 6 can successfully operate. What, however, about the selective operation in tasks with unlimited viewing times such as the original Stroop test, or a whole report task with extended exposure durations, or even a reading task? How is the decay of irrelevant information brought about in these types of tasks? There are at least three possible answers to this question.

The first stems from the results of an experiment from Haber and Standing (1970) on icon duration. In that experiment, Ss adjusted a click to the apparent initiation and the apparent termination of a brief visual stimulus. The interclick interval was taken as a measure of the subjective duration of the flash. The physical duration of the flash was the main independent variable. The data showed that visual storage from brief pulses lasted up to 250 msec after the pulse ended, but that longer pulses had less persistence. Mainly based on the results of this experiment, Dick (1974) states: 'One could imagine two polar theoretical positions: in the first it is assumed that the icon begins when the stimulus is terminated. . . . The second position is that the Icon begins when the stimulus is initiated and runs its course whether the stimulus is present or not' (Dick, 1974, p. 579). If the time-course of activation of the logogens is equated with the time-course of the icon, or, if it is assumed that the time-course of activation of a logogen is monotonically related to the time-course of the icon, the model presented in chapter 6, together with this second theoretical position as an additional assumption is capable of accounting for the selection of information with extended exposures.

It seems that Haber and Hershenson (1974) adopt the second theoretical position and assume that the icon lasts for no more than 250 msec, which is also the minimum duration of an eye fixation. According to these authors, Haber's and Standing's (1970) data suggest, 'that the icon lasts about one quarter of a second, either from a continual representation of the stimulus as it remains on view, or as a persistence after the stimulus ends' (Haber and Hershenson, 1974, p. 168). From the minimum duration of a fixation (250 msec), and from the interval of time over which the icon decays (250 msec), it follows that the icon will always have disappeared before an eye movement can occur. (For further — and adverse — comments on this issue, see Dick, 1974, p. 584.)

Dick's (1974) point of view with regard to this issue is less clear, but a number of remarks favouring the second theoretical position can be found.

> Basically, the most consistent interpretation seems to be that some portions of the physical stimulus may be irrelevant for identification . . .; i.e., we might use only the first few milliseconds of a fixation to take in information for form analysis. A number of investigations have supported the contention . . . . To acquire more information, we must make a second fixation . . . , unless the stimulus is subthreshold. (Dick, 1974, p. 579)

> the icon might be viewed as an artifact of the tachistoscopic procedure, since in the natural environment the duration of the stimulus is seldom restricted. From this point of view, the persisting icon would be redundant, since the physical energies are available long enough for complete processing. The data on duration of exposure, however, suggest that the physical presence of the stimulus is redundant and that the icon is used for identification and form perception. (Dick, 1974, p. 583)

> There are situations, of course, in which the entire stimulus will fall on the fovea. When this occurs, a second fixation will not serve to move the stimulus to more sensitive positions of the retina. It is in this case that a second function of a second fixation is most apparent, that of generating a second icon, allowing for a 'second look' at the stimulus. (Dick, 1974, p. 584)

Recently, Di Lollo (1980) made a strong case in favour of this position. In a series of five experiments, evidence was obtained for an inverse relationship between duration of stimulus and duration of visible persistence. Di Lollo concludes that visual persistence can be regarded better as an outcome of neural activity at an early phase of visual information processing. In his extensive review, Coltheart (1980), however, seriously doubts whether 'iconic memory' and 'visible persistence' are the two sides of one coin. He argues that these phenomena have fundamentally different properties and therefore do not reflect a single underlying process.

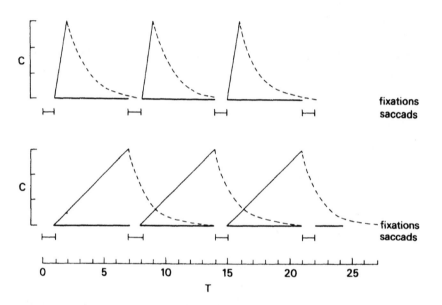

Figure 7.1 *Hypothetical time-course of activation of groups of logogens during three fixations. Upper panel: decay of counts during the fixation. Lower panel: decay of counts during the saccadic eye movement and the next fixation (for further explanation see text). Horizontal axes give time in units of 50 msec (T); vertical axes give count level (C)*

Of course, with regard to the model described in chapter 6, this second theoretical position – the icon is initiated when the stimulus starts, but runs its course independently of objective exposure conditions – is very attractive. At present, the evidence in favour seems rather ambiguous, however (see Coltheart, 1980). Nevertheless, the upper panel of Figure 7.1 shows how, according to this point of view, the hypothetical time-course of activation of groups of logogens during a number of fixations should look.

A second possible answer to the question of how the irrelevant information decays under conditions with extended exposures starts from the observation that fixation durations under normal viewing conditions are rather short. The average fixation duration found in reading research is between 250 and 300 msec, and the average duration of a saccadic eye movement is between 25 and 50 msec (see Haber and Hershenson, 1974, p. 220). Kahneman (1973) mentions fixation durations averaging between 200 and 225 msec for reading and between 300 and 350 msec for the observation of pictures (p. 58).

So, in a way, conditions with extended exposures can be regarded as conditions in which a fast series of stationary, 'tachistoscopic' stimuli is presented. The decay of the irrelevant information can then take place during and after the saccadic eye movement. More generally, during the $(n + 1)^{th}$ fixation, or during a saccadic eye movement, the irrelevant information taken in together with the relevant information in the nth fixation, can decay sufficiently to make response initiation possible (the discrepancy in time between the moment of fixating the relevant information and the moment of initiating the response can then be seen as contributing to the well-known 'eye-voice span').

For this solution, the assumption that neither a saccadic eye movement nor a later fixation can erase or wipe out the contents of the logogen system is essential. If the time-course of activation of the logogens is equated with the time-course of the icon, or if it is assumed that the time-course of activation is monotonically related to the time-course of the icon, the further assumption that neither a saccadic eye movement nor a later fixation can erase or wipe out the icon resulting from a previous fixation is essential. In chapter 1 the effect of a patterned masking field on the contents of iconic memory was discussed. In short, both Scheerer (1973) and Turvey (1973) provided evidence that a patterned mask interrupts the processing of the stimulus by erasing the icon, if the interval between stimulus onset and mask onset is greater than 100 msec. This can be taken to mean that a saccadic eye movement or a following fixation, both following the onset of the first fixation after an interval far greater than 100 msec, can act as a patterned mask and erase the icon. However, there is at least some evidence that a saccadic eye movement does not erase the icon (see Davidson et al., 1973; Dick, 1974, p. 584).

It seems, furthermore, rather doubtful to equate the effects of an

193

experimenter-controlled patterned mask, that is unrelated to the previous stimulation, with the effects of a subject-controlled second fixation of the same scene. A second fixation moves portions of the stimulus first projected on less sensitive locations on the retina to more sensitive parts, thereby increasing the clarity or the quality of the icon for these portions. As far as the logogen system is concerned, it seems reasonable to assume that this results in an increase in counts for the logogens receiving their input from this portion of the stimulus. A second fixation, however, also moves portions of the stimulus first projected on the more sensitive parts to less sensitive parts. It seems not unreasonable to assume that this results in a gradual decrease of the clarity or of the quality of the icon for these portions of the stimulus, and that, as far as the logogen system is concerned, this results in a gradual decrease in counts for the logogens receiving their inputs from this portion of the stimulus. (This assumption suffices to explain the effects of distance from the fixation point obtained by Eriksen and Eriksen (1974), by Gatti and Egeth (1978) and by Merikle and Gorewich (1979), in terms of the model presented in chapter 6. See also Goolkasian (1978) for relevant results.)

According to this point of view, the optimal moment for initiating an eye movement is when the iconic representation is of maximum clarity. Refixations would serve two functions. First, new information, or old information with increased clarity, is presented to the logogen system. Second, old information is taken away or reduced in clarity, thereby making the selection of information possible. It will be clear that in order for this selection mechanism to work, the increase of the counts of the logogens corresponding to the new information must be relatively late or slow as compared with the decrease in counts of the logogens corresponding to the old information. There is evidence, however, that the visual sensitivity to stimulation is reduced not only during a saccadic eye movement (25 to 50 msec), but over an interval of time ranging from about 50 msec before until 50 msec after the movement (see Latour, 1962; Haber and Hershenson, 1974, p. 209). Therefore, this requirement seems to be met. In the lower panel of Figure 7.1, one of the several ways which, according to this point of view, the hypothetical time-course of activation of groups of logogens during a number of fixations could be presented is sketched.

While the first two answers to the question of how irrelevant information decays under conditions with extended exposures are mutually exclusive — that is, either the upper panel or the lower panel or neither of the two panels of Figure 7.1 gives an adequate representation of the hypothetical time-course of activation of the logogens – the last mechanism to be discussed is compatible with both. This mechanism for reducing the count level of logogens corresponding to irrelevant information is suggested by the results of an experiment by Klein (1964). In this experiment, Klein showed that reading the word prior to colour-naming on the Stroop conflict card required only a little more time than naming only the colours. Klein comments on this task: 'All Ss . . . save one, said it felt easier than the standard single-response task. Typical comments were: "The meaning disappeared and I could spend the time searching for the color-name." "Getting it out of your system, you can concentrate on the color" ' (p. 583).

It seems, therefore, that the act of selecting a logogen followed by the execution of its response can make the response conflict disappear. In terms of the modified logogen model which was presented in the previous chapter, this finding can be described by stating that the execution, vocal or subvocal, of the response has as a result the decrease of the count level of the logogen. Morton (1969a) suggests a comparable mechanism for logogens that have made their response available. 'Since this system operates during reading and listening to continuous speech, it is necessary to assume that the value of the count decays very rapidly with time, returning to its original value in something of the order of 1 second. Otherwise words with a structural similarity to the ones spoken would become available uncontrollably' (p. 166).

Before Morton's assumption can be incorporated into the modified logogen model as described in the previous chapter, two modifications are necessary. First, because in that model responses do not become available in a passive way, but have to be selected, it has to be assumed that this rapid count decay of a logogen takes place after the logogen is selected. Second, because the decay of counts is already one of the features of this model, the selection of a logogen must result in a faster count decay in order to have any positive effect. (To this issue we will return later on.) Therefore, a decay time of 1 second, as Morton suggests, seems rather long. Also the results found by Klein (1964) and mentioned above suggest a faster count decay. Furthermore, a much faster decay of the count level of a logogen once selected follows if the time-course of activation of non-selected logogens is equated with the time-course of the icon. For the present, we base the third possible answer to the question of how the count level of the irrelevant logogen decreases under conditions with extended exposures, on the assumption that the act of executing a logogen's response results in a fast decrease of the count of that logogen. Therefore, the execution of an irrelevant response will result in a fast count decay of the logogen from which the response stemmed. (From a tuning-fork resonance metaphor, it can become clear that this assumption is not incompatible with, and does not explain, a repetition effect.)

It is possible to invent other answers to the question of how the counts decay with extended exposures. It is also possible to relate this point of view to other areas in visual perception research (Troxler effect, Stabilized Images, Single-cell Recordings, etc.; see, for example, Cornsweet, 1970). These issues will not be further pursued, however. One of the first two answers — for ease of exposition we will take decay during a fixation — together with the last answer — a fast decrease of the counts of a logogen whose response is executed — suffices to account for the selection of information with extended exposures.

One important issue remains to be mentioned with regard to the passive decay of irrelevant information. In chapter 6 (Figures 6.1 and 6.2) and also in Figure 7.1 in this chapter it is suggested that the time-course of activation of the logogens starts at a count level 0 and returns to the same level later on. It must be clear that as far as the model described in chapter 6 is concerned, this assumption is not necessary. The count level can start to increase from any level, C, and return to that level (or to another level, given certain further assumptions) later on. Assume that the increase in activation for the relevant logogen starts from count level C_r and for the irrelevant logogen from count level C_i.

Equation (2) from chapter 6 then has to be written as

$$(C_r + R\,e^{-\alpha ts}) - (C_i + I\,e^{-\alpha ti}) = \delta. \tag{1}$$

This equation can be rewritten as

$$R\,e^{-\alpha ts} - I\,e^{-\alpha ti} = \delta - (C_r - C_i). \tag{2}$$

For $C_r = C_i$ this equation reduces to

$$R\,e^{-\alpha ts} - I\,e^{-\alpha ti} = \delta \tag{3}$$

and this is equation (2) from chapter 6, used for the numerical example. This argument shows that as far as the model in chapter 6 is concerned, it is not necessary to assume that count levels start with and return to 0. In order to generalize the model, it is no longer necessary, therefore, to assume that the hypothetical time-course of activation of groups of logogens during a number of fixations as depicted in Figure 7.1 in this chapter starts with and returns to 0. (The Y-axes, representing counts (C) in Figure 7.1 are not numbered!) The assumption of a complete decay of counts within a fixation or during the saccadic eye movement and the next fixation is therefore not needed. Any exponential decay, to whatever level, is sufficient as far as the model in chapter 6 is concerned. (At this point it is worthwhile to briefly return to the assumption mentioned in chapter 6, that (a) external activation and (b) internal activation, simply add. One way of interpreting C_r and C_i is as the effects caused by a context (that is, internal activation). Equation (1) then shows how both kinds of activation add. Equation (2) then shows how context, according to the model described in chapter 6, exerts its effects. A number of testable predictions can be derived. This topic, however, is outside our line of argument and therefore will not be further discussed.)

(b) One response vs several responses

The model presented in the previous chapter was constructed in order to explain the data obtained with a modified Stroop task, a task requiring only one response per trial from the Ss. In the model it was supposed that the Ss had to perform the following sequence of operations: (a) locating the relevant information, (b) selecting the relevant response, and (c) execution of the response. A large number of experimental tasks, however, for instance, whole report tasks (see chapter 1) and partial report tasks (see chapter 3), require a number of responses on a single trial. This section is concerned with the problem of how the model has to be extended in order to be capable of accounting also for the results of multiple response tasks.

The two problems of major importance concern (a) the transition from parallel to serial operations, and (b) the time needed for each of the operations. In chapter 4, in the section 'related models', an outline of a general visual information processing model was already given. Two stages, parts, or sets of operations, were distinguished: (a) processing (i.e. identification or categorization) of visual information, and (b) further operations performed upon the processed information. In fact, locating the relevant information, selecting the relevant response, execution of the relevant response, and storage of information in a more enduring memory, are examples of further operations performed upon the processed information. Now it seems clear that this set of operations is needed in order to perform whole report and partial report tasks. In whole report tasks the elements have to be reported in their correct position, and in partial report tasks a specified subset of elements has to be reported. So, in both tasks identity information and position information are needed. Therefore, relevant information has to be located, relevant responses have to be selected, and selected responses have to be executed, or representations of the selected responses have to be stored in memory for report later on. (We return to the question of immediate vs delayed report in the next section. For the present we will use the word 'responding' for the operation performed upon the selected information, whether it is immediate execution or storage in a more enduring memory.) Starting from this model, the first problem can be formulated more precisely. Based on the results of chapter 2, the conclusion was already reached that processing of visual information is performed in parallel (additional evidence was presented in chapters 4 and 5). Therefore, the general problem of the transition from parallel to serial processing amounts to the question: is the transition between parallel and serial operations (a) between processing and locating of information, (b) between locating and selecting, or (c) between selecting and responding to the information? The second problem mentioned above concerns questions such as (a) how much time is needed for locating the relevant information, (b) how much time is needed for selecting the responses and (c) how much time is needed for responding?

In order to find some answers to these questions, it seems appropriate to start with the work of Sperling (1967, 1970), who considered and rejected a number of visual information processing models for whole and partial report tasks and suggested and supported one such model. Though Sperling's model is a precategorical selection model (see chapter 3), it is worthwhile to consider it in detail because up to now it gives the most complete account of the findings with these tasks. A reformulation of this model into a postcategorical selection model can then possibly provide the answers wanted.

Two experimental findings are basic for this model.

The first observation was already mentioned in chapter 1. In order to measure the time needed for processing the individual elements, Sperling (1967) used a whole report task and varied the exposure durations of the display over an interval from 10 to 200 msec. The visual display was at offset immediately followed by a visual noise mask (see chapter 1). The experiment showed that each 10 to 15 msec increase in exposure duration enabled the subjects to report one additional letter, up to about three or four letters. (For comparable results, see, for example, Sperling, 1963; Van der Heijden, 1971.) Because of the discrepancy between this processing rate (1 element per 10 to 15 msec) and the known rate of overt responses and of subvocal rehearsal (1 element per 150 to 300 msec), a buffer-memory between processing and responding has to be postulated: the recognition buffer-memory (Sperling, 1967).

The second observation was already discussed in Appendix B of chapter 1. In order to investigate the issue of serial vs parallel processing, Sperling (1967) examined the rate at which information was acquired about individual letters in the display. Figure 1.3 gives a set of five 'growth curves' that are nearly identical to the curves found by Sperling (1967). Sperling (1967) concludes: 'The observation that all locations begin to be reported at better than chance levels even at the briefest exposures, may be interpreted as evidence of an essentially parallel process for letter-recognition' (p. 290).

These two observations with their interpretations, together with the known facts about the visual image (Sperling, 1960) and about subvocal rehearsal (Sperling, 1963), led Sperling to the following model:

1 The visual representation of the stimulus is placed in VIS (Visual Information Storage): a high capacity, fast decaying, very short-term memory for unidentified visual information.

2 A scan component determines the sequence of locations from which information is entered into subsequent systems, or, decides which areas of the visual field contain information on which further processing should be performed.

3 Processing capacity is directed to the locations selected by the scan component.

4 The visual input from the selected locations is processed; that is, the visual images of the letters are converted into 'programs of motor-instructions'. The first observation mentioned above is reflected in the assumption that these programs can be set up very fast (for example, 50 msec for 3 letters). The second observation is reflected in the assumption that a number of motor programs can be set up simultaneously.

5 The programs, once set up, are stored in the recognition buffer-memory.

6 The execution of the programs constitutes vocal or subvocal rehearsal.

Sperling (1967) comments on this model:

The important idea embodied in the recognition buffer-memory is that the program of motor-instructions for a rehearsal can be set up in a very short time (e.g., 50 msec for 3 letters) compared to the time necessary to execute it (e.g., 500 msec for 3 letters). The recognition buffer is efficient partly because the programs for rehearsing several letters can be set up in it simultaneously. However, the major gain in speed derives from the assumption that setting up a program to rehearse a letter is inherently a faster process than executing the program, i.e. rehearsing the letter. (p. 291)

This feature of the model is indeed of great importance. While recent research on the effect of a patterned noise masking stimulus has shown that the representation of a visual display cannot be erased at any time, as Sperling (1963, 1967, 1970) assumes (see also the discussion in chapter 1), a noise masking stimulus certainly reduces the interval of time during which the visual representation is available and usable (see, for example, Coltheart, 1972, pp. 13-14; Haber and Hershenson, 1974, pp. 131-4). So it remains true that the number of elements named with brief exposures followed by a noise masking stimulus is too large to be accounted for by a model in which a direct translation of the visual image of the letters into a vocal or subvocal response or into a written response is assumed (see Sperling, 1967, model 1 and model 2). The experiment reported in chapter 1 gives a clear example; with an effective stimulus duration (exposure duration + duration of the visual image) of 200 msec, about 2.5 elements can be recalled. With an implicit speech rate of about 200 msec per element (Landauer, 1962; Sperling, 1967), and a direct translation from the visual image into a vocal or subvocal response, 2.5 x 200 = 500 msec effective exposure duration should be necessary.

There is, however, one serious problem with Sperling's (1967, 1970) model. In whole report experiments and in partial report experiments, the Ss have to report the elements in their correct position. The recognition buffer-memory, however, contains only programs of motor instructions, and no information about the place in the visual image from which the program originated. In other words, all spatial information is lost in the recognition buffer-memory. So, the execution of the programs without a further provision will not result in a correct placement of the remembered items. (This is exactly the same problem as found in Morton's account of the Stroop test.) There are at least two possible extensions of this model that can remove this deficiency.

In the first, it is assumed that in one way or another the spatial information is retained in this buffer, while the visual representation has already disappeared (for instance, spatially tagged programs). This, however, leads to considerable complications of the model. If the Ss are, for instance, requested to name the elements in the correct order, a second selection mechanism, or another 'scan component', operating on the contents of the recognition buffer, is necessary, in order to ensure that the programs are executed in the correct order.

A more parsimonious assumption is that the first and original scan component translates the spatial order in a temporal order, and that this temporal order of the motor programs in the buffer is used to reconstruct the spatial order. (With this assumption a second selection mechanism is also necessary, but simpler mechanisms suffice as compared with the first alternative.) But now, the assumption that the elements are processed in parallel (the programs of motor-instructions are set up simultaneously) causes severe difficulties. If the programs are set up in parallel in the recognition buffer-memory, and, if this buffer contains nothing else than these programs, then there is no useful temporal order information from which the spatial order can be reconstructed.

A way out of this problem can be found if Sperling's (1967, 1970) conclusion that the 'growth curves' of the individual elements (cf. figure 1.3) suggest parallel processing, is rejected. There are two important arguments against Sperling's conclusion.

First, these curves do not necessarily represent the processing of the elements. According to Sperling's model, after the processing of the elements, the programs of motor instructions are stored in a memory. As argued in the previous paragraphs, these programs then have to be selected later on for execution. Therefore, the last event in the chain of operations is not processing, but the selection of a program from the recognition buffer-memory and its subsequent execution. Thus, the curves give the probability that a given program is selected from the recognition buffer-memory for execution. Only if all programs stored in the buffer are selected and executed without errors — and this will probably be the case only with a small number of programs stored — these curves also represent the probability that a program has entered the buffer (in Sperling's terms, the probability that the element is processed). Because this will not be the case in general, it is better to state that the 'growth curves' represent the last stage in the processing chain; that is, the probability that a given program is selected from the recognition buffer-memory.

Second, there is no compelling evidence that these curves represent the operation of a mechanism that works in parallel. (This issue was already extensively discussed in chapter 2.) In a footnote (cf. Sperling, 1967, p. 290) Sperling admits:

> An alternative interpretation is that the scan is serial but the order
> varies from trial to trial and/or there is great variability in the
> processing time per item. We tentatively consider that interpretation
> to be unlikely because (a) the modal scan pattern is highly
> repeatable from session to session and (b) parallel processing of

other aspects of the stimulus is occurring, e.g., of its orientation, overall length, brightness, etc.

The value of Sperling's arguments is rather doubtful, however. Also, with serial processing, but especially with a serial selective operation, a highly repeatable modal scan pattern is to be expected. The argument that other aspects of the stimulus are processed in parallel is weak, and completely loses its force if it is assumed that the 'growth curves' represent the selection of the programs from the recognition buffer-memory instead of the processing of the elements. The last argument can also be countered by stating that (a) the processing of the information occurs in parallel, but that (b) the individual growth curves represent a serial operation performed upon the processed information.

In conclusion, it seems better to interpret these curves as representing the serial selection of the programs instead of as representing the parallel processing of the information. But if the programs are serially selected from the recognition buffer-memory, why then do we need the first scan component? If it is assumed that there are no limitations as far as the processing of information is concerned, and if it is, furthermore, assumed that the recognition buffer-memory contains sufficient information for locating the correct responses, then this scan component can be dismissed.

If this point of view is accepted, then it is not very difficult to reformulate Sperling's precategorical selection model in such a way that it corresponds with the postcategorical selection model presented in the previous chapter. The latter model comprised four stages: (1) processing, (2) locating, (3) selecting, (4) responding. The six stages in Sperling's model must then be reinterpreted as follows:

1 The visual representation of the stimulus activates the logogen system (a system of transducers linking visual features with programs of motor-instructions). This system can be considered a high capacity, fast decaying very short-term memory for visual information (the visual features) and for identified information (the programs). This is our version of Sperling's (1967) recognition buffer-memory (processing).

2 A scan component determines the sequence of locations from which information has to be selected (locating or postcategorical filtering).

3 Capacity (or 'effort' or 'resources') is directed to these locations in the order determined by the scan component.

4 The programs corresponding to these locations are selected one after another. As stated in chapter 6, this stage is thought to require effort or capacity (selecting).

5 The selected programs are stored in a buffer memory (responding).

6 The subsequent execution of the programs in the order of being stored constitutes vocal or subvocal rehearsal.

As far as the parallel vs serial processing issue is concerned, it seems that the transition from parallel to serial operations has to be placed between stage 2 and stage 3. On the one hand, more relevant elements, for instance, a row of letters, can be located simultaneously. On the other hand, the capacity is used, according to this conceptualization, for the selection of a relevant program, that is, for maintaining the count level of a relevant logogen until a further operation, responding, is possible. Stages 3 and 4, therefore, form, in fact, one stage in the present model. Because the order in which the programs enter the buffer is thought to be essential for reconstructing spatial order information, a serial selection operation is necessary.

For further information about the duration of each operation performed upon the processed information, we can again start with Sperling's (1967, 1970) interpretation of the results of this whole report experiment. In this experiment the maximum exposure duration was 200 msec. On each trial a stimulus card containing five elements was presented, followed by a patterned noise mask. As stated, Sperling implicitly assumes, that all programs stored in the buffer are correctly selected and executed. This assumption may indeed be tenable if only a small number of elements is stored. If it can be assumed that none of the elements is forgotten, it is correct to interpret within Sperling's model the function that relates amount of elements reported to exposure duration as representing the amount of elements processed as a function of exposure duration. Sperling furthermore assumes that this function reflects only the processing of the elements, that is, the setting up of the programs. In other words, it is assumed that locating the elements, direction of capacity to relevant locations and storage of the programs in the buffer requires only a negligible amount of time, or, can be performed in parallel with the processing of the elements.

Sperling's interpretation can readily be rephrased in terms of the postcategorical selection model just described. As will be clear, the prime difference between Sperling's model and this model is in stage 4; Sperling's 'parallel processing of the elements' is replaced by 'serial selection of programs of motor-instructions'. It is therefore possible to maintain Sperling's assumption that, at least in whole report tasks, all operations except stage 4 (serial selection of programs) require a negligible amount of time, or can be performed in parallel with the serial selection of programs. Furthermore, we must then conclude that under optimal conditions, when no forgetting of selected programs is to be expected, the function relating amount of elements reported to exposure duration reflects the serial selective operation.

Fortunately, it can be shown that a series of selective operations, as specified by the model described in the previous chapter, really results in a function relating amount of elements reported to exposure duration, as found by Sperling (1967). As stated in chapter 1, this function (see Sperling, 1967, fig. 3b; Sperling, 1970, fig. 3b) can be described with

$$X = -\beta/\alpha \, e^{-\alpha t} + \beta/\alpha \qquad (1)$$

where X is the number of elements reported, t equals the exposure time and α and β can be interpreted as processing parameters. According to the postcategorical selection model described in the previous chapter, responding can start when the count of the selected logogen exceeds the logogen next highest in count by a given amount δ. We assume that the time-course of activation of all logogens activated is identical. For ease of exposition, we assume that the selection of the first program is started at time t = 0, when the count level of each of the activated logogens is given by

$$Ce^{-at} = C,$$

and that the count levels of the logogens are already decreasing (see section a). The first selected program can then be responded to on time t when the count level of the non-selected logogens is given by

$$Ce^{-at} = C - \delta.$$

If the second selection is started at the same time t, the second substitute response, that is, the storage of the program, can start at time t when the count level of the non-selected logogens is given by

$$Ce^{-at} = C - 2\delta.$$

In general, the Xth program can be stored at time t, when the count level of the non-selected logogens is given by

$$Ce^{-at} = C - X\delta. \qquad (2)$$

This equation can be rewritten as

$$X = -\frac{C}{\delta} e^{-at} + \frac{C}{\delta} \qquad (3)$$

and equation (3) is of the same form as equation (1) describing Sperling's obtained results (and the results we obtained in the whole report experiment; see chapter 1).

But there is more. Equation (3) can easily be rewritten as

$$X = C \left(\frac{1}{\delta} - \frac{1}{\delta} e^{-at} \right). \qquad (4)$$

In this form it is apparent that the rate of increase of X as a function of time, t, as well as the limiting value of X, increases with increasing C. In chapter 6, in order to explain the asymmetry in Stroop interference, a greater value of C was used for words than for colours (that is, 100 and 80). Therefore, in whole report experiments a faster rate of increase and a higher limiting value have to be found with words than with colours.

Now, Allport (1973) showed, that the function for arrays of unrelated common words of three to six letters in length was essentially the same as the function for unrelated consonants. Mackworth (1963a) showed that the rate of increase and the maximum level ultimately reached were indeed appreciably greater for letters than for colours. (Allport (1973) used a patterned mask, Mackworth (1963a) a homogeneous post-exposure field, but our analysis of whole report tasks in chapter 1 shows that there are no essential differences between these two procedures.) Completely in line, Allport (1977) states: 'stimuli which require to be "named" rather than "read" (Fraisse, 1964), such as Landolt Cs, yield a substantially less steep masking interval function, and a lower span (Allport, 1968)' (Allport, 1977, p. 507). So, also in this more detailed way, the results of the modified Stroop test and the results of whole report experiments can be related to each other. This considerably strengthens our point of view.

In conclusion, it seems that the extended version of the postcategorical selection model presented in the previous chapter can give an adequate account of the data obtained under optimal conditions in a whole report experiment. The important feature of the model is that in whole report experiments programs, once selected, are not immediately executed (a very slow operation), but are stored in one or another memory in the order in which they are selected (a very fast operation).

A number of further remarks have to be made.

The first concerns the implications of the model presented in this section for the interpretation of the parameters in the equation found in chapter 1

$$\frac{\Delta X}{\Delta T} = -aX + b. \tag{5}$$

In chapter 1, parameter b was tentatively interpreted as a 'processing parameter' and parameter a as a 'forgetting parameter'. This interpretation was taken as a background for further theorizing in chapters 2 and 3. In chapter 1 also, a number of alternative interpretations were advanced that could not be ruled out given the evidence presented (see chapter 1, Appendix C). In particular, the evidence discussed in chapter

3 suggested that a different interpretation might be more appropriate. The analyses presented in the previous paragraphs — in this analysis the postcategorical selection model discussed in chapter 6 was generalized — can be used in establishing more firmly which alternative interpretation is most likely. Two assumptions are at the basis of this choice of interpretation: (a) in whole report tasks the same selection mechanism operates as in the Stroop test and in related types of tasks, and (b) under optimal conditions in whole report tasks — small number of elements presented and short exposure durations — no forgetting of selected and stored programs occurs. In Appendix C of chapter 1 a model consistent with these assumptions was described. This model can be represented with the equation

$$\frac{\Delta X}{\Delta T} = a\,(L - X). \tag{6}$$

This equation represents the rate of the serial selection of identified information (programs) for storage in memory and X represents the number of programs already selected and stored (see chapter 1, Appendix C, II). From $L = {}^{b}/a$ (see chapter 1, Appendix C) and from equation (3), it follows that L in equation (6) equals ${}^{C}/\delta$. (Alternatively, solving (6) with $L = {}^{C}/\delta$ gives equation (3) if $X = 0$ for $t = 0$.) So the limit L in (6), ${}^{C}/\delta$, represents the total number of selective operations that can be performed, given that at the start of the first selective operation the count level of the logogens equals C and given that no resetting of count levels takes place (that is, no fixation shifts). 'Optimal exposure conditions' can now be defined more precisely as conditions excluding fixation shifts. Within this condition, 'optimal exposure conditions' possibly presuppose one 'perceptual group' (see Kahneman and Henik, 1977). It seems that much of the perceptual grouping effects in whole report experiments found by these authors can be explained in terms of the model with the assumption: postcategorical filtering takes a negligible amount of time for a next element within a perceptual group and an appreciable amount of time for a next element in a different perceptual group.

It is conceivable that this model gives only an adequate account of what happens within one fixation, while only a composite model, involving processing and forgetting, adequately describes the results of experiments involving a series of fixations (see chapter 1, Appendix C, c). It seems that only further investigations involving eye-movement recording can shed light on this problem. Therefore this issue will not be further pursued.

The second issue to be discussed concerns the mathematical

description of partial report experiments. In chapter 3 two models were worked out in detail, a precategorical selection model and a postcategorical selection model. It can be shown (and it is not difficult to see) that, given the present view, the equations of the precategorical selection model give an adequate description of what happens in partial report experiments. The interpretation has to be drastically changed, however. Instead of precategorical selection, postcategorical selection consisting of two stages: (a) postcategorical filtering, and (b) selection. Furthermore, no forgetting of selected and stored programs is assumed. So, as far as partial report experiments are concerned, our 'resource limited' selection model leads to the most efficient of the two selection models presented in chapter 3 (see Figure 3.1).

The third remark concerns the STM notions used and discussed in chapter 1. Our original interpretation of equation (5) led to a STM conception involving fixed capacity limits. Also, in our original interpretation of equation (6), we suggested that L could be conceived as the limit of the memory that has to hold the names of the identified elements (cf. chapter 1, Appendix C). In chapter 1 it was stated that recent research on STM had rendered such 'slot notions' very unlikely. The slot notion does justice neither to the fact that STM capacity is very dependent on the content of the presented material nor to the associative character of STM.

The model described in the previous paragraphs is more in accordance with these recent developments in STM research. First, the dependence of STM capacity on the content of the presented material (that is, letters, digits, colours, etc.) can be accounted for in terms of this model if it is assumed that different kinds of material have different effects on the logogens as far as the maximum count levels, C, are concerned. The higher this value of C, the more selective operations can be performed. Second, the way in which the associative character of STM can be accounted for depends upon how the logogen system is further conceptualized. If the logogen system is regarded as a system independent of other memories (especially of long-term memory or secondary storage), then additional assumptions are necessary for explaining associative facilitation and interference. It is more parsimonious, however, to identify the logogen system with (or as part of) long-term memory or secondary storage or to redefine it as a lexicon (that is, a combined logogen system and semantic system; see, for example, Allport, 1977). It is, then, to be expected that properties of secondary storage also become apparent in STM research. This point of view is in line with Norman's (1968) and Shiffrin's and Schneider's (1977) general information processing models. To this issue we will briefly return in the last section of this chapter: the outline of a single-store model.

The next issue to be discussed can be called perceptual and semantic dissociation. In the last decade a number of highly interesting observations have been made under conditions with very short exposures of words followed by a patterned noise mask. For instance, it has been shown that under conditions where Ss were unaware that anything had been displayed (that is, the Ss were unable to report a word's identity or its presence), Ss could make better than chance responses on a forced choice semantic judgment task (Marcel and Patterson, 1978). Related observations have been reported by Wickens (1972), Marcel (1974) and Allport (1977).

It is not too difficult to explain this phenomenon in terms of our model. We defined logogens as transducers, linking visual codes (in a 'visual' domain) with verbal codes (in a 'verbal' domain). Upon presentation of a visual word the logogen is activated. If a pattern mask is then presented, the input side of the logogen (that is, the code in the 'visual' domain) is destroyed or replaced. There is no reason, however, to assume that this has any effect on the time-course of activation of the logogen, as far as the output side is concerned (that is, on the verbal code in the 'verbal' domain). If the pattern mask follows after a very short interval of time upon the word stimulus, then, as a result of temporal integration in the visual domain, Ss do not see the word and are unaware of its presence and so cannot report a seen word. The verbal code (possibly more verbal codes; see chapter 6, 'The anatomy of a logogen'), detached from its visual features is available, however, and can exert its effects. If the interval of time between stimulus onset and mask onset is made somewhat larger, Ss see the word and can report the word. If more letters (see, for example, Sperling, 1967) or more words (for example, Allport, 1977) are presented simultaneously under conditions of severe backward masking, then it depends on the selection time per letter or word and on the interval between stimulus onset and mask onset, how much can be reported of the letters or words seen. The words or letters that cannot be reported, have, however, exerted their effects during the selection of the other items. (It will be clear that, given the conceptualization presented in 'The anatomy of a logogen' in chapter 6, more refined accounts can be given of the phenomena observed under conditions with severe backward masking.) Allport (1977) presents a completely different explanation for these results (cf. also Chapter 4). According to his opinion, under conditions of severe backward masking words are not seen because there is not sufficient time to compare a lexical code against the visual code and to integrate the two into a seen word. He assumes, as we do, that the lexical code is not disturbed by the pattern mask. The masking interval function is explained along the same lines. The comparison process is resource-limited, and it depends upon the interval of time between stimulus onset and mask onset, how many items can be compared, integrated and seen. In chapter 4 we discussed Allport's point of view and we pointed at two weaknesses. There are two further problems with Allport's proposal. (a) Ss state that they see the items under backward masking but cannot report them. 'The Ss commented spontaneously that, despite the high contrast of the letters presented under backward masking, they seemed to appear for such a brief duration that there was very little time to identify them before the mask appeared' (Liss, 1968, p. 329). So Ss speak about letters they saw and could not identify, and not about 'complex, letterlike forms', or, a number of black 'squiggles' (Allport, 1977, p. 528). (b) Under severe backward masking Ss cannot report reliably the item presented. Often semantic errors are made. Allport (1977) (and others) compare these errors with errors made by brain-damaged phonemic dyslexics. It is extremely difficult to see how such an inaccessible lexical code can be used as an adequate starting point in a time-consuming (resource-limited) comparison process.

One further remark has to be made in this connection. There is nothing in the conceptualization proposed in chapter 4 and in subsequent chapters (see especially chapter 6, 'The anatomy of a logogen') that excludes the possibility of starting a locating process with verbal, semantic or lexical codes (that is, the reversed order of operations as suggested in postcategorical filtering). According to our point of view, however, these codes are not compared with the visual code, but linked with the visual code and no resources are needed to relate them. So the present point of view is not incompatible with the results of Allport's (1977) experiment in which Ss successfully selected animal names from among other words under conditions of severe pattern masking. The present point of view is even not incompatible with a conceptualization of the reading process starting with verbal codes or semantic codes (generated by context, for instance). Again, however, no comparison of codes is involved. If the visual code appears, the word is seen and read, if the visual code does not appear, the word is not seen or read. If reading starts with verbal or semantic codes, then thinking becomes reading if the appropriate visual codes are available. In such a view, reading is not so much 'externally guided thinking' (Neisser, 1967), but reading is 'seeing what is thought'.

The last issues to be discussed concern the effect of responding (the storage of the selected programs in a memory) on the count level of the logogen selected, and two related issues: (a) selection of information in acquired dyslexia, and (b) an 'inhibition strategy' of selective attention. In the previous section it was already suggested that the execution of the response results in a fast count decay of the logogen from which the response stems. In the model described in this section, vocal or subvocal responding is replaced by a faster operation: storage of the selected program in a memory. In order for the model to work in the way described, it remains necessary to assume that this substitute operation also results in a fast count decay of the logogen responded to. In the present model, the selection of a logogen is effected by maintaining its count level until its count exceeds the count level of the logogen next highest in count by a certain amount δ. This results, at the moment of responding, in a relatively high count level for this logogen as compared with the count levels of the other logogens. Unless it is assumed that responding results in a fast decrease of the count level of this logogen, the selection of the next logogen will be severely interfered with. Let us call this assumption the 'count level assumption'.

This type of interference can possibly be observed in certain kinds of acquired dyslexia. Levine and Calvanio (1978) investigated three patients with lesions of the left occipito-temporal lobes and the clinical picture of alexia-simultanagnosia. These patients identified single letters and single letters followed by a pattern mask as normal subjects. They could successfully report a single letter from a trigram if told in advance which position to report, but faced great difficulties if told after exposure of the stimulus. Furthermore, when presented with three letters simultaneously, they could name only one or two letters, even with very long exposures. It seems that this is exactly the pattern of results that, according to our model, has to be expected if responding after selection has no further effect on the count level of the selected logogen. The first item responded to then remains highly available, and strongly interferes with the selection of subsequent items.

It is interesting to note that Levine and Calvanio (1978) attempt an explanation of the observed phenomena in terms of Sperling's (1967) three-component-model. In their opinion 'perceptual analysis — the read-out of information from iconic storage into the visual recognition buffer — is impaired' (Levine and Calvanio, 1978, p. 79). It was exactly this stage in Sperling's (1967) model that we replaced in the present section by 'serial selection of programs of motor-instructions'. So, in terms of our model, Levine and Calvanio state that serial selection is impaired. The 'count level assumption' mentioned above then perhaps makes explicit one possible reason why serial selection is impaired.

Shallice and Warrington (1977) observed seemingly similar results in two patients who could read words but not their constituent letters (literal dyslexia). Performance was impaired with stimuli in which more than one item of the same category was simultaneously present in the visual field (e.g. a letter in letters). Reading an item surrounded by items from another category (e.g. a letter in numbers) was nearly un-impaired.

We already discussed and criticized Shallice and Warrington's prime reason for rejecting an explanation in terms of implicit response inter-ference (chapter 6). In fact, the 'category effect' just mentioned, seems an important indicator of response competition. (See chapter 5, experi-ment IV: strong interference if a relevant item is presented together with another relevant item and virtually no interference if presented together with an irrelevant item.)

It is not clear whether for the behaviour of these patients the same explanation as for Levine and Calvanio's (1978) patients is the most adequate. The general pattern of results obtained as well as some specific remarks suggest this explanation ('having named four of one row of letters with the same name', p. 33). The 'category effect', however, indicates that there are also severe difficulties during the 'selection stage' (that is, during solving the response conflict). Ss have to name only one item, and if this item is surrounded by items of the same category, performance is impaired. Furthermore, their patient P.T. possibly faced difficulties with what we called 'post-categorical filtering' (see Shallice and Warrington, pp. 33 and 34: scanning ability).

In some sense, we can agree with Shallice and Warrington's (1977) explanation of the results: 'It is suggested that their impairment arises from a specific defect at the level at which visual input is selected for meaningful analysis' (p. 31), because it is the selection stage that is stressed in their explanation. Whether this explanation has to be made explicit in terms of 'post-categorical filtering', 'selection' (that is, solving the response conflict), or in terms of levels of activation that decay too slowly, is not clear.

In principle, the 'count level assumption' also suggests a second 'selection mechanism' or 'selection strategy' that Ss can use in perform-ing Stroop-like tasks. In chapter 6 we described a 'selection strategy': selectively maintaining the count level of the logogen corresponding with the relevant response until its count is highest and exceeds the

211

count level of the next highest logogen by an amount δ. The 'count level assumption' suggests as an alternative an 'inhibition strategy': selectively inhibiting the count level of the logogen corresponding to the distractor response by what we called 'responding'. Neill (1977, 1978) has proposed the latter alternative. Lowe (1979) further investigated Neill's claim that there are inhibitory mechanisms in selective attention. Furthermore, Logan and Zbrodoff (1979) presented highly relevant data in relation to this issue.

Logan's and Zbrodoff's (1979) data are the most clear-cut. If it is assumed that, after inhibition, the inhibited response is temporarily less available, then their data strongly suggest that Ss use the selection strategy if conflicting trials (that is, trials with incongruent stimuli) are relatively infrequent, while they use the inhibition strategy if conflicting trials are relatively frequent. (In Logan's and Zbrodoff's terminology: strategies vary from 'selective attention to the reported dimension' with relatively infrequent conflicting trials to 'dividing attention between reported and unreported dimensions' and 'selective attention to the unreported dimension' if conflicting trials are relatively frequent.) A similar trend can be found in Lowe's (1979) data. Effects hinting at an inhibition strategy are found in experiments in which only incongruent Stroop stimuli are used (Exp. I, II, IV group I). Effects hinting at a selection strategy are found in experiments in which also neutral stimuli are used (Exp. III, IV group II and III). Also, Neill (1977, 1978) obtained his evidence for an inhibition strategy in experiments in which only incongruent stimuli were used. In our experiments, reported in chapters 4 and 5 and further discussed in chapter 6, conflicting trials were relatively infrequent (also neutral and congruent stimuli were included in a block of trials). It is, therefore, reasonable to assume — and this was one of our basic assumptions in chapter 6 — that in these experiments Ss used the selection strategy.

While the picture is far from clear (see especially Lowe, 1979), it seems that Ss can use the inhibition trick, and flexibly use that strategy that, according to some criterion is most adapted to the relevant aspects of the task environment. What exactly that criterion is is as yet not clear. It must be clear, however, that in general the inhibition strategy is of limited use. Especially if there are more than one conflicting irrelevant responses, if the irrelevant response is equally 'strong' as the relevant response and if the irrelevant response is 'weaker' than the relevant response the inhibition strategy seems inadequate. Only if there is *one* competing response, and if that response is 'stronger' than the relevant response does the inhibition strategy seem to be of any use.

(c) Immediate responding vs delayed responding

In the Stroop task and in the modified visual probe experiments, Ss are instructed to respond as fast as possible with one of the alternative responses. In the model described in the previous chapter, responding was equivalent to the immediate execution of the program of motor instructions from the relevant logogen. In the previous section of this chapter it was already argued that with whole report experiments the immediate, vocal or subvocal, sequential execution of the relevant responses is impossible. It was concluded there that a faster operation has to be postulated as a substitute for vocal or subvocal responding and that a store is needed in which the results of this substitute operation can be kept until the response can be given. (Comparable suggestions can be found in Phillips, 1971; Sperling, 1963, 1967, 1970; Mackworth, 1972; Geyer and Kolers, 1974. Also, in Coltheart, 1972; Estes, 1973; Geyer, 1970; Posner and Keele, 1967; Standing et al., 1969; Walsh, 1971; Mitchell, 1976; Mewhort and Beal, 1977; and Mewhort and Campbell, 1978, suggestions about a store between the iconic representation and vocal or subvocal responding can be found.) Two issues now have to be made more specific: (1) The nature of the substitute operation (this operation was called 'responding'), and (2) The characteristics of the intermediate store. In the previous section some suggestions about these issues were already advanced. The last stages of the model proposed there were:

the programs corresponding to the scanned locations are selected one after another (selecting);

the selected programs are stored in a buffer memory (responding);

the subsequent execution of the programs in the order of being stored constitutes vocal or subvocal rehearsal.

There are, however, several ways in which these suggestions can be made more specific. In general, two ways are: (a) in terms of a multi-store model, that is, a model in which more stores are postulated and in which it is assumed that the information is transferred from one store to another; (b) in terms of a single-store model, that is, a model in which only one memory system is postulated, and in which, therefore, this transfer of information does not occur.

1 The outline of a multi-store model

Both Sperling (1967, 1970) and Morton (1970) — their models have been extensively discussed previously — provide examples of a multi-store model. Sperling (1967, 1970) postulates (at least) three different memory systems: (a) visual information storage (VIS), (b) the recognition buffer-memory, and (c) auditory information storage (AIS). The relation between the first two memory systems was already discussed in the previous section. About the relation between the second and the third memory system, Sperling remarks:

> In vocal rehearsal, the motor instructions designated by the recognition buffer-memory are executed, and a spoken letter results. . . . The sound produced by a vocal rehearsal is heard and remembered in auditory short-term memory. In principle, although not in detail, the auditory scan is exactly analogous to the visual scan. The auditory scan selects some contents of auditory memory (e.g., the sound representation of one letter) and converts them into the address of a motor program. The address is remembered in the recognition buffer-memory, the program is executed by the rehearsal component, and the sounds are re-entered into auditory memory. By means of this rehearsal loop, information can be retained for a very long time in auditory short-term memory . . . most adults seem to have evolved a shortcut, which I have designated 'subvocal rehearsal'. In subvocal rehearsal, the subvocal output of the rehearsal component is entered into the auditory short-term memory just as though it had been a vocal output. (Sperling, 1970, pp. 200-1; cf. also Sperling, 1967, p. 291)

Morton (1970) also postulates three different memory systems; a) a visual memory system, b) the logogen system and c) a response buffer. The first stages of Morton's logogen model were already discussed previously. His conception of the relation between the last two systems is similar to Sperling's. 'Following response availability, we can then go on actually to make the response, but, of course, need not. In the interval between responses being made available and their being produced they are in a Response Buffer. . . . Silent rehearsal is seen as the circulating of such information from the Response Buffer back to the Logogen System' (pp. 213-14).

The drawbacks of both models were already extensively discussed. In both models there is no provision that gives at least the possibility of maintaining spatial order information in whole report experiments in which a number of elements (letters or digits) are presented simultaneously. At the output side of the logogen system in Morton's model only responses are available and these responses are detached from the physical features (see chapter 5). Furthermore, there is no provision in the model that ensures that the spatial order information in a stimulus is reflected in a temporal order in the Response Buffer from which the spatial order information can be regained.* In the previous section of this chapter the same problem was encountered with Sperling's (1967, 1970) model. It was argued there that this model was also, and for the same reason, incapable of accounting for the results of whole report experiments. At the level of the recognition buffer-memory spatial order information is lost, and, furthermore, because of the assumption that the programs of motor instructions are set up in parallel in this memory, spatial order information cannot be reconstructed from temporal order information.

In the model we proposed, these deficiencies were overcome by postulating (a) that the relevant logogens are selected one after another (cf. Section (b) of this chapter); and (b) that physical features — in whole report experiments a.o. the spatial position — are used for selecting the relevant elements (see chapters 4, 5 and 6). Therefore, the introduction of a buffer-memory — a response buffer or a recognition buffer-memory — separate from the logogen system, together with the assumption that the temporal order information is maintained and used for reconstructing spatial order information, suffices to complete the model as a multi-store model. In this multi-store model 'responding' has to be interpreted as storage of the program in this memory. The subsequent vocal or subvocal execution of the response constitutes rehearsal. This rehearsal serves the same function as in Sperling's and Morton's model: the circulating of the information between an intermediate memory system (the recognition buffer-memory (Sperling, 1967, 1970) or the response buffer (Morton, 1970)) and the categorizing system (the recognition buffer-memory (Sperling, 1967) or the logogen system (Morton, 1970)) in a continuous loop until the response is called for. (In Sperling's 1967 model the recognition buffer-memory serves both functions of converting the image of a letter in a program of motor instructions and of the storage of these instructions. In Sperling's 1970 model the first function is taken over by a 'scan component'.)

---

*For sequentially presented information, Morton's (1970) model provides an adequate explanation because it is assumed that the items in the store are ordered temporally (see Morton, 1970, p. 238).

2 The outline of a single-store model

As an alternative, the model described in section (b) can be further specified in terms of a single-store model. Such a specification seems to result in a simpler model. Such a model was proposed by Norman (1968) among others. (Schneider and Shiffrin, 1977, and Shiffrin and Schneider, 1977, present a similar model.) His model contains a storage system with two different modes of activation, (a) a permanent excitation, called long-term or secondary store, and (b) a temporary excitation called short-term or primary memory. The model assumes that the storage system is organized in such a way, that the sensory code can make direct access to the stored information. As will be clear, this dual-storage system is similar to our version of the logogen system described in chapter 6. Norman's long-term or secondary storage has the same function as the logogen system and the temporary activation of the logogen system is similar to Norman's short-term or primary memory.

That the multi-store model as described above is not the most parsimonious model becomes apparent if the issue of what is stored in the intermediate memory is considered. In Sperling's (1967) model this is 'programs of motor instructions' (p. 291). Morton's Response Buffer contains the same code. 'The supposed origin of the response is termed a logogen, which is the part of the system that produces or leads directly to the instructions to the articulators' (see Morton, 1970, p. 206), and 'the Response Buffer is the only way to the response mechanisms' (p. 238). So, also in this model, instructions to the articulators, or some code that leads directly to these instructions, are stored in the intermediate memory. In line with these two models we also assumed that in the multi-store model programs of motor instructions are stored in the intermediate memory. In chapter 6, however, we defined a logogen as a transducer, in which programs of motor instructions are activated by stimulus features. According to this point of view the program of motor instructions is an essential part of a logogen and not the product of a logogen. Therefore, if the model is specified as the multi-store model described in the previous paragraphs, it must be assumed that either a part or a copy of a part of a logogen is stored in the intermediate memory. Such assumptions, however, state nothing else than that programs of motor instructions are displaced from one short-term store (the activated logogen system as described in chapter 6) to another short-term store (the intermediate memory as described in this chapter). In a model such a duplication of stores is only justified if it can be shown that only with the combination of stores an adequate model results. The postulate of a second short-term store is superfluous, however, if it can be shown that one store and one operation performed upon the information in that store can serve the same functions.

Now it seems that in a single-store model, in which the activated logogens serve as the intermediate memory, two incompatible demands are imposed as far as the count level of the logogens is concerned. On the one hand, if the activated logogens have to serve as a memory for motor instructions until delayed responding is possible then the count level of the relevant logogens has to be maintained. On the other hand, in order for the selection mechanism described to work, the count level of a selected logogen has to decrease as fast as possible. Therefore, in section (b) of this chapter it was assumed that the substitute operation for responding, the storage of the selected program in a memory, resulted in a fast count decay of the logogen. In a multi-store model, no problem exists, because the simple assumption that the count level decreases in the logogen system, but is maintained in the intermediate memory, suffices. In a single-store model, however, we have to explain how we can have the cake and eat it.

One way of reconciling these two apparently incompatible requirements — a fast decay of the count level and the maintaining of the count level in one and the same store — can be found if it is realized that both requirements do not have to be met at the same time. If 'responding' results in a fast decrease of the count level of the logogen selected, then the fast selection of the next logogen is possible. If later the count level of the logogen responded to increases again, the count level is also maintained in the same store.

In neurophysiology, units showing such an oscillating level after stimulation are described. With prolonged stimulation, but also after stimulation during a small interval of time, these units show a damped oscillation, ultimately reaching an asymptotic activity level. It is thought that these cyclical changes in activity over time result from the operation of recurrent self-inhibitory connections (see, for example, Cornsweet, 1970, pp. 410-16). For the single-store model, such units can serve as a model for the building blocks of the logogen system. If it is assumed that 'responding' after selection causes an oscillating activity level in the logogen responded to in one or another way, then both requirements, (a) a fast immediate decrease of the count level, and (b) an increase of the count level later on, can be met.

In order to see how a model containing such units can account for other phenomena found with visual information processing tasks, the model has to be specified in more detail and additional assumptions are necessary. For the moment it seems premature to work out such a model. According to the knowledge of the present author, only Dyer (1974) presents some experimental evidence that in a Stroop task, the 'activity corresponding to the word stimulus may vary cyclically over time' (p. 10). It is, nevertheless, worthwhile to see that, given a number of necessary assumptions, a single-store model containing a mechanism as described, can show a number of interesting properties.

We give the following examples of such derived properties.

(a) Only the logogens selected and responded to show this oscillating activity level around their background level, while the count level of the non-selected logogens simply returns to the background level. In this way, the selected logogens become differentiated from the non-selected logogens.

(b) The oscillation of the count level of the selected logogens around their background level continues also when there is no further external stimulation of the logogens. In this way, the information about the identity of the selected elements remains stored in memory after stimulation has ceased.

(c) The order in which the count levels of the selected logogens the first time exceed their background level again is the same as the order in which these logogens were originally selected and responded to. Therefore, the order of selection is maintained in the logogen system and, in principle, the reconstruction of spatial order is possible. Furthermore, this ordered reappearance of the count levels above the background level makes it possible that the programs of motor instructions are executed in the order of their counts (see chapter 6), thereby maintaining the correct temporal order of selection.

There are a number of ways in which other phenomena can be accounted for. These issues will not be further pursued, however. The above remarks, however vague, make it clear that it seems possible to account for most of the observed facts found with whole report and partial report tasks in terms of a single-store model. Such a model can readily be related to a number of powerful general information processing models (see chapter 4, related models) and, because such a model is more parsimonious in its assumptions than the multi-store model, it should be preferred. (See Grossberg, 1978, especially pages 203-4, for a number of important, related ideas.)

Bibliography

Allen, T.W., Marcell, M.M., and Anderson, P. (1978), Modality specific interference with verbal and nonverbal stimulus information, 'Memory & Cognition', 6(2), 184-8.

Allport, D.A. (1968), The rate of assimilation of visual information, 'Psychonomic Science', 12(6), 231-2.

Allport, D.A. (1971), Parallel encoding within and between elementary stimulus dimensions, 'Perception & Psychophysics', 10(2), 104-8.

Allport, D.A. (1973), Word recognition and the recognition buffer, paper presented to Experimental Psychology Society, London, January.

Allport, D.A. (1977), On knowing the meaning of words we are unable to report: the effects of visual masking, in S. Dornic (ed.), 'Attention and Performance VI', Hillsdale, N.J., Lawrence Erlbaum Associates.

Allport, D.A. (1979), Word recognition in reading, in P.A. Kolers, M.E. Wrolstad and H. Bouma (eds), 'Processing of Visible Language I', New York, Plenum Press.

Atkinson, R.C., Holmgren, J.E., and Juola, J.F. (1969), Processing time as influenced by the number of elements in a visual display, 'Perception & Psychophysics', 6(6a), 321-6.

Attneave, F. (1959), 'Application of Information Theory to Psychology', New York, Holt, Rinehart & Winston.

Averbach, E., and Coriell, A.S. (1961), Short-term memory in vision, 'Bell System Technical Journal', 40, 309-28.

Averbach, E., and Sperling, G. (1961), Short term storage of information in vision, in C. Cherry (ed.), 'Information Theory', London, Butterworth, 196-211.

Banks, W.P., Bachrach, K.M., and Larson, D.W. (1977), The asymmetry of lateral interference in visual letter identification, 'Perception & Psychophysics', 22(3), 232-40.

Biederman, I., and Tsao, Y.C. (1979), On processing Chinese ideographs and English words: some implications from Stroop-test results, 'Cognitive Psychology', 11, 125-132.

Bjork, E.L., and Murray, J.T. (1977), On the nature of input channels in visual processing, 'Psychological Review', 84, 5, 472-84.

Bouma, H. (1970), Interaction effects in parafoveal letter recognition, 'Nature', 226, 177-8.

219

Broadbent, D.E. (1958), 'Perception and Communication', London, Pergamon Press.

Broadbent, D.E. (1970), Stimulus set and response set: two kinds of selective attention, in D.I. Mostofsky (ed.), 'Attention: Contemporary Theories and Analysis', New York, Appleton-Century-Crofts.

Broadbent, D.E. (1971), 'Decision and Stress', London, Academic Press.

Brown, J. (1958), Some tests of decay theory of immediate memory, 'Quarterly Journal of Experimental Psychology', 10, 12-24.

Brown, J. (1964), Short term memory, 'British Medical Bulletin', 20, 8-11.

Clark, S.E. (1969), Retrieval of color information from preperceptual memory, 'Journal of Experimental Psychology', 82, 263-6.

Cohen, G., and Martin, M. (1975), Hemisphere differences in an auditory Stroop test, 'Perception & Psychophysics', 17, 79-83.

Colegate, R.L., Hoffman, J.E., and Eriksen, C.W. (1973), Selective encoding from multielement visual displays, 'Perception & Psychophysics', 14, 217-24.

Collins, A.M., and Loftus, E.F. (1975), A spreading-activation theory of semantic processing, 'Psychological Review', 82, 407-28.

Coltheart, M. (1972), Visual information processing, in P.C. Dodwell (ed.), 'New Horizons in Psychology 2', Harmondsworth, Penguin.

Coltheart, M. (1975a), Iconic memory: a reply to professor Holding, 'Memory & Cognition', 3(1), 42-8.

Coltheart, M. (1975b), Doubts about iconic memory: a reply to Holding, 'Quarterly Journal of Experimental Psychology', 27, 511-12.

Coltheart, M. (1980), Iconic memory and visible persistence, 'Perception & Psychophysics', 27(3), 183-228.

Coltheart, M., Lea, C.D., and Thompson, K. (1974), In defense of iconic memory, 'Quarterly Journal of Experimental Psychology', 26, 633-41.

Compton, R.P., and Flowers, J.H. (1977), Pictorial interference with geometric shapes and achromatic shades, 'Perception & Psychophysics', 22, 303-9.

Conrad, C. (1974), Context effects in sentence comprehension: a study of the subjective lexicon, 'Memory & Cognition', 2, 130-8.

Cornsweet, T.N. (1970), 'Visual Perception', New York, Academic Press.

Craik, F.I.M., and Lockhart, R.S. (1972), Levels of processing: a framework for memory research, 'Journal of Verbal Learning and Verbal Behavior', 11, 671-84.

Crowder, R.G., and Morton, J. (1969), Precategorical acoustic storage (PAS), 'Perception & Psychophysics', 5, 365-73.

Dallas, M., and Merikle, P.M. (1976a), Semantic processing of non-attended visual information, 'Canadian Journal of Psychology', 30(1), 15-21.

Dallas, M., and Merikle, P.M. (1976b), Response processes and semantic-context effects, 'Bulletin of the Psychonomic Society', 8(6), 441-4.

Dalrymple-Alford, E.C. (1972), Sound similarity and color-word interference in the Stroop task, 'Psychonomic Science', 28, 209-10.

Dalrymple-Alford, E.C., and Budayr, B. (1966), Examination of some aspects of the Stroop color-word test, 'Perceptual and Motor Skills', 23, 1211-14.

Davidson, M.L., Fox, M.J., and Dick, A.O. (1973), Effect of eye movements on backward masking and perceived location, 'Perception & Psychophysics', 14, 110-16.

Den Heyer, K., and Barrett, B. (1971), Selective loss of visual and verbal information in short-term memory by means of visual and verbal interpolated tasks, 'Psychonomic Science', 25, 100-3.

Deutsch, J.A., and Deutsch, D. (1963), Attention: some theoretical considerations, 'Psychological Review', 70, 80-90.

Dick, A.O. (1971), On the problem of selection in short-term visual (iconic) memory, 'Canadian Journal of Psychology', 25, 250-63.

Dick, A.O. (1972), Parallel and serial processing in tachistoscopic recognition: two mechanisms, 'Journal of Experimental Psychology', 96, 60-6.

Dick, A.O. (1974), Iconic memory and its relation to perceptual processing and other memory mechanisms, 'Perception & Psychophysics', 16 (3), 575-96.

Di Lollo, V. (1980), Temporal integration in visual memory, 'Journal of Experimental Psychology: General', 109, 75-97.

Donders, F.C. (1969), On the speed of mental processes, in W.G. Koster (ed. and trans.), 'Attention and Performance II', Amsterdam, North-Holland.

Dyer, F.N. (1971), The duration of word meaning responses: Stroop interference for different preexposures of the word, 'Psychonomic Science', 25, 229-31.

Dyer, F.N. (1973a), The Stroop phenomenon and its use in the study of perceptual, cognitive, and response processes, 'Memory & Cognition', 1(2), 106-20.

Dyer, F.N. (1973b), Interference and facilitation for color naming with separate bilateral presentations of the word and color, 'Journal of Experimental Psychology', 99, 314-17.

Dyer, F.N. (1974), Stroop interference with long preexposures of the word: comparison of pure and mixed preexposure sequences, 'Bulletin of the Psychonomic Society', 3, 8-10.

Dyer, F.N., and Severance, L.J. (1972), Effects of irrelevant colors on reading of color names: a controlled replication of the 'reversed Stroop' effect, 'Psychonomic Science', 28, 336-8.

Dyer, F.N., and Severance, L.J. (1973), Stroop interference with successive presentations of separate incongruent words and colors, 'Journal of Experimental Psychology', 98, 438-9.

Egeth, H.E. (1967), Selective attention, 'Psychological Bulletin', 67, 41-57.

Egeth, H., Jonides, J., and Wall, S. (1972), Parallel processing of multi-element displays, 'Cognitive Psychology', 3, 674-98.

Egeth, H., Atkinson, J., Gilmore, G., and Marcus, N. (1973), Factors affecting processing mode in visual search, 'Perception & Psychophysics', 13(3), 394-402.

Eriksen, C.W., and Collins, J.F. (1969), Temporal course of selective attention, 'Journal of Experimental Psychology', 80, 254-61.

Eriksen, B.A., and Eriksen, C.W. (1974), Effects of noise letters upon the identification of a target letter in a nonsearch task, 'Perception & Psychophysics', 16, 143-9.

Eriksen, C.W., and Hoffman, J.E. (1972a), Temporal and spatial characteristics of selective encoding from visual displays, 'Perception & Psychophysics', 12, 201-4.

Eriksen, C.W., and Hoffman, J.E. (1972b), Some characteristics of selective attention in visual perception determined by vocal reaction time, 'Perception & Psychophysics', 11, 169-71.

Eriksen, C.W., and Hoffman, J.E. (1973), The extent of processing of noise elements during selective encoding from visual displays, 'Perception & Psychophysics', 14, 217-24.

Eriksen, C.W., and Rohrbaugh, J.W. (1970), Some factors determining efficiency of selective attention, 'American Journal of Psychology', 83, 330-43.

Eriksen, C.W., and Schultz, D.W. (1979), Information processing in visual search: a continuous flow conception and experimental results, 'Perception & Psychophysics', 25(4), 249-63.

Eriksen, C.W., and Spencer, T. (1969), Rate of information processing in visual perception: some results and methodological considerations, 'Journal of Experimental Psychology Monograph', 79 (no. 2, part 2).

Estes, W.K. (1972), Interactions of signal and background variables in visual processing, 'Perception & Psychophysics', 12(3), 278-86.

Estes, W.K. (1973), Phonemic coding and rehearsal in short-term memory for letter strings, 'Journal of Verbal Learning and Verbal Behavior', 12, 360-72.

Estes, W.K. (1974), Redundancy of noise elements and signals in visual detection of letters, 'Perception & Psychophysics', 16(1), 53-60.

Estes, W.K. (1978), Perceptual processing in letter recognition and reading, in E.C. Carterette and M.P. Friedman (eds), 'Handbook of perception, Vol. IX', New York, Academic Press.

Estes, W.K., and Taylor, H.A. (1964), A detection method and probabilistic models for assessing information processing from brief visual displays, 'Proc. Nat. Ac. Sci.', 52, 446-54.

Estes, W.K., and Taylor, H.A. (1966), Visual detection in relation to display size and redundancy of critical elements, 'Perception & Psychophysics', 1, 9-16.

Estes, W.K., and Wessel, D.L. (1966), Reaction time in relation to display size and correctness of response in forced-choice visual signal detection, 'Perception & Psychophysics', 1, 369-73.

Estes, W.K., and Wolford, G.L. (1971), Effects of spaces on report from tachistoscopically presented letter strings, 'Psychonomic Science',

25, 77-80.

Fraisse, P. (1969), Why is naming longer than reading?, 'Acta Psychologica', 30, 96-103.

Gardner, G.T. (1973), Evidence for independent parallel channels in tachistoscopic perception, 'Cognitive Psychology', 4, 130-55.

Gatti, S.V., and Egeth, H.E. (1978), Failure of spatial selectivity in vision, 'Bulletin of the Psychonomic Society', 11(3), 181-4.

Geyer, J.J. (1970), Models of perceptual processes in reading, in H. Singer and R.B. Ruddell (eds), 'Theoretical models and processes of reading', Newark, International Reading Association, 47-94.

Geyer, J.J., and Kolers, P.A. (1974), Reading as information processing, in M.J. Voight (ed.), 'Advances in Librarianship', New York, Academic Press.

Gholson, B., and Hohle, R.H. (1968), Verbal reaction times to hues vs hue names and forms vs form names, 'Perception & Psychophysics', 3, 191-6.

Goolkasian, P. (1978), Reading and detecting color-word stimuli presented at various retinal locations, 'The Journal of Psychology', 100, 167-81.

Graves, R.S. (1976), Are more items identified than can be reported?, 'Journal of Experimental Psychology, Human Learning and Memory', 2(2), 208-14.

Grossberg, S. (1978), Behavioral contrast in short term memory: serial binary models or parallel continuous memory models?, 'Journal of Mathematical Psychology', 17, 199-219.

Gumenik, W.E., and Glass, R. (1970), Effects of reducing the readability of the words in the Stroop Color-Word Test, 'Psychonomic Science', 20, 247-8.

Haber, R.N. (1964a), A replication of selective attention and coding in visual perception, 'Journal of Experimental Psychology', 67, 402-4.

Haber, R.N. (1964b), Effects of coding strategy on perceptual memory, 'Journal of Experimental Psychology', 68, 357-62.

Haber, R.N. (1966), Nature of the effect of set on perception, 'Psychological Review', 73, 335-51.

Haber, R.N., and Hershenson, M. (1974), 'The Psychology of Visual Perception', London, Holt, Rinehart & Winston.

Haber, R.N., and Standing, L.G. (1969), Direct measures of short-term visual storage, 'Quarterly Journal of Experimental Psychology', 21, 43-54.

Haber, R.N., and Standing, L.G. (1970), Direct estimates of the apparent duration of a flash, 'Canadian Journal of Psychology', 24, 216-29.

Harris, C.S., and Haber, R.N. (1963), Selective attention and coding in visual perception, 'Journal of Experimental Psychology', 65, 328-33.

Henderson, L.A. (1974), A word superiority effect without orthographic assistance, 'Quarterly Journal of Experimental Psychology', 26, 301-11.

Hintzman, D.L., Carre, F.A., Eskridge, V.L., Owens, A.M., Shaff, S.S., and Sparks, M.E. (1972), 'Stroop' effect: input or output phenomenon?, 'Journal of Experimental Psychology', 95, 458-9.

Hoffman, J.E. (1975), Hierarchical stages in the processing of visual information, 'Perception & Psychophysics', 18(5), 348-54.

Holding, D.H. (1975), Sensory storage reconsidered, 'Memory & Cognition', 3(1), 31-41.

Holmgren, J.E., Juola, J.F., and Atkinson, R.C. (1974), Response latency in visual search with redundancy in the visual display, 'Perception & Psychophysics', 16(1), 123-8.

Humphreys, G.W. (1978), The use of category information in perception, 'Perception', 7, 589-604.

Humphreys, G. (in press), On varying the span of visual attention: evidence for two modes of spatial attention, 'Quarterly Journal of Experimental Psychology (Human, Experimental Section)'.

Jacobson, J.Z. (1973), Effects of association upon masking and reading latency, 'Canadian Journal of Psychology', 27(1), 58-69.

Jacobson, J.Z. (1974), Interaction of similarity to words of visual masks and targets, 'Journal of Experimental Psychology', 102(3), 431-4.

Jacobson, J.Z., and Rhinelander, G. (1978), Geometric and semantic similarity in visual masking, 'Journal of Experimental Psychology: Human Perception and Performance', 4(2), 224-31.

Kahneman, D.H. (1968), Method, findings and theory in studies of visual masking, 'Psychological Bulletin', 70, 404-25.

Kahneman, D. (1973), 'Attention and Effort', Englewood Cliffs, N.J., Prentice-Hall.

Kahneman, D., and Henik, A. (1977), Effect of visual grouping on immediate recall and selective attention, in S. Dornic (ed.), 'Attention and Performance VI', Hillsdale, N.J., Lawrence Erlbaum Associates.

Keele, S.W. (1972), Attention demands of memory retrieval, 'Journal of Experimental Psychology', 93, 245-8.

Keele, S.W. (1973), 'Attention and Human Performance', Pacific Palisades, Calif., Goodyear.

Keele, S.W., and Neill, T. (1978), Mechanisms of attention, in E.C. Carterette and M.P. Friedman (eds), 'Handbook of Perception, Vol. IX', New York, Academic Press.

Keren, G. (1976), Some considerations of two alleged kinds of selective attention, 'Journal of Experimental Psychology: General', 105, 349-74.

Kinsbourne, M., and Innis, N. (1972), Visual search through short digit sequences is selfterminating, 'Acta Psychologica', 36, 54-9.

Kintsch, W. (1970), 'Learning, Memory, and Conceptual Processes', New York, Wiley & Sons.

Kirk, R.E. (1968), 'Experimental Design: Procedures for the Behavioral Sciences', Belmont, Calif., Brooks-Cole Publishing Co.

Klein, G.S. (1964), Semantic power measured through the interference of words with color-naming, 'American Journal of Psychology', 57, 576-88.

Kolers, P.A., and Smythe, W.E. (1979), Images, symbols and skills,

'Canadian Journal of Psychology', 33(3), 158-84.

Krueger, L.E., and Shapiro, R.G. (1979), Letter detection with rapid serial visual presentation: evidence against word superiority at feature extraction, 'Journal of Experimental Psychology: Human Perception and Performance', 5, 657-73.

Krumhansl, C.L. (1977), Naming and locating simultaneously and sequentially presented letters, 'Perception & Psychophysics', 22(3), 293-302.

Landauer, T.K. (1962), Rate of implicit speech, 'Perceptual and Motor Skills', 15, 646.

Latour, P.L. (1962), Visual threshold during eye-movements, 'Vision Research', 2, 261-2.

Lema-Stern, S., and Gottwald, H.L. (1979), Effects of semantic cues in dichoptic presentation, 'Bulletin of the Psychonomic Society', 13(4), 215-18.

Levine, D.N., and Calvanio, R. (1978), A study of the visual defect in verbal alexia-simultanagnosia, 'Brain', 101, 65-81.

Lindsay, P.H., and Norman, D.A. (1977), 'Human Information Processing', New York, Academic Press.

Liss, P. (1968), Does backward masking by visual noise stop stimulus processing?, 'Perception & Psychophysics', 4, 329-30.

Logan, G.D. (1976), Converging evidence for automatic perceptual processing in visual search, 'Canadian Journal of Psychology', 30, 193-200.

Logan, G.D. (1978), Attention in character-classification tasks: evidence for the automaticity of component stages, 'Journal of Experimental Psychology: General', 107, 1, 32-63.

Logan, G.D., and Zbrodoff, N.J. (1979), When it helps to be misled: facilitative effects of increasing the frequency of conflicting stimuli in a Stroop-like task, 'Memory & Cognition', 7 (3), 166-74.

Lowe, D.G. (1979), Strategies, context, and the mechanism of response inhibition, 'Memory & Cognition', 7(5), 382-9.

Luria, S.M. (1967), Colorname as a function of stimulus-intensity and duration, 'American Journal of Psychology', 80, 1-13.

Mackworth, J.F. (1962), The visual image and the memory trace, 'Canadian Journal of Psychology', 16, 55-9.

Mackworth, J.F. (1963a), The relation between the visual image and post-perceptual immediate memory, 'Journal of Verbal Learning and Verbal Behavior', 2, 75-85.

Mackworth, J.F. (1963b), The duration of the visual image, 'Canadian Journal of Psychology', 17, 62-81.

Mackworth, J.F. (1972), Some models of the reading process: learners and skilled readers, 'Reading Research Quarterly', 7, 701-33.

Marcel, A.J. (1974), Perception with and without awareness, paper presented to a meeting of the Experimental Psychology Society, Scotland.

Marcel, T., and Patterson, K. (1978), Word recognition and production: reciprocity in clinical and normal studies, in M.J. Requin (ed.), 'Attention and Performance VII', Hillsdale, N.J., Lawrence Erlbaum

Associates.

Merikle, P.M., and Glick, M.J. (1976), Processing order in visual perception, 'Quarterly Journal of Experimental Psychology', 28, 17-26.

Merikle, P.M., and Gorewich, N.J. (1979), Spatial selectivity in vision: field size depends on noise size, 'Bulletin of the Psychonomic Society', 14(5), 343-6.

Mewhort, D.J.K., and Beal, A.L. (1977), Mechanisms of word identification, 'Journal of Experimental Psychology: Human Perception and Performance', 3, 629-40.

Mewhort, D.J.K., and Campbell, A.J. (1978), Processing spatial information and the selective-masking effect, 'Perception & Psychophysics', 24(1), 93-101.

Mewhort, D.J.K., Merikle, P.M., and Bryden, M.P. (1969), On the transfer from iconic to short-term memory, 'Journal of Experimental Psychology', 81, 89-94.

Miller, G.A. (1956), The magical number seven, plus or minus two, 'Psychological Review', 63, 81-97.

Mitchell, D.C. (1976), Buffer storage modality and identification time in tachistoscopic recognition, 'Quarterly Journal of Experimental Psychology', 28, 325-37.

Morin, R.E., Konick, A., Troxell, N., and McPherson, S. (1965), Information and reaction time for 'naming' responses, 'Journal of Experimental Psychology', 70, 309-14.

Morton, J. (1964a), The effects of context on the visual duration threshold for words, 'British Journal of Psychology', 55, 165-80.

Morton, J. (1964b), The effects of context upon speed of reading, eye-movements and eye-voice span, 'Quarterly Journal of Experimental Psychology', 16, 340-54.

Morton, J. (1969a), Interaction of information in word recognition, 'Psychological Review', 76, 165-78.

Morton, J. (1969b), Categories of interference: verbal mediation and conflict in card sorting, 'British Journal of Psychology', 60(3), 329-46.

Morton, J. (1970), A functional model for memory, in D.A. Norman (ed.), 'Models of Human Memory', New York, Academic Press.

Morton, J. (1977), Word Recognition, in J. Morton and J.C. Marshall (eds), 'Psycholinguistics series II', London, Elek.

Morton, J. (1979), Facilitation in word recognition: experiments causing change in the logogen model, in P.A. Kolers, M.E. Wrolstad and H. Bouma (eds), 'Processing of Visible Language I', New York, Plenum Press.

Morton, J., and Chambers, S.M. (1973), Selective attention to words and colours, 'Quarterly Journal of Experimental Psychology', 25, 387-97.

Neely, J.H. (1977), Semantic priming and retrieval from lexical memory: roles of inhibitionless spreading activation and limited-capacity attention, 'Journal of Experimental Psychology: General', 106, 226-54.

Neill, W.T. (1977), Inhibitory and facilitatory processes in selective attention, 'Journal of Experimental Psychology: Human Perception and Performance, 3, 444-50.

Neill, W.T. (1978), Decision processes in selective attention: response priming in the Stroop color-word task, 'Perception & Psychophysics', 23(1), 80-4.

Neisser, U. (1964), Visual search, 'Scientific American', 210 (June), 94-102.

Neisser, U. (1967), 'Cognitive Psychology', New York, Appleton-Century-Crofts.

Nelson, D.L. (1979), Remembering pictures and words: appearance, significance, and name, in L.S. Cermak and F.M. Craik (eds), 'Levels of Processing in Human Memory', London, Erlbaum.

Nickerson, R.S. (1972), Binary-classification reaction time: a review of some studies of human information-processing capabilities, 'Psychonomic Monograph Supplements', 4, 17 (whole no. 65).

Norman, D.A. (1968), Towards a theory of memory and attention, 'Psychological Review', 75, 522-36.

Norman, D.A. (1976), 'Memory and Attention: An Introduction to Human Information Processing' (2nd edn), New York, Wiley.

Norman, D.A., and Bobrow, D.G. (1975), On data limited and resource-limited processes, 'Cognitive Psychology', 7, 44-64.

Phillips, W.A. (1971), Does familiarity affect transfer from an iconic to a short-term memory?, 'Perception & Psychophysics', 10, 153-7.

Posner, M.I. (1969), Abstraction and the process of recognition, in J.T. Spence and G. Bower (eds), 'The Psychology of Learning and Motivation', vol. 3, London, Academic Press.

Posner, M.I. (1973), Coordination of internal codes, in W.G. Chase (ed.), 'Visual Information Processing', London, Academic Press.

Posner, M.I., Boies, S.J., Eichelman, W.H., and Taylor, R.L. (1969), Retention of visual and name codes of single letters, 'Journal of Experimental Psychology', Monograph 79, 1-16.

Posner, M.I., and Keele, S.W. (1967), Attention demands of movement, in 'Proceedings of the 16th International Congress of Applied Psychology', Amsterdam, Swets & Zeitlinger.

Posner, M.I., and Snyder, C.R.R. (1975a), Attention and cognitive control, in R.L. Solso (ed.), 'Information Processing and Cognition, The Loyola Symposium', Hillsdale, N.J., Lawrence Erlbaum Associates.

Posner, M.I., and Snyder, C.R.R. (1975b), Facilitation and inhibition in the processing of signals, in P.M.A. Rabbitt and S. Dornic (eds), 'Attention and Performance V', London, Academic Press.

Posner, M.I., and Warren, R.E. (1972), Traces, concepts, and conscious constructions, in A.W. Melton and E. Martin (eds), 'Coding Processes in Human Memory', Washington D.C., Winston.

Proctor, R.W. (1978), Sources of color-word interference in the Stroop color-naming task, 'Perception & Psychophysics', 23, 413-19.

Raymond, B., and Glanzer, M. (1967), Continuity of exposure length effects in tachistoscopic perception, 'Psychonomic Science', 7, 287-8.

Regan, J. (1978), Involuntary automatic processing in color-naming tasks, 'Perception & Psychophysics', 24(2), 130-6.

Reicher, G.M. (1969), Perceptual recognition as a function of meaningfulness of stimulus material, 'Journal of Experimental Psychology', 81, 275-80.

Rommetveit, R., and Blakar, R.M. (1973), Induced semantic-associative states and resolution on binocular-rivalry conflicts between letters, 'Scandinavian Journal of Psychology', 14, 185-94.

Rumelhart, D.E. (1970), A multicomponent theory of the perception of briefly exposed visual displays, 'Journal of Mathematical Psychology', 7, 191-218.

Sanders, A.F. (1975), Some remarks on short-term memory, in P.M.A. Rabbitt and S. Dornic (eds), 'Attention and Performance V', London, Academic Press.

Saraga, E., and Shallice, T. (1973), Parallel processing of the attributes of single stimuli, 'Perception & Psychophysics', 13, 261-70.

Scheerer, E. (1973), Integration, interruption and processing rate in visual backward masking, 'Psychologische Forschung', 36, 71-93.

Schmit, V., and Davis, R. (1974), The role of hemisphere specialization in the analysis of Stroop stimuli, 'Acta Psychologica', 38, 149-58.

Schneider, W., and Shiffrin, R.M. (1977), Controlled and automatic human information processing: I. Detection, search, and attention, 'Psychological Review', 84(1), 1-66.

Schulz, D.W., and Eriksen, C.W. (1977), Do noise masks terminate target processing?, 'Memory & Cognition', 5, 90-6.

Schulz, T. (1979), Components of the reaction time Stroop-task, 'Psychological Research', 40, 377-95.

Selfridge, O.G. (1959), Pandemonium: a paradigm for learning, in 'The Mechanics of Thought Processes', London, HMSO.

Seymour, P.H.K. (1977), Conceptual encoding and locus of the Stroop effect, 'Quarterly Journal of Experimental Psychology', 29, 245-65.

Shallice, T., and Warrington, E.K. (1977), The possible role of selective attention in acquired dyslexia, 'Neuropsychologia', 15, 31-41.

Shiffrin, R.M. (1975), The locus and role of attention in memory systems, in P.M.A. Rabbitt and S. Dornic (eds), 'Attention and Performance V', London, Academic Press.

Shiffrin, R.M., and Gardner, G.T. (1972), Visual processing capacity and attentional control, 'Journal of Experimental Psychology', 93, 72-82.

Shiffrin, R.M., Gardner, G.T., and Allmeyer, D.H. (1973), On the degree of attention and capacity limitations in visual processing, 'Perception & Psychophysics', 14, 231-6.

Shiffrin, R.M., and Geisler, W.S. (1973), Visual recognition in a theory of information processing, in R. Solso (ed.), 'The Loyola Symposium: Contemporary Viewpoints in Cognitive Psychology', Washington D.C., Winston.

Shiffrin, R.M., and Schneider, W. (1977), Controlled and automatic human information processing: II. Perceptual learning, automatic attending, and a general theory, 'Psychological Review', 84(2),

127-90.

Shulman, G.L., Remington, R.W., and McLean, J.P. (1979), Moving attention through visual space, 'Journal of Experimental Psychology: Human Perception and Performance', 5, 522-6.

Sichel, J.L., and Chandler, K.A. (1969), The color-word interference test: the effects of varied color-word combinations upon verbal response latency, 'Journal of Psychology', 72, 219-31.

Singer, M.H., Lappin, J.S., and Moore, L.P. (1975), The interference of various word parts on color naming in the Stroop test, 'Perception & Psychophysics', 18, 191-3.

Sperber, R.D., McCauley, C., Ragain, R.D., and Weil, C.M. (1979), Semantic priming effects on picture and word processing, 'Memory & Cognition', 7(5), 339-45.

Sperling, G. (1960), The information available in brief visual presentations, 'Psychological Monograph', 74(11).

Sperling, G. (1963), A model for visual memory tasks, 'Human Factors', 5, 19-31.

Sperling, G. (1967), Successive approximations to a model for short-term memory, 'Acta Psychologica', 27, 285-92.

Sperling, G. (1970), Short-term memory, long-term memory and scanning in the processing of visual information, in F.A. Young and D.B. Lindslay (eds), 'Early Experience and Visual Information Processing in Perceptual and Reading Disorders', Washington, National Academy of Sciences.

Sperling, G., Budiansky, J., Spivak, J.G., and Johnson, M.C. (1971), Extremely rapid visual search: the maximum rate of scanning letters for the presence of a numeral, 'Science', 174, 307-11.

Standing, L., Haber, R.N., Cataldo, M., and Sales, D.B. (1969), Two types of short-term visual storage, 'Perception & Psychophysics', 5, 193-6.

Sternberg, S. (1967), Two operations in character-recognition: Some evidence from reaction-time measurements, 'Perception & Psychophysics', 2, 45-53.

Sternberg, S. (1969), Memory-scanning: mental processes revealed by reaction-time experiments, 'American Scientist', 1969, 4, 421-57.

Stirling, N. (1979), Stroop interference: an input and an output phenomenon, 'Quarterly Journal of Experimental Psychology', 31, 121-32.

Stroop, J.R. (1935), Studies of interference in serial verbal reactions, 'Journal of Experimental Psychology', 18, 643-62.

Taylor, D.A. (1976), Stage analysis of reaction time, 'Psychological Bulletin', 83(2), 161-91.

Taylor, D.A. (1977), Time course of context effects, 'Journal of Experimental Psychology: General', 106(4), 404-26.

Townsend, J.T. (1972), Some results on the identifiability of parallel and serial processes, 'British Journal of Mathematical and Statistical Psychology', 25, 168-99.

Townsend, J.T. (1974), Issues and models concerning the processing of a finite number of inputs, in B.H. Kantowitz (ed.), 'Human

Information Processing: Tutorials in Performance and Cognition', Hillsdale, N.J., Lawrence Erlbaum Associates.

Townsend, J.T., Taylor, S.G., and Brown, D.R. (1971), Lateral masking for letters with unlimited viewing time, 'Perception & Psychophysics', 10(5), 375-8.

Townsend, J.T., and Roos, R.N. (1973), Search reaction time for single targets in multiletter stimuli with brief visual displays, 'Memory & Cognition', 1(3), 319-32.

Townsend, V.M. (1973), Loss of spatial and identity information following a tachistoscopic exposure, 'Journal of Experimental Psychology', 98, 113-18.

Treisman, A.M. (1960), Contextual cues in selective listening, 'Quarterly Journal of Experimental Psychology', 12, 242-8.

Treisman, A.M. (1969), Strategies and models of selective attention, 'Psychological Review', 76, 282-99.

Treisman, A.M., Russell, R., and Green, J. (1975), Brief visual storage of shape and movement, in P.M.A. Rabbitt and S. Dornic (eds), 'Attention and Performance V', London, Academic Press.

Treisman, A.M., Sykes, M., and Gelade, G. (1977), Selective attention and stimulus integration, in S. Dornic (ed.), 'Attention and Performance VI', Hillsdale, N.J., Lawrence Erlbaum Associates.

Treisman, A.M., and Gelade, G. (1980), A feature-integration theory of attention, 'Cognitive Psychology', 12, 97-136.

Turvey, M.T. (1973), On peripheral and central processes in vision: inferences from an information-processing analysis of masking with patterned stimuli, 'Psychological Review', 80, 1-52.

Turvey, M.T. (1975), Perspectives in vision: Conception or Perception, in D.D. Duane and M.B. Rawson (eds), 'Reading, Perception and Language', Baltimore, York Press.

Turvey, M.T., and Kravetz, S. (1970), Retrieval from iconic memory with shape as the selection criterion, 'Perception & Psychophysics', 8, 171-2.

van der Heijden, A.H.C. (1971), The processing of tachistoscopic displays as a function of effective stimulus duration, 'Acta Psychologica', 35, 233-42.

van der Heijden, A.H.C. (1975), Some evidence for a limited capacity parallel selfterminating process in simple visual search tasks, 'Acta Psychologica', 39, 21-42.

van der Heijden, A.H.C., and Eerland, E. (1973), The effect of cueing in a visual signal detection task, 'Quarterly Journal of Experimental Psychology', 25, 496-503.

van der Heijden, A.H.C., and Frankhuizen, J. (1975), Studies in Stroop Interference. A comparison of the effect of naming responses to irrelevant colors and of reading responses to irrelevant words, unpublished report, Psychological Institute, University of Leiden.

van der Heijden, A.H.C., and Menckenberg, H.W. (1974), Some evidence for a selfterminating process in simple visual search tasks, 'Acta Psychologica', 38, 169-81.

Vanthoor, F.L.J., and Eijkman, E.G.J. (1973), Time course of the iconic memory signal, 'Acta Psychologica', 37, 79-85.

Von Wright, J.M. (1968), Selection in visual immediate memory, 'Quarterly Journal of Experimental Psychology', 20, 62-8.

Von Wright, J.M. (1970), On selection in visual immediate memory, 'Acta Psychologica', 33, 280-92.

Von Wright, J.M. (1972), On the problem of selection in iconic memory, 'Scandinavian Journal of Psychology', 13, 159-71.

Walsh, T. (1971), The joint effect of forward and backward visual masking: some comments on Uttal's character in the hole experiment, 'Perception & Psychophysics', 10, 265-6.

Warren, R.E. (1972), Stimulus encoding and memory, 'Journal of Experimental Psychology', 94, 90-100.

Warren, R.E. (1974), Association, directionality and stimulus encoding, 'Journal of Experimental Psychology', 102, 151-8.

Warren, R.E., and Lasher, M.D. (1974), Interference in a typeface variant of the Stroop test, 'Perception & Psychophysics', 15, 128-30.

Waugh, N.C., and Norman, D.A. (1965); Primary memory, 'Psychological Review', 72, 89-104.

Wheeler, D.D. (1970), Processes in word recognition, 'Cognitive Psychology', 1, 59-85.

Wickelgren, W.A. (1979), 'Cognitive Psychology', Englewood Cliffs, N.J., Prentice-Hall.

Wickens, D.D. (1972), Characteristics of word encoding, in A.W. Melton and E. Martin (eds), 'Coding Processes in Human Memory', Washington D.C., Winston.

Wolford, G.L., Wessel, D.L., and Estes, W.K. (1968), Further evidence concerning scanning and sampling assumptions of visual detection models, 'Perception & Psychophysics', 3(6), 439-44.

Woodworth, R.S., and Schlosberg, H. (1954), 'Experimental Psychology', New York, Holt.

Author index

Subject index

For Product Safety Concerns and Information please contact our EU
representative GPSR@taylorandfrancis.com Taylor & Francis Verlag GmbH,
Kaufingerstraße 24, 80331 München, Germany

Batch number: 08153780

Printed by Printforce, the Netherlands